The Metaphysics of Representation

The Metaphysics of Representation

J. ROBERT G. WILLIAMS

OXFORD
UNIVERSITY PRESS

OXFORD
UNIVERSITY PRESS

Great Clarendon Street, Oxford, OX2 6DP,
United Kingdom

Oxford University Press is a department of the University of Oxford.
It furthers the University's objective of excellence in research, scholarship,
and education by publishing worldwide. Oxford is a registered trade mark of
Oxford University Press in the UK and in certain other countries

First Edition published in 2019

Impression: 1

Published in the United States of America by Oxford University Press
198 Madison Avenue, New York, NY 10016, United States of America

British Library Cataloguing in Publication Data

Data available

Library of Congress Control Number: 2019949406

ISBN 978–0–19–885020–5

DOI: 10.1093/oso/9780198850205.001.0001

Printed and bound in Great Britain by
Clays Ltd, Elcograf S.p.A.

Preface

This is a book about the nature of representational facts: representation in language, in thought, in action and perception. My hypothesis is that the metaphysics of these states is hierarchical. Certain facts about action and perception are metaphysically prior to, and independent of, the others. They constitute a first layer of representational facts. They are part of the basis that grounds facts about what a perceiver-actor believes and desires. Belief and desire constitute a second layer of representational facts. Facts about mental content then form part of the basis that grounds facts about what the words we speak mean. So linguistic representation is a third layer of representational facts. The story in the chapters to follow starts with the central case of mental content. After that, it looks above and below: building up to linguistic content, and finally laying the foundations in perception and action.

The story I tell is deeply influenced by David Lewis's account of mental and linguistic representation. He never set out his account in full detail, and for years I've been puzzled about how the details were supposed to go.[1] What follows is not an attempt at Lewis exegesis, but an improvisation on a Lewisian theme. The most striking global divergence from Lewis is that I cannot see how to make the account fly without an appeal to the first layer

---

[1] A major difficulty, exegetically, is to understand how the story in Lewis (1974) was supposed to be adjusted in the light of the objections in Lewis (1983)—the bubble puzzle of my chapter 1. Though I thought I understood how Lewis's remedy for underdetermination challenges, involving an appeal to naturalness, was to go (see Williams 2007, 2015 for my take on this), I did not see how this would go in the case of mental content, until a cluster of papers in the early 2010s made a connection between a role for naturalness in the epistemology of induction and radical interpretation. These were published as Weatherson (2013), Pautz (2013), and Schwarz (2014) (an earlier draft of the Weatherson paper proposed a much bolder version of a connection between induction and natural properties ('inductive dogmatism'), which was influential on me). The brief discussions in each of these papers left plenty of room for further worries and development, as we'll see in chapter 4, but at least the form of a naturalness-based resolution of the key underdetermination puzzle was in view. I still don't fully understand how Lewis himself would square this story with his coarse-grained approach to mental content, and I am puzzled as to why, if this was his picture, he didn't come out and articulate directly the view that Weatherson (2013) very plausibly attributes to him.

of representation—an autonomous account of perceptual and action-guiding content.[2] Here, it is not Lewis, but the 'naturalising' tradition that provides the setting. My original plan was to tackle this first layer of representation using resources drawn from Dretske's work, but I was fortunate that, at a late stage in this project's development, Karen Neander published a book-length treatment of perceptual representation which suited my purposes beautifully.

Accordingly, there are two traditions woven together in the story I am about to tell. The first tradition is that of 'teleoinformational' accounts of representation: roughly, that a state represents that p iff that state has the function to be caused by the fact that p. The second are 'interpretationist' accounts of representation, roughly: a state of an agent represents that p if the most rationalizing overall interpretation of that agent maps that state to the content that p. To keep the story flowing in the main text, I will confine discussion of this background context and my methodological assumptions to this preface.

Interpretationist Ancestry

In this section I offer brief sketches of three central precedents for the interpretationist side of my account (the second and third layers of representation). I review the approaches of Quine, Davidson and Lewis, before comparing and contrasting them to each other and the approach to be developed here.

W.V. Quine didn't think we should talk about meaning, but he had a theory about what we were up to when we ascribed reference and truth to bits of language.[3] His work is one of the sources for interpretationist treatments of content. When dealing with self-ascriptions of reference and truth, his favoured approach appealed to disquotation schemata: 'Willard' refers to Willard, 'is a rabbit' is true of something iff that thing is a rabbit. Accordingly, 'Willard is a rabbit' is true iff Willard is a rabbit. The key here is simply to say that by adding and removing quotation marks, we can characterize the extension of reference and truth.

---

[2] See Pautz (2013) for a take on this, focused on the role for perceptual content.
[3] The locus classicus for Quine on radical translation is his (1960). My view of Quine is heavily influenced by the way that Hartry Field explains and co-opts the Quinean account in the essays collected in Field (2001).

One can't in general disquote (in L) expressions taken from a language other than L. The claim:

- 'est un chien' is true of something iff that thing est un chien

is neither a sentence of French, nor of English. So Quine faced a challenge to make sense of ascriptions of reference and truth to sentences beyond one's 'home language'. In order to handle this, he appealed to translation. If we can appeal to the fact that the French phrase 'est un chien' translates into English as 'is a dog', then we could reason as follows:

- For predicate F and G where G translates F, F is true of something iff G is true of that thing.
- 'is a dog' is true of something iff that thing is a dog.
- 'is a dog' (in English) translates 'est un chien' (in French).
- Therefore: 'est un chien' is true of something iff that thing is a dog.

So the general Quinean strategy for handling content (truth and reference as applied to linguistic expressions) is to translate-and-deflate.

But what is this translation relation? You might think: x (in English) translates y (in French) iff x and y are synonymous. But Quine thought synonymy disreputable (remember: he thought we were not to talk about meaning). So what he proposed instead is a set of constraints on acceptable translation. Now, in everyday translation, we have a lot of data to work from—we can ask bilinguals, we have dictionaries to consult, and so forth. But Quine also asked about *radical* translation, where we had *no* antecedent knowledge or resources about the target language to draw upon, and so the whole task of constructing the interpretation had to proceed on an austere basis. For Quine, the austere basis was just the patterns of assent and dissent of speakers of the language to sentences in a variety of circumstances. And so the fundamental Quinean challenge was set up: what are the principles constraining translation, that are available even to a radical translator? Quine suggested things like: make sure to make 'observational sentences' true, and: attribute the same logic to the target that you yourself endorse.

Do such principles uniquely determine the translation? Quine suggested that the answer was no: various deviant translation schemes were in principle possible, and while they would be less convenient for us to use, there would be nothing *in principle* wrong with using them. Thus we get the characteristic Quinean principle of inscrutability of reference: there are acceptable translations, from the radical-translation perspective, where 'Willard' refers to a small furry creature on Alpha Centauri, not the eminent Harvard Professor.

Donald Davidson worked with interpretations, not translations.[4] And he was interested not just in isolated ascriptions of reference and truth to bits of language, but with what makes a systematic, compositional semantic theory for a target language (e.g. English, French) correct. Far more than Quine, he also took seriously the task of explaining when it was correct to say that an individual believed this or desired that. It's not so clear that Quine thought belief-and-desire talk worth saving, though conditioned behaviours and in particular inclinations of speakers to assent to or dissent from a given sentence are made to stand in for those attitudes on occasion. Just as Quine developed a theory of radical translation, Davidson developed a theory of radical interpretation—a set of constraints for fixing an interpretation applicable even in cases where we have no prior information about our interpretee's language or attitudes.

Davidson proposed that the radical interpreter start with access to a certain relation between the interpretee and sentences of their language—that S is 'held true' by Sally in thus-and-such circumstance, or that Sally 'prefers-true' S over T. In early versions of the theory, starting from patterns in the sentence Sally holds true, he extracts from this some 'target' T-sentences like: 'Grass is green' is true iff grass is green. One side of a target T-sentence will be a sentence held-true, the other a description of the circumstances under which they are held true. As Davidson presents it, the fundamental job is now to find a law-like theory that generates all these T-sentences. He argued this should take the form of an axiomatized 'T-theory', with axioms specifying the interpretation of each atomic part of a sentence in the language, from which the target biconditionals are will be derivable. So, our fix on the correctness of a T-theory is just that it generate the target T-sentences.

So what does it take for 'Willard' to refer to Willard, for Davidson? It is for the correct T-theory for English to contain this as an axiom. What is it for Sally to believe that Willard is a rabbit, or that grass is green? It is for her to hold-true sentences S, S*, sentences in a language the correct T-theory for

---

[4] The essays collected in Davidson (1984) lay out his theory of radical interpretation, though see also Davidson (1980), which sets up radical interpretation in a somewhat different but very clear way. My favourite secondary text is the detailed and dense discussions in Lepore and Ludwig (2005), and see Williams (2008a, 2013) for my own discussions of aspects of Davidson's approach.

which canonically generates the T-sentences: S is true iff Willard is a rabbit; S* is true iff grass is green.

David Lewis, like Davidson, worked with interpretations.[5] Like Davidson, he took the task to be to identify a correct interpretation, in the absence of prior information about what language the interpretees speak or about their attitudes—so this is still the project of radical interpretation. Unlike Quine and Davidson, Lewis proposed an account of the content of psychological attitudes that was independent of and prior to the content of public language. In order to get a fix on the attitudes, Lewis appeals to the interpretee's behaviour and sensory input, and says that the correct interpretation of Sally is the one that best rationalizes her behaviour and depicts her as responding rationally to her sensory evidence. In order to get a fix on language, Lewis built on this, appealing to shared attitudes in a linguistic community, which link sentences to particular contents—the contents of the beliefs conventionally associated with utterances of that sentence. These sentence-proposition pairings played for Lewis much the same role that target-T-sentences did for Davidson, with Lewis's highly developed theory of conventions replacing the primitive appeals to 'holding true S in context *c*' in Davidson. For Lewis, the correct semantic theory pertaining to a set of utterances is the one that best captures the conventionally established sentence-proposition pairs. There was no need to take the further step of reading off the subject's attitudes from the semantic theory, since the fix on the attitudes was established prior to the interpretation of language.

Quine, Davidson, and Lewis's treatments of representation are ancestors of my own. But the differences between them are as striking as the similarities. Quine's account is a long way from what I propose below. Not only is Quine's a 'wordfirst' story—going straight in at my third layer, theorizing the representational properties of public language—but it's a framework with a fundamentally different shape. For Quine, the starting point is a home

---

[5] Key texts for Lewis are (1969, 1974, 1975, 1983, 1984, 1992, and 1994a). A source of much confusion has been the way, in the very accessible (1984) paper, Lewis takes up some assumptions of his dialectical opponent, Putnam (1980). These include a focus on linguistic content to the exclusion of mental content, and a focus on assigning sentences the right truth values, rather than the right truth conditions. The role for metaphysically fundamental properties in responding to Putnam was clearly laid out in that paper, but in the context of a theory that is not Lewis's own. In the literature that follows, the Putnam-Lewis hybrid is often appealed to or evaluated—three examples are Weatherson (2003), Williams (2007), and Dunaway and McPherson (2016). In Williams (2015), I survey some of the issues in understanding the role of eligibility in Lewis's theory.

language—perhaps the language of the theorist, as cleaned up for the purposes of serious theorizing. And from that point it is a sentence-to-sentence relation of translation that is the key piece of ideology. Only indirectly do we get a fix on a language-world relation, as the product of translation to, and disquotation within, that home-language. This has some striking consequences. We have no way of making sense, for example, of a possible language that refers to things inexpressible in (untranslatable into) our home language. I take that to be a bug, not a feature. More generally, translation is an activity performed by real-life flesh-and-blood people, for Quine. We're not necessarily radical translators—but the project of para-phrase that Quine and the Quineans offer in presenting their favoured philosophical gloss on ordinary talk *is* just the business of proposing trans-lations into our favoured, regimented language. Radical translation, then, is just the limit of this everyday practice, an attempt to illuminate the con-straints by taking a familiar activity to its hypothetical limit.

Davidson is a more direct source of my project, since he makes the key move of theorizing interpretation, not translation. Further, he targets both the second and third layers of representation I presented above (belief and desire, and language), but in his theory, the representational properties of thought and talk are entirely interdependent. He embraced the surprising corollary that only language-using creatures can have beliefs or desires (bad news for the dolphins). It is not clear to me to what extent flesh-and-blood interpretation is Davidson's focus, as flesh-and-blood translation was for Quine. Sometimes, it sounds like radical interpretation was the limiting case of our actual practice of interpreting others—his remarks on the limits of intelligible variation in conceptual scheme, the role of 'learnability' as a motivation for the focus on T-theories, as well as his writings on prior and passing theories, suggest something like this. That would also give a ration-ale for some of the constraints he proposes, like the focus on compositional interpretations that are 'learnable', since flesh and blood interpreters obvi-ously will reach for such things. But at other times, it sounds like he is telling us, not about a possible process by which we may interpret others, but about what *correct interpretation* is—the nature of the truths about what people think and what their words mean, at which we are aiming.

With Davidson, and against Quine, Lewis's project is focused on correct interpretation. He is clear, moreover, that his theory is a theory of what makes an interpretation correct, not how flesh and blood creatures may go about the practical task of interpreting others. Indeed, the theory is an element of Lewis's overall metaphysical agenda to locate the world as it is presented to us (full of values, meaning, content, dispositions, laws and causes) within the austere Humean mosaic of microphysical events that Lewis posited as the fundamental description of reality. Against both Quine and Davidson, Lewis has a theory that makes room for non-linguistic or pre-linguistic creatures to have representations. That is a drastic extension of the scope of the theory, as small children and animals, collectives and artificial beings now potentially fall within the scope of the theory. This is a very good thing. Whereas Davidson took sentential attitudes (holding-true, preferring-true, in a context) as explanatory bedrock, Lewis uses his independent fix on mental content to characterize a community-wide 'holding true' relation, via conventions that link sentences to beliefs with determinate content. In all these matters, I regard Lewis as having made decisive advances.

The accounts I offer of the second and third layers of representation are, at heart, implementations of the Lewisian strategy. I inherit, then, many of his contrasts to Quine and Davidson. I finish this section, though, by identifying the three central ways that I will be diverging from Lewis.

First, Lewis thought he could run his account of belief and desire appealing to Sally's behaviour and sensation—non-representational properties of Sally which are supposed to rationalize and be rationalized by her beliefs and desires. I do not think this can work. It is this difference that creates the context for my treatment of the first layer of representation—perception and action.

Second, at the heart of Lewis's autonomous account of mental representation was a notion of 'rationalization', about which he said very little. His theory is schematic at this absolutely central point. So Lewis gives us not a single theory, but a space of theories, parameterized by the different possible accounts of rationalization. I'm going to crack this open, lay out a theory, and derive consequences. In particular, on my reading of the key notion, radical interpretation predicts very many interesting conditionals of the form: if our cognitive architecture is thus-and-so, then mental content will pattern in thus and such ways. This allows me to link up the foundational picture I advocate with work elsewhere in the theory of mind.

Third, while I adopt from Lewis the appeals to linguistic convention, I extend its reach. For example, I work with conventional relations to attitudes-types other than belief, allowing me to connect the foundational theory to contemporary work on expressivist semantics. And (in a move echoing Davidsonian themes). I will consider ways in which these conventions themselves have an influence on (some cases of) mental representation.

There is a final piece to put on the table, which will also be my bridge to the next set of topics. This is the complex picture that Stalnaker (1984, Ch. 1) calls the 'causal-pragmatic picture' of content. Stalnaker starts by considering a view on which

> to desire that P is to be disposed to act in ways that would tend to bring it about that P in a world in which one's beliefs, whatever they are, were true. To believe that P is to be disposed to act in ways that would tend to satisfy one's desires, whatever they are, in a world in which P (together with one's other beliefs) were true. (p.15)

This pair of claims goes around in a tight little circle, since belief content is appealed to in explaining the content of desires, and vice versa. The reaction of Davidson and Lewis is to pool beliefs and desires together into a single 'interpretation', and then try to pin down conditions under which this joint interpretation is correct. Stalnaker doesn't think that this will work.[6] He proposes a different view: the content of desires is characterized as above, but the content of belief is independently constrained by 'indication' relations:

> We believe that p just because we are in a state that, under optimal conditions, we are in only if P, and under optimal conditions, we are in that state because P, or because of something that entails P. (p.21)

Such states count as *beliefs*, for Stalnaker, because of their dispositional connections to action, but their content is fixed independently by the above, which he labels 'causal connections'. With their content nailed down, we can then appeal to this to give a more interpretationist take on the content of desire.

I do not think that Stalnaker's way of carving things up can be right. Suppose Sally believes that around eighty per cent of UK citizens think the government is entitled to keep people under video surveillance in public areas, because of what she reads in the British Social Attitudes survey. Tracing back the causal history of this belief, we find that this information

---

[6] His argument for this asks us to imagine a deviant interpretation of Mary on which all beliefs, desires and emotions that (in fact) are directed at her neighbour Fred, are reinterpreted as concerning Albert. Stalnaker notes, plausibly, that this deviant reinterpretation will satisfy the pair of conditions introduced above.

is in the survey due to results obtained through systematic sampling of the population. But it would be wrong-headed to say that these samples have the distribution of opinions they do *because of the overall distribution of attitudes in the population*. Even under optimal conditions, Sally can believes what she does on the basis of evidence that supports a generalization, without that general fact itself being part of what explains her belief. So prima facie, the envisaged story about how belief content is fixed looks way too strong (and Stalnaker concedes it is the merest sketch).

Still, I agree with Stalnaker that the best foundational story will combine interpretational elements and broadly naturalistic or causal elements. In the next section, I'll outline the relevant context for this second half of my account.[7]

Teleoinformational Ancestry

The other heritage on which I draw is work on informational/teleosemantic accounts of content. I'll again sketch the approaches of three key figures, to provide a context against which to explain the approach I will be taking.

Fred Dretske's account of content is based on a prior theory of what it is for a state of the world to carry information about another. His original (1981) characterization is the following: a state *s* carries the information that *p* when the existence of *s* raises the probability of *p* to 1. So, for example, badger tracks may carry the information that a badger passed by, if the existence of the tracks raises the probability of badger-visitation to 1. In Dretske's early work, in basic cases beliefs are to be states which during a 'learning phase' (or, if innate, as a result of evolution) became selectively sensitive to distal information about some object. To a first approximation, the information to which they became selectively sensitive is then content of the belief. In later developments of these ideas (1988), he claims that such beliefs are states whose *function* is carry information. If a state actually carries the information that *p*, then *p* must be the case (it raises the probability of *p* to 1)—but a state which has the function of carrying the information that *p* is compatible with *p* failing to obtain—it just has to be in

---

[7] Notice the appeal to 'optimal conditions' in Stalnaker's characterization of the content of belief—this is central to his analysis having any plausibility, since beliefs can be false, and a false belief will not be a state we are in because P. Compare the role, within the teleoinformational tradition (e.g. Millikan 1984), of a state which is in the *normal conditions for discharging its proper function*.

circumstances where it fails to fulfil its function. And so we have in Dretske the distinctive combination of information and function (teleology) that characterizes this tradition.

One very obvious difficulty for Dretske is that in any ordinary sense, the probability of tracks-without-badger will be non-zero (they could always be clever fakes, or the tracks of a maimed fox). So Dretske proposed to conditionalize the probability not just on the existence of s, but also on the obtaining of relevance conditions R. Maimed foxes and clever fakes aren't relevant possibilities, so the tracks can indeed carry badger-visitation information.[8]

A Dretskian, filling out this approach, needs to tell us about what kinds of *probability* are involved, what makes a possibility *relevant* and what it takes for a state to have a function to carry information (indeed, what it takes for a state to have any function whatsoever). But further, what has been given is really a story about a certain range of *atomic* beliefs, focused first and foremost on the content of de re perceptual beliefs, where the idea that a false belief is a *malfunctioning* belief is most plausible. More needs to be said to extend this to logically complex beliefs, and theoretical, mathematical, and moral beliefs. And the account does not promise any obvious generalization to the content of desire, or even language.[9]

Ruth Millikan (1984, 1989a, 1989b) builds a metaphysics of representation out of functions. For Millikan a 'proper function of x' is feature of x that is selected for or maintained in the evolution of an organism. There are then going to be some conditions (which may be statistically rare) in which this feature has beneficial effects for an organism—these beneficial effects being the reason why it was selected for. These are the 'normal conditions' for x's function. Proper functions and normal conditions are Millikan's key theoretical tools.

Millikan invites us to consider a system of states of two kinds: producers and consumers. In the cases relevant to us, think of the producers as being

---

[8] Dretske also conditionalizes on background knowledge, but envisages a hierarchical structure, so that a basic range of belief are related to information defined without the need to conditionalize on K; knowledge that is grounded in this fashion then becomes the K for further levels of information, etc.

[9] Dretske offers a quite different story about desire, appealing to the conditions which would cause a state's extinction. For another way of building on this set, see Stalnaker (1984), whose causal-pragmatic picture of the foundations of mental content involves a broadly Dretskian treatment of the content of belief, supplemented by an *interpretationist* treatment of the content of desire (the desires of an individual being whatever makes most rational sense, given what the individual's beliefs are, of what the individual brings about in action).

states of belief, and the consumers as anything within the cognitive system the performance of which is conditional on what the current belief-state is— for example, the formation of intention or action. The consumer states have various functions—say, to secure food, shelter, reproduction. Sometimes these efforts secure food, shelter or produce offspring, and so are to be beneficial to us as biological organisms. As with all functions, there are normal conditions under which the benefits (e.g. consuming some delicious berries) are realized—and these include not only e.g. that it's the right time of year for the berries to be edible, but that we've correctly identified what we put into our mouth as a berry. Thus: the normal conditions for producing these benefits include a certain correlation between producer states and states of the external world. It is this that Millikan identifies with representation. This is just one part of Millikan's intricate and challenging work on representation, which extends to accounts of the contents of desire and of public language, as well as states of belief.

Karen Neander was also one of the prime movers of the movement to put biological teleology at the heart of the metaphysics of representation. Millikan and Neander independently developed a historical-evolutionary account of what it takes for a state of a biological organism to have a function.[10] They each deploy this notion of 'normal, proper function' in analysing representation.

In her most recent monograph, Neander (2017) concentrates on the representational content of perceptual states. The scope of this account is far more focused than either Dretske or Millikan. The shape of the story she offers of representation in sensory-perceptual states echoes that of Dretske's: for s to represent that p is for it to have the function to carry the information that p—this contrasts with Millikan whose teleosemantic metaphysics gave no role for information. But Neander makes the metaphysics of functions bear much more of the load than Dretske did, and accordingly thins down the notion of 'carrying information' to the point where it is simply a causal relation. The details will be laid out later, but roughly, according to Neander a sensory-perceptual state s represents that p when it has the function to be produced by the fact that p.

Neander's teleoinformational account has an elegant simplicity. The simplicity is a direct result of its constrained scope, since it looks unpromising for

---

[10] Neander has been a pioneer in this field, with her dissertation work on an etiological theory of functions circulating since the early 1980s, before appearing as her (1991b). See also her (1991a, 1995, and 2004).

any representational states except those most closely connected to states of the world. Beliefs with universal content are again a nice example of this (compare the discussion of Stalnaker above), and in Neander's formulation examples are even easier to come by: the causes of the belief that *the sun will rise tomorrow* do not include tomorrow's sunrise. These are hardly malfunctioning belief systems, and so it cannot be plausibly said that such beliefs have the function to be caused by the state of affairs described by its content. If one was targeting a teleoinformational theory of belief content in general, as with Millikan and (in principle) Dretske, then this would be a severe problem, and Millikan and Dretske's more complex theories contain resources in anticipation of the generalization. The trade-off is nicely illustrated by Dretskian information. On the one hand, a state of the head could in principle carry information about the future or about universal generalizations, even those do not figure among its causes. On the other hand, this additional power is bought at the cost of appeal to probabilities and a distinction among relevant and irrelevant possibilities—and that loads up his account with new commitments, each of which is a new vulnerability.

My account of the first layer of intentionality—the intentionality of perception and intention—is teleoinformational. Unlike Dretske and Millikan, I do not have the ambition to extend this style of account to ground the content of beliefs in general, still less desires and public language—as we have seen, I offer an interpretationist account of the second and third layers of representation. Neander's more bottom-up approach suits my needs perfectly—I need a simple, robust, and focused teleoinformational theory, not one adapted for generalization.

My account of perceptual representation is directly borrowed from Neander. I extend the scope of the account beyond perception to include action-guiding states as well. Unlike others in this tradition, I need to show how to shape these representational raw materials into the specific facts about perception and intention that are required by my interpretationist story about second-layer representation (belief and desire).

The teleosemantic tradition is shaped by a methodological assumption from which I want to distance myself. Dretske, Millikan, and Neander all think that a successful metaphysics of representation would be a naturalistic one, grounding representational facts in the kind of properties that feature in natural science. My project here is to offer a metaphysics that grounds representational facts in the non-representational world. Grounding representational facts in a non-representational and naturalistic world is compatible with this aim. But I do not presume from the start that all the resources we will need are to be found in the natural sciences.

Metaphysics, Not Conceptual Analysis

My target is to answer questions about the nature of representation, not to chart the contours of our concept of representation. Consider the following, schematic in P, B, and E:

- Sally perceives that there is a red square in front of her iff P(Sally, the event of there being a red square in front of Sally).
- Sally believes that the temperature is rising iff B(Sally, the proposition that the temperature is rising).
- 'Socrates was Greek' expresses that Socrates was Greek in Sally's language iff E('Socrates was Greek', Sally, the proposition that Socrates was Greek).

My aim in what follows is to develop a way of filling in such biconditionals, so that *what it is* for the facts mentioned in the left-hand side to obtain is for the facts on the right-hand-side of to obtain. But the biconditionals that result need not be analytic or conceptual truths, and so it will be possible to doubt their truth without conceptual confusion. My project is thus distinct, for example, from the task that Gibbard (2012) sets himself, which is explicitly an attempt to theorize the *concept* of representation.[11] In this I'm in agreement with those teleosemanticists who emphasize that they aim for theoretical identifications, not conceptual analyses.[12] Lewis famously

---

[11] Gibbard's project is driven by the thesis that truths about belief and linguistic meaning analytically entail normative claims concerning the conditions under which it is appropriate to form beliefs or utter/accept sentences. Representation, for Gibbard, is a 'normative concept'. And as is familiar from work in metaethics in the past century (including Gibbard's own), naturalistic or descriptive *conceptual* analyses of *normative* concepts are problematic. This is how Gibbard reads the 'normativity challenge' arising from Kripke's (1982) take on Wittgenstein on rule-following. I do not engage with Kripke's normativity challenge below, because it does not arise for the metaphysical rather than conceptual analysis of representation. (The *underdetermination* challenges arising from that same work, however, matter to me.) An excellent entry point to the vast literature on normativity and meaning is Hattigiandi (2007).

[12] See Millikan (1989b), but contrast Neander (1991a). Notice that it would be a further step to relativize the theoretical identification to perceptual or belief content *in particular creatures*. Without this, and assuming theoretical identifications are committed to the biconditionals holding of necessity, such identifications are still susceptible to counterexamples that involve merely possible creatures.

offered 'analytic' reductions of many mental concepts, as well as grounding (species-relative) theoretical identifications. I'm not sure whether he thought his theory of content was an analytic reduction, and so am not certain whether my embrace of the opposing conception marks a point at which he and I diverge.

While a conceptual analysis is by nature non-revisionary, a metaphysical story about representation might be revisionary or non-revisionary of pre-theoretic opinion. But even if we're up for revisionism in principle, it is a perfectly good objection to a theory of any kind (including a metaphysical one) that it entails some q, where q is patently false. In the first chapter, for example, I'll be pointing out that one metaphysics of representation entails that it is impossible for us so much as to form determinate beliefs about the world outside a local space-time-bubble that surrounds us—and so impossible, roughly, for you to determinately believe that objects persist unperceived. This strikes me as an absurd result, and so I cry foul, and revise the theory. My reason is: it is possible for me to believe that this table in front of me continues to exist unperceived. The theory under discussion entails something obviously false, so the theory is false.

Inevitably, such judgements of obvious falsity rely on our prior opinion about the matter in question (prior, but not necessarily pre-theoretic). So one reaction of a theorist to my cry of reductio can be to push ahead with the unrevised theory and instruct me to *revise* my prior opinion. In both the interpretationist and teleoinformational traditions, there are famous instances of this. Quine and Davidson as I read them say that there is no fact of the matter concerning whether 'Willard' refers to a Harvard professor or a small furry creature on Alpha Centauri. Neander and Millikan say that a perfect atom-by-atom duplicate of a human being arising from a quantum fluctuation in a swamp rather than from evolutionary history would not perceive or believe anything. Such localized revisionism, though, is possible only against the backdrop of a lot of pre-theoretic opinion held fixed. One doesn't do a good job in keeping Neurath's boat afloat if one tries to replace the planks all at once. So I need no special rationale, nor the backing of a mysterious faculty of intuition establishing dialectical fixed points, when I let prior opinion on representation be my guide most of the time. The possibility of a dialectical opponent 'biting a bullet' is so ubiquitous as to be banal.

My project is the nature of representation, not the nature of *attributions* of representation. A real flesh-and-blood interpreter might have a certain explanatory project (predicting what a certain biological system might do, capturing high-level generalizations about its operation) and might find certain attributing representational states helpful in the service of that project. We might call this 'adopting the intentional stance'.[13] A focus on the conditions under which we (flesh and blood theorists) attribute representations allows for distinctive pragmatic element. There may be a good case to be made, for certain sophisticated systems, that a real-life interpreter should start with the null hypothesis that the target has the same beliefs or belief-formation tendencies that they themselves possess, and diverge from this only as the evidence demands.

Daniel Dennett is for many the paradigm 'interpretationist', so it's important to appreciate that our projects have a different subject-matter. Dennett, I think, is concerned with representation-attribution.[14] Dennett's appeal to stances, explanatory projects, and projections of our own attitudes make perfect sense if construed as concerning the cash value of the claims made by flesh and blood interpreters. But all this is very different if one tried to squeeze them into the metaphysical project that I am targeting. Read as a piece of metaphysics, an appeal to an interpreter's projects and beliefs would be bizarre. Truths about each individual's beliefs would obtain only relative to another's perspective, and those perspectives would be constituted in part by the others' attitudes, generating a morass of circularities. Read as intended, the account makes sense, but does not speak directly to the questions of the nature of representation.[15] As Lewis (1974: 333–4) put it:

[13] The term is Daniel Dennett's. See the essays collected in his (1978) and (1987).

[14] Certainly this is the way Dennett often writes, and the way he is often understood. For the latter, see for example, Tollefsen (2015) who, in co-opting Dennett's framework for the purposes of theorizing about group agents, emphasizes the role of conceptual and attributional questions.

[15] Daniel Elstein has persuaded me that one interesting version of radical interpretation is an expressivist or quasi-realist strategy. Expressivists characteristically start not by tackling the basic propositions in a target area (e.g. [Harry ought not to be late again]) but instead concentrate on what adopting attitudes to those propositions amounts to (viz. [Sally believes that Harry ought not be late again]). Upon analysis, it is claimed that the latter are more fundamentally attitudes other than belief, e.g. [Sally desires* that Harry not be late], for some desire-like attitude, desire*. And on this proposed analysis, the problematic terminology has disappeared from the content. What appeared to be normative beliefs are really some other attitudes to mundane non-normative content. Just so, one might leverage the Dennett-style comments on the practices of interpretation to offer an illuminating analysis of what 'Sally believes that Harry believes that grass is green' amounts to—perhaps this is that Sally finds it useful to adopt the intentional stance towards Harry and, for the purposes of predicting his behaviour, works with an interpretation of him which includes a probability measure that maps the proposition [that grass is green] to a high number. The latter description forswears attributing attitudes directly to Harry, or any appeal to the correct interpretation, in favour of characterizing those interpretations that are useful for Sally for a certain purpose. Now, even if correct, it is not clear that this strategy allows us to evade the question of what properties/relations 'ought' or 'believes' picks out. Expressivists often present their work as conceptual analysis, and for instance in the case of the 'moral ought', they take their analysis to be compatible with e.g. utilitarianism being the true (and non-normatively formulated) description

the question is not how we determine the facts, but how the facts determine the facts.

The Role of Empirical Data in This Project

The reader will find few appeals to empirical results in cognitive science, biology, psychology, or linguistics in the pages to follow. Though the teleoinformational tradition—and the work of Neander that I borrow—does draw upon this, I won't be engaging with that aspect of the data. That is not because I think these things are philosophically irrelevant; on another day, for another project, I think it entirely appropriate to dive into the details. I think, for example, that it is fascinating to consider how the Neander-style teleoinformational account of content that I endorse can be applied or adapted to recent work in AI and cognitive science on the 'predictive mind' model of perception. But there are trade-offs in each research project, and by suppressing certain questions, one focuses more intently on others. The question I set myself here is a 'how possible' one. How is it possible for facts about philosophically central sorts of representation to arise in a fundamentally non-representational world? I offer an account of one way that it could happen. That account will work for creatures with a certain kind of belief/desire psychology, one that relates in the ways I will go on to describe to perception, action, and language. As we will see, articulating this in adequate detail already generates a landscape that I find fascinating to explore.

Let's suppose you agree that my project has been successful on its own terms. Then there will be a further question—is this the way it works in us flesh and blood human beings? Is it the way it works in frogs? Does it go for the hyperintelligent aliens inhabiting some distant planet? It could turn out that the model I worked with is a good description of some or all such cases, but more likely, it will need tailoring. (So I here again distance myself from the 'analytic' version of a project like mine, where the models I construct in

---

of the property the concept picks out. So in the case we are concerned with, the demand to say what the representation relation *is* does not go away, even if the strategy Elstein suggests was viable. And, to emphasize again, this is not the strategy that I am pursuing. Dennett has often emphasized a kind of 'soft realism' in his approach: it allows for the *objectivity* of belief and desire attributions (they are 'real patterns' to be discovered, albeit for creatures with the right kind of idiosyncratic interests). This does not rule out the expressivist reading of his project, any more than the objectivity of morality is a problem for a Hare-style expressivist about morality.

the armchair have special authority because they are laying out what is implicit in the very concept of belief/desire/representation, etc.). It would be nice if the tailoring proved to be modest, involving 'more of the same', for example, further kinds of first-layer teleoinformational states, a more complex interpretation with more subtly interrelated attitude types in the second layer, and refinements at the third layer to suit the latest developments in linguistic semantics. Perhaps the surgery will need to be more radical. So be it! Theorists need to speculate to accumulate, and I am happy with the theoretical gamble involved in the how-possible project in which I am engaged.

There is a place in my project where some more specific and contingent assumptions become important. Though the second-layer story about belief and desire is compatible with many different assumptions about the underlying cognitive architecture of the states which carry this kind of content, we get much more specific predictions about certain species of belief/desire (singular thought, general thought, normative thought, etc.) when we add in specific assumptions. So at various points I'll be assuming that beliefs and desires have vehicles with language-like 'conceptual' structure, which enter into inferential relations. Together with the general radical interpretation framework, this allows me to derive results about what the posited 'concepts' pick out. What I'm aiming to establish in these sections are conditionals: that if such-and-such a cognitive architecture is present, then so-and-so content will be assigned. Those conditionals are of interest to those who have independent arguments for the cognitive architecture in question, for they can perform modus ponens and derive the results. Those initially neutral on the architecture but sympathetic to the conclusions about content derived, on the other hand, can view this as indirect support for the cognitive architecture in question—an explanatory/predictive success.

The Scope of the Project

My three layers leave much unsaid. You won't find a discussion either of photographs nor memories in what follows, but memories and photographs represent the world. Along with memories, there are many other mental states that are not discussed—among them affective intentional states like fearing the blob or hoping for a win, and objectual states like admiring Nelson or attending to a laser-pointer. Some of these states may be analysed into combinations of the representational states I cover, plus other material. Some of them could be given their own grounding using the resources herein deployed (it's natural to try out a teleoinformational account for memories as a widening of the first layer, and to try covering additional intentional attitudes by adding extra dimensions to the interpretations grounded at the second layer). But it may be that new ideas are needed.

The human-made world is replete with further representations beyond the words and sentences that are my focus. There are non-verbal signals where a version of my favoured approach to sentences—conventional expression of thoughts—has long been a popular option. Other artefacts may be better treated by an extension of the teleoinformational approach: photographs, prima facie, seem more informational and less conventional. Within linguistic representation alone, there are plenty more challenges to explore. Consider stretches of dialogue, which surely have representational properties whose relation to the representational properties of the words and sentences used is complex (consider the mechanisms by which anaphor is fixed, or co-indexing of variables). Or consider novels and stories: what is represented to be the case by a written work of fiction surely relates in some way to what its sentences say, but the generation of fictional truths is a complex business that is rightly a topic of study in its own right. And who's to say what the best story would be about the representational content of a (more or less abstract) painting? But again and again, in thinking through such cases it is natural to draw on a toolkit of experience, intention, belief, desire, and language.[16] So I think of my chosen topics as the essential core. If we can get the nature of these kinds of representation right, that will be a platform for generalization and reduction, and a necessary foil for any autonomous treatment of the metaphysics of other sorts of representational phenomena.

---

[16] On conventional signals, see Lewis (1969). On information and photographs, see Cohen and Meskin (2006). On dialogue-level semantic interpretation, see Heim (1982). On truth in fiction, see Lewis (1978), and Walton (1990).

Acknowledgements

The research leading to these results has received funding from the European Research Council under the European Union's Seventh Framework Programme (FP/2007-2013)/ERC Grant Agreement n. 312938. I would like to thank the funders, as well as my school and faculty at the University of Leeds, for their support.

I owe a debt to the *Nature of Representation* research team who over the years have worked with me and discussed these issues: Thomas Brouwer, Jennifer Carr, Laura Crosilla, Ed Elliott, Daniel Elstein, Will Gamester, Rachel Goodman, Simon Hewitt, Gail Leckie, and Nick Tasker. Conversations with Andy McGonigal and Adam Pautz were also particularly significant in determining where to take this project. While I was writing the first draft, Thomas Brouwer, Paolo Santorio and Jack Woods gave me detailed and valuable feedback in real time, which had a big influence on how I put it together. Two referees for Oxford University Press wrote insightful and helpful reports that shaped the final version. Thomas Brouwer has repeatedly provided line-by-line comments which improved both the substance and the presentation of the book. Thanks to Josh Dever and Brian Weatherson for their commentary on two key chapters during the 2018 metasemantics workshop in Tokyo. Much of the material in this book has been presented at conferences and colloquia in various forms over the last five years, and I haven't missed a chance to talk it over with friends and visitors. Philosophy is best when it's shared, and I look forward to thanking each of you in person.

To everyone who helped me think about thinking and talk about talking: thank you. Elizabeth Barnes, Ross Cameron, and Jason Turner, who did all that and more: thank you. To my family, to the fell runners of the north of England, and to Paula: thank you.

Contents

Contents

Introduction

A Manifesto and a Plan

0.1 A Manifesto

The experience of running downhill. The desire to drink coffee in the morning. The belief that everything is grounded in the physical. The intention that guides your hand as you reach out to grasp the door handle. The words 'all emeralds are green'.

All these phenomena have the spooky feature of 'aboutness'. The words are a blast of sound localized in a particular place and time. But they represent a general fact about the universe we inhabit, and their truth or falsity depends on how the world is in the farthest reaches of the universe. A desire itself (let's assume) is a certain configuration of your brain, but it represents a certain possible state of the world that you then set about bringing into being. We have one thing (states of our brain, other biological systems, artefacts) representing others (hills, coffee, emeralds).

What is representation? How do the more primitive aspects of our world come together to generate it? How do these different kinds of representation relate to one another? These are the questions to which I will present answers. In doing so, I am engaged in metaphysics: seeking to identify the metaphysical foundations for a particularly striking kind of fact, and articulate how those facts are grounded in that basis.

The story I tell is in three parts:

(1) The most primitive layer of representation is the 'aboutness' of sensation/perception and intention/action, which are the two most basic modes in which an individual and the world interact. This layer of representation consists in states of our head which, if functioning properly, are produced by particular aspects of our environment (perception) or bring about changes in our environment (action/intention). It is to be analysed, say I, into a combination of teleology ('the function of x is to...') and causation ('x is produced by y/y

The Metaphysics of Representation. J. Robert G. Williams, Oxford University Press (2019).
© J. Robert G. Williams.
DOI: 10.1093/oso/9780198850205.001.0001

brings about x'). We can understand how this kind of representation can exist in a fundamentally physical world so long as we have an independent, illuminating grip on functions and causation.[1]

(2) The next layer of representation is the 'aboutness' of (degrees of) belief and desire. Where the representational content of perception and action was tightly bound to visible or manipulable features of the immediate environment, beliefs and desires can represent anything (certainly anything you can think of!). This sort of representation consists in states of our head which evolve in response to incoming information from perceptual states, and which combine to produce states of intention and, ultimately, bodily action. I say: what it is for Sally to believe or desire is for the correct interpretation of her to attribute those beliefs/ desires to her. In spelling out what it takes for a belief/desire interpretation to be correct, I rely on the layered structure. The correct interpretation of an agent, say I, is the one which makes their action-guiding states, given their perceptual evidence, most reasonable.

(3) The final layer of representation I cover is the 'aboutness' of words and sentences. Here I step outside the head to consider the representational features of a very special class of human creations: linguistic artefacts. Here we find representational facts such as: the name 'Sally' refers to a certain person, 'running' denotes a particular feature things may have, and when combined, 'Sally is running' is true only if the world is a certain way. Sentences express contentful attitudes, and by appealing to this, we can give an illuminating account of the conditions under which a compositional interpretation of a public language like English is correct, and so ground facts about the semantic content of the words we use. Further, the way in which sentences express beliefs, desires, etc. can itself be reduced to facts about community-wide patterns of attitudes, allowing us to characterize the third layer of representation by means of the second layer.

0.2 A Plan

Chapter 1

This chapter sets out the metaphysics of the mental content of belief and desire that is the focus of the first five chapters of the book: Radical

---

[1] I'll be assuming that the 'aboutness' of perception includes coarse-grained *propositional* content.

Interpretation. This says that the correct interpretation of an agent is that which best rationalizes the agent's actions given their evidence. Radical Interpretation therefore combines two ingredients to ground mental content: a set of base facts involving an agent's action and evidence, and a relation of rationalization. The chapter makes progress on the second of these, with the 'bubble puzzle' being used to argue that the relation of rationalized involved must be a substantive one. The best rationalizing interpretation of an agent will make that agent as morally and epistemically good as possible.

Chapter 2

This chapter is one of three that draws out the consequences of Radical Interpretation for how concepts represent the world. The focus in this chapter is on logical concepts: conjunction, negation and universal generalization. This connects Radical Interpretation as a foundational theory of mental content to *inferentialism*, where commitment to certain kinds of rules of inference or coherence are cited to explain why our connectives mean what they do. Radical Interpretation, together with auxiliary assumptions about cognitive architecture and epistemology, predicts these patterns. One of the upshots is an explanation of how quantification over absolutely everything is possible, rebutting long-standing underdetermination puzzles.

Chapter 3

This chapter continues to draw out the consequences of Radical Interpretation for how concepts represent the world. A claim associated with David Lewis is that metaphysically fundamental properties are 'reference magnets'—that if usage is equipoised between two candidate referents, the one that is 'closer to the metaphysical fundamentals' is the one that gets to be the referent. This chapter examines how such a thesis might arise as a *prediction* of Radical Interpretation. It looks to epistemology of inference to the best explanation to make a connection between concepts used in explanations and naturalness.

Chapter 4

This chapter continues to draw out the consequences of Radical Interpretation for how concepts represent the world. This chapter introduces a famous puzzle about the normative concept *wrongness*. It appears to have a distinctive referential stability: we can be completely mistaken in what we think makes an act morally right or wrong, but somehow we remain locked onto the moral subject matter. This chapter derives this stability as a prediction of Radical Interpretation.

Chapter 5

This chapter evaluates whether the Radical Interpretation as it has been developed so far can be a reductive foundational metaphysics of mental representation. One can be worried about this from two angles: first, whether it really qualifies as foundational metaphysics; second, whether what it targets is the whole of mental representation. Both challenges are addressed. Among other things, it is shown how the metaphysics of *reference and truth conditions* of the previous chapters can be extended to a metaphysics of *sense*.

Chapter 6

This chapter is one of three that sets out a metaphysics of linguistic representation. In this chapter the basic features of the approach are laid out. The base facts for linguistic representation are conventional associations between sentences and propositions (the propositions being the contents of beliefs conventionally expressed by the sentences). The correct linguistic interpretation is then selected as the best theory of this data. The chapter considers two preliminary objections to the approach: an alleged need for a prior and independent identification of words and language-using population, and an inability to handle declarative sentences that fail to express beliefs. Both charges are rebutted.

Chapter 7

This chapter continues the development of a metaphysics of linguistic representation. This chapter examines a key ingredient: linguistic convention. The focus is on a tension between the apparently individualistic character of the metaphysics of mental representation given by Radical

Interpretation, and the presupposition of shared mental content apparently presupposed by appeals to linguistic convention. By considering the way in which beliefs about others' beliefs influence the metaphysics of mental content, the tension is resolved.

Chapter 8

This chapter continues the development of a metaphysics of linguistic representation. This chapter focuses on the way that correct linguistic interpretation is selected. The correct interpretation is the best theory of the linguistic conventions, and the best theory optimizes simplicity (elegance) and fit with the data. It is argued that elegance should be understood relative to the language-users' pooled conceptual repertoire, and the combined theory of representation in language and thought is wielded to resolve indeterminacy puzzles.

Chapter 9

The metaphysics of linguistic representation is built atop mental representation, and the metaphysics of mental representation is built atop facts about how an agent acts and what they experience. This chapter turns to the last, foundational elements of this account. This chapter argues that facts about how an agent acts and experiences are themselves representational; trying to do things in terms of raw sensation or behaviour won't work. Within a broadly Bayesian account of the rationalization of belief-change and choice, it identifies some representational facts that would do the job.

Chapter 10

This chapter outlines a metaphysics of the representational content of action and perception. This is built on a teleoinformational account of perceptual content borrowed from Neander, which is here generalized to give an account of the content of action-guiding states. The key ingredient of such stories is an account of biological function, and this chapter lays out and responds to a central challenge to such approaches.

PART I

RADICAL INTERPRETATION

My account of the metaphysics of representation has three layers, and I start in the middle. In the next five chapters, I present an account of Radical Interpretation, and the way that it transforms primordial representational facts about what agents perceive and how they act, into representational facts about what they believe and desire.

The Metaphysics of Representation. J. Robert G. Williams, Oxford University Press (2019).
© J. Robert G. Williams.
DOI: 10.1093/oso/9780198850205.001.0001

1

Radical Interpretation as a Metaphysics of Mental Content

1.1 The Metaphysics of Mental Representation Must Say What Makes an Interpretation Correct

Interpretations of persons—functions that map points in the history of that person ('person stages') to a set of beliefs and desires—are ten a penny. There is, for example, one abstract interpretation that maps you-right-now inter alia to a belief that the Earth is run by lizard people. Another attributes to you an overwhelming desire to count the grains of sand in the Sahara. Most of these interpretations bear no relation to what you in fact believe or desire, and make no sense of what you say and do. They are, after all, just pieces of mathematical machinery.

Somewhere among this space of abstract interpretations, however, for each of us there is one that gets things right—there is one which maps you right now to those beliefs and desires that you do in fact possess, for example. The following is obviously true:

- the correct interpretation of x maps x-at-t to a belief that p iff x believes p at t

The same goes, *mutatis mutandis*, for representational attitudes of other types (degrees of belief, desires, planning states etc.). The boring way to understand this is to presuppose that we have a grip on belief and desire, and to take such biconditionals to define what it is for an interpretation to be correct, with direction of explanation flowing from right to left. By contrast, the direction of explanation on my account flows from left to right. We promise an illuminating, independent account of correctness, and then use these same biconditionals to explain what it is for a person to believe, desire, plan, etc.

The Metaphysics of Representation. J. Robert G. Williams, Oxford University Press (2019).
© J. Robert G. Williams.
DOI: 10.1093/oso/9780198850205.001.0001

Reframing the metaphysical questions as concerning the correctness of abstract interpretations begs no questions. The following pair of (very schematic) accounts which illustrate two very different theories that can be presented in this framework:

- The correct interpretation of an agent x is that one which maps x at t to a set of beliefs and desires that best accounts for x's dispositions to act at t, given courses of experience x undergoes up to t.
- The correct interpretation of an agent x is that one which maps an inner state s of x to a belief that p iff the state's function within x's cognitive system is to carry the information that p, for the purposes of controlling behaviour.

Note the differences between these two accounts:

(a) The first is compatible with the space of abstract interpretations mapping whole time-slices of agents to beliefs/desires. The second has to work with interpretations that map individual states of a person to beliefs (some other clauses would be needed if we wanted to ground desire-content too).

(b) In the first, the basis of correct interpretation includes dispositions to act and courses of experience undergone. (It also includes, implicitly, the reidentification of the agent over time and across counterfactual scenarios.) In the second, the basis are facts about the teleology of components of cognitive systems, and specifically, information-carrying functions.

(c) In the first, as well as this base facts about action and experience, there is an extra story about how the correct interpretation is selected by this basis (it's the one that 'best accounts for' those base facts). In the second part of the story, all the work is done by the 'iff'.

Generalizing from these cases, I say that a metaphysics of mental representation (at the second, belief-and-desire layer) will give a story in two parts. In the first part, which we may call *Framing*, it gives further details about a relevant space of abstract interpretations. Here we need to answer questions such as the following:

- What kinds of things get interpreted? That is, what is the domain of the functions that are the abstract interpretations?

- What is ascribed by an interpretation? That is, what is the co-domain of the functions that are the abstract interpretations?

With the domain and co-domain spelled out, the space of abstract interpretations can be defined as the set of arbitrary mappings from one to the other.

The second part of the story, which we may call *Correctness*, is where we give an illuminating account of what the world has to be like for one of these abstract interpretations to be the correct interpretation of an individual. In giving this account, one will of course cite certain facts about the individual—this could be almost anything, in principle, from their inner cognitive processing, to their causal relations to the surrounding relation, to features of the species to which they belong, to facts about what they perceive or how they choose to behave. The facts cited are what I'll call the *basis* for correct interpretation. The account of how those facts select an interpretation I'll call the *selectional story*.

The framing I myself favour is state-based. To a first approximation, you can take this to be the kind of 'language of thought' model of the vehicles of mental representation for which Fodor has long argued. Thus: agents are in certain brain states, which play distinctive functional roles. On the basis of those functional roles, they are classified by type. I assume that agents have both 'flat-out' beliefs and degrees of belief; they have degrees of desire, and 'flat-out' future-directed intentions.[1] Beyond this, I often work with the further hypothesis that these states have language-like structure, being built out of word-like atomic concepts. An interpretation will map these states onto (truth conditional) propositional content, in virtue of mapping the atomic concepts onto contents, and containing rules for fixing the content of complex concepts and whole states out of the contents of their parts. Overall, then, we can think of interpretations associating a pair of an attitude-type and structured attitude-content to each relevant brain state of the subject at each time.[2] It is a nice question about whether we use other representational

---

[1] Here I am thinking of future directed intentions or planning states as described in (Bratman 1987).

[2] For those wishing for a specific model of the structured content to work with: take a labelled parse-tree isomorphic to the syntactic structure of the sentence-like vehicle of thought, with the nodes labelled with the content assigned by the interpretation to the part of the vehicle corresponding to that node (compare Lewis 'General Semantics'). For the most part, I'll work with the assumption that assigning referents for the parts will suffice to determine truth conditions for the whole, so the nodes are labelled e.g. with objects (for singular concepts)

formats instead or in addition, such as map-like structures,[3] but I won't consider the issue further, but simply flag up my assumptions as and where they become important. Once you've chosen a framing, you need to check whether the original formulation of the project needs refinement to fit with the framing choices. Here's an appropriate revised version for mine:

- the correct interpretation of x maps brain-state s of x-at-t to the pair <belief, p> iff x has a belief at t with the structured propositional content p.[4]

This framing differs markedly from, and is much more committal than, the one that Lewis favoured. He worked with *stage-based* interpretations, where the domain of interpretation consists of temporal stages of agents (e.g. Sally at 2pm on Tuesday), and the co-domain consists of an overall attribution of beliefs and of desires (e.g. a probability-utility pair). I think this account falls prey to a famous old objection (Block 1978) which I relitigate in a coda to this chapter. For the rest of this chapter, this shouldn't make a difference, so I set the issue aside. There is plenty of room for further discussion about the details of the framing. Might some states encode comparative confidence in propositions, rather than flat-out degrees of belief? Do we need flat-out-beliefs and plans in addition to degrees of belief and desire, or can either be reduced to the other?[5] Does an interpretation need to specify risk attitudes, as well as beliefs and desires, in order to rationalize behaviour?[6] These are excellent questions, but I want a tractable model to work with, and so I stick to the four listed.

---

and properties (for general concepts) and the top node is labelled with a function from possible worlds to truth values.

[3] See Camp 2007 on map-like representation.

[4] Why not stick with the simpler 'x believes-at-t that p'? In order to be syntactically well-formed, p should be used in sentence-position throughout, so the proposal would be that the correct interpretation of x maps brain-state s of x-at-t to the pair <belief, the proposition that p> iff x believes-at-t that p. The most important worry to have here is over the fineness of grain. I hold both the following: the belief that Hesperus is shiny and the belief that Phosphorus is shiny are distinct; the beliefs have the same structured propositional content. So construed, the formulation in this footnote won't fly, but the one in the text will. See chapter 5 for much relevant discussion.

[5] Some of my personal favourites from the belief vs. degrees of belief debate include Bratman (1992), Christensen (2004), Clarke (2013), Greco (2015), Ross and Schroeder (2014), and Holton (forthcoming).

[6] Buchak (2013) defends a tripartite rational psychology of probabilities, utilities, and risk-attitudes.

Turning to Correctness, the metaphysics of mental representation I am exploring is a version of Radical Interpretation, and a slight elaboration of the first option introduced above:

- The correct interpretation of an agent x is that one which best rationalizes x's dispositions to act in the light of the courses of experience x may undergo.

The basis thus includes actual and counterfactual experiences and dispositions to act, and the selectional story appeals to better and worse rationalizations. This will be refined later, with further information on rationalization in this chapter, hypotheses about structured states playing a large role in the next few chapters, and more detail about the basis being given in the chapters on source intentionality. But equally significant are the things it does not contain. For example, there's no relativization to any actual or ideal interpreter or 'interpretative stance'. Insofar as it's an objective (non-stance-relative) matter how an agent acts and what they experience, and an objective matter what rationalizes what to what degree, then it'll be an objective matter what the correct interpretation is, and so an objective matter what the agent believes and desires.

My favoured story about correctness, as stated, does not reduce the representational facts about belief/desire to purely physicalistic, naturalistic or even non-representational facts. The fact that I perceive the presence of a red ball, or the fact that your limbs moving along a certain trajectory counts as you hailing a taxi, are themselves representational facts. Whether or not a cluster of beliefs and desires rationalizes certain choices, in a certain context, is prima facie a normative fact, and whether normative facts are physicalistic or naturalistic is very much *sub judice*. It is not something I will take a stand on here. I offer it as an account of how one kind of intentionality—that of perception and action—gets transformed, via normative truths, into the intentionality of belief and desire. As indicated in the introduction, I favour supplementing Radical Interpretation with a naturalistic account of the intentionality of experience and action, and together the two stories reduce the representational to the non-representational. But Radical Interpretation as presented here need not be yoked to that broader project. One might, as Adam Pautz (2013) has advocated, combine this story of the transformation of perceptual and agential content into belief/desire content with the claim that conscious experience is primitively intentional.

The story about the metaphysics of representation just given defines a theoretical agenda. This is to get clear on each of these three elements: experience, action, and rationalization. It is rationalization that will be our primary focus in the rest of this chapter.

1.2 Radical Interpretation Comes in Two Varieties: Structural and Substantive

Radical Interpretation tells us: the correct interpretation of an individual is one which best rationalizes their dispositions to act in the light of the courses of experience they undergo. But what is it for an interpretation to rationalize such things? There are thinner and thicker ways of understanding the phrase 'rationalization', and this generates two very different versions of Radical Interpretation.

The first option is to appeal to *structural* rationality. A structurally rational agent is one whose mental states are patterned in the right way.[7] For example, a paradigm constraint of structural rationality is formal consistency of belief. One violates this if one simultaneously believes that grass is green and believes that it is not green. Another paradigm of structural rationality is means-end coherence between beliefs/desires/actions. One violates that if one desires above all to get smarties, believes the only way in one's power to get smarties is to open the cupboard, yet fails to open the cupboard.

Such rational constraints are 'structural' in that they're insensitive to the specific contents of attitudes involved. It's not anything to do with grass or greenness that makes it problematic to believe that grass is green and that grass is not green. Schematically, for any p, it's problematic to believe that p and that not-p. Likewise for the means-end constraint. Schematically, for any proposition q and act A, it's problematic to desire (above all) to bring about q, believe that the only way in one's power to bring about q is to A, and yet fail to A. Structural rational constraints are characteristically topic-neutral, relying only on very abstract and formal specifications of the

---

[7] My own thinking is shaped by the distinctions made in the literature about the normativity of (structural) rationality, as in e.g. Kolodny (2005). It might help to think of structural rationality as those constraints where Kolodny's accusation that they amount to a mere 'fetish for mental neatness' makes sense, whether or not it is ultimately cogent.

relations between attitudes/acts/experiences, for example, their logical forms (e.g. that the content of one belief is the negation of another).[8]

Structural rationality constraints lend themselves to formal modelling. For a concrete example of this consider (a minimal version of) Bayesianism.[9] The Bayesian starts from a distinctive take on the space of abstract interpretations. The version I'll consider takes interpretations to map person-stages to an assignment of degree of belief in each proposition (probability) and degree of desirability in each proposition (utility). My Bayesian's proposal for structural rational constraints includes:

- rationality constraints on beliefs over time: that they are updated by conditionalization on content extracted from experience;
- rationality constraints on beliefs at a time: that they are probabilistic (i.e. satisfy the axioms of probability theory);
- rationality constraints on final/instrumental desires and beliefs: that they fit means-end constraints articulated by (Jeffrey-style) decision theory; and
- rationality constraints on choices: that the agent chooses to do the thing they most desire to do, among the things they think they're able to do.

This gives us a candidate metaphysics of representation: Structural Radical Interpretation Bayes-style. An interpretation will be correct if and only if it comes closest to making the agent's dispositions to act (at t) dispositions to select the option that maximizes expected desirability (at t), and to making

---

[8] I believe in a real distinction between structural and substantive rationality. If the reader is sceptical that there is a principled distinction here, that is all to the good, since it would provide another reason for being dissatisfied with Structural Radical Interpretation. This does leave a lot of room for discussion about how to draw a principled line between structural and more substantive rationality. For example, it is not clear whether logical concepts should have a specially privileged role. Non-logical concepts such as chance and belief are at the heart of constraints such as the Principal Principle (Lewis 1980) and Reflection (van Fraassen 1984) discussed in the Bayesian tradition. On the other side, I have argued for a generalized Bayesianism where logical content has no privileged role (Williams 2018b)—and of course, the thinner the constraints of structural rationality are, the less of a constraining role they will play in Radical Interpretation.

[9] See Jeffrey (1965) for an articulation and explanation of Bayesianism in this sense. Joyce (1999) generalizes Jeffrey to encompass causal decision theory (cf. also Lewis 1981). In Jeffrey and Joyce, probabilities and utilities (beliefs and desires) are defined over all propositions (or at least, all within a certain algebra). This makes it much more attractive for my purpose than Savage-style frameworks which posit an exogenous distinction between the objects of belief, choice, and value (Savage 1954). See Elliot (2017, sec. 4).

the beliefs and desires attributed evolve under the impact of experiences in the way the Bayesian demands.

These Bayesian constraints do not rule out wild initial belief states. It is rational, so far as the above constraints go, to have high conditional confidence that the world will explode tomorrow, given the course of experience you have undergone to this point. That means they do not rule out wild subsequent belief states, since given that wild belief state and your course of experience, the rational thing to believe is that the world will explode tomorrow.

Nor do Bayesian constraints rule out wild final desires, e.g. basic desires for a saucer of mud or indifference to what happens to you on future Tuesdays. That is by design: the core Bayesian story as articulated above was developed as a theory of the formal patterns that a well-run mind should exhibit, not about the particular contents that we have most reason to believe or desire. It would be a surprise if one could rule out wild initial belief states or desires on the basis of formal features alone. Perhaps some have aspired to this (Carnap 1950), but it would be headline news if they really succeeded. I will take Bayesian structural rationality to be in this respect representative of structural rationality accounts more generally.

Yet there's something crazy about a basic desire for a saucer of mud, or future-Tuesday indifference, and about humdrum experience triggering paranoid beliefs—something deeper and more alien than what's wrong with commonplace false beliefs or unwholesome desires. In addition to constraints of rationality based on purely formal patterns among our attitudes, perhaps there are rational constraints that are sensitive to the particular contents we think or want. These would be constraints of substantive rationality.

This generates our second option. Substantive Radical Interpretation is a metaphysics of content on which the correct interpretation of an agent is the one that does the best job of making her substantively as well as structurally rational. This is what Lewis (1974, 1992) explicitly advocates, as recent authors such as Pautz (2013), Weatherson (2013), and Schwartz (2014) have emphasized. Unfortunately, Lewis never told us much about what these constraints of substantive rationality were, beyond a few examples similar to those I have just mentioned: the saucer of mud, future-Tuesday indifference. What metaphysics of representation we get out will depend on what account of substantive rationality we feed in.[10]

---

[10] One reaction here would be to implement the *Canberra plan* on the notion of rationality—in effect, to engage in conceptual analysis of the notion of 'rationality', on the basis of what

The view I will be developing here is Substantive Radical Interpretation. Some of the work to be done is in describing what substantive rationality constraints amount to, and using this to predict and explain results in the philosophy of mind. But before I get into this level of detail, the next couple of sections will review the reasons that structural rational interpretation, when not supplemented with anything else, is untenable, and locate Substantive Radical Interpretation as a natural reaction to this problem.

1.3 The Bubble Puzzle Demonstrates that Structural Radical Interpretation Won't Work

Structural Radical Interpretation does not work: perhaps the correct interpretation meets all its constraints, but David Lewis (1983) very briefly sketched an argument that wildly inaccurate interpretations do so too. I will describe my favoured version of this 'bubble' argument here.[11] There are more famous 'underdetermination' arguments, but many of those don't have direct application to this setting, as they target language (third-layer representation, in my scheme) or are more modest in their conclusion, as they leave the truth conditions of thoughts untouched.[12] The bubble puzzle, in my view, is where the action is.

We can think of the bubble argument as a black box which takes as input any sensible interpretation of Sally (Original) and outputs a deviant variant (Paranoid). Original and Paranoid coincide on what attitudes Sally adopts concerning the goings-on in a local space-time bubble surrounding her. If Original ascribes to Sally a belief that there is a house in the road they are standing in, so does Paranoid. If Original ascribes to Sally a desire to purchase that house she is confronting, so does Paranoid.

In our ordinary case, our beliefs and desires concerning the local bubble are a piece in a much larger jigsaw. Exit the road, and you continue to believe

---

strikes us as obvious truths both about particular cases of rational and irrational states and of more general platitudes. Such an approach always leaves us open to the question: why should we care about 'mental content' so characterized, if for all we said its features are set by idiosyncratic contours of our notion of rationality. I much prefer to start with something systematic.

[11] I give full details in the context of both evidential and causal decision theory in Williams (2016d).
[12] For other underdetermination arguments, see e.g. Quine (1960), Davidson (1977, 1979), Wallace (1977), Putnam (1980, 1981), and Kripke (1982). I'll be returning to many of these below.

that there's a house on the corner—that it persists unperceived. Your desire to purchase it also (often) persists even once you've turned the corner. In line with this, we suppose that Original ascribes to Sally many beliefs and desires that are about the goings-on outside her local bubble.

Paranoid diverges from this, depicting Sally as believing that outside her bubble, all is void. It also depicts her as supremely indifferent to this fact, caring only about how things are patterned within the bubble. So they differ:

- **Belief differences**: Both interpretations ascribe to Sally a belief (on Monday, standing in the road) that it contains a house, and both ascribe a belief (on Tuesday, on the train heading south) that there was a house on the corner of that road the day before. But Paranoid, unlike Original, says that Sally believes that no house exists on Tuesday (since it would be outside her bubble, and outside her bubble all is void).
- **Desire differences**: Both interpretations ascribe to Sally a desire (on Monday, standing in the house) to purchase that very house, and attribute a desire (on Tuesday, on the train) to be able to enjoy property rights over a house in that location when she visits it in future. But Paranoid, unlike Original, fails to ascribe to Sally the desire (on Tuesday, on the train heading south) to *presently* own that house.

Now Original and Paranoid agree on the content of Sally's attitudes insofar as they concern matters inside her local bubble. So according to Paranoid, on the train on Tuesday, Sally does possess:

- a desire that she be in possession of a key which would open the front door to that house, were she in its presence;
- a desire to live in that house in future; or
- a desire for congratulatory messages to appear on her social media stream.

She wants to be in a world where her local bubble at all times is exactly as if she purchased the house. Similarly for her beliefs and expectations: she is confident that if she retraced her steps to that same road, she would see the house—she believes her bubble was and will be exactly as if there is a house on that corner.

Both Original and Paranoid make Sally opinionated about the world outside her bubble. A third interpretation, Deviant, depicts Sally as agnostic between these two world-views. It ascribes to her beliefs and desires only when those are attributed by both the others, and where they diverge represents Sally as indifferent and agnostic.

Thus we have some deviant bubble-interpretations of Sally. And here's the payoff: if we demand only that we make her structurally rational, in the way formalized by the Bayesian canon, we cannot eliminate the Deviant or Paranoid interpretation. Structural Radical Interpretation makes it indeterminate at best which of these is the correct interpretation of Sally. So it makes it indeterminate at best whether Sally believes in a regular world outside her bubble, believes that outwith the bubble all is void, or is agnostic between those hypotheses.

I've asserted that Structural Radical Interpretation cannot discriminate between Original, Deviant, and Paranoid. Those prepared to take my assertion on trust can skip the next section, where I argue for it. On the other hand, enthusiasts will want to supplement the next section with Williams (2016d) where the formal details underpinning what I say below are set out.

1.4 The Grid and the Bubble

Here's the plan. The first task will be to construct an evidence-action grid. Picture this as an enormous spreadsheet. The columns correspond to possible evidence, and the rows correspond to possible actions, in a way to be spelled out shortly. We'll then place every possible world in exactly one cell of the grid—the grid is a partition of logical space. I'll then argue that two interpretations of Sally which agree over the credibility and desirability of each cell in term will be just as structurally rational as each other (relative to any evidence and any set of actions). I argue that Original, Paranoid, and Deviant all agree on the credibility and desirability of each cell. So they are structurally-rationally equivalent. That then implies that Structural Radical Interpretation has no resources to rule out Paranoid and Deviant as incorrect interpretations of Sally.

First, the columns and rows of the grid. Each column is labelled by distinctions between possibilities implicit in the possible evidence streams our agent could receive. For example, suppose the only two possible evidential histories for Sally are ones where she sees a red sphere and then blinks out of existence, and ones where she sees a green sphere and then blinks out of existence. These two evidential histories overlap (each being compatible with a world where both a green and red sphere exist), but neither entails the other. The columns are then labelled not by the evidential histories, but by the distinctions implicit in the pattern of overlap and non-overlap in the evidential histories:[13]

	Red sphere exists but no green sphere	Green sphere exists but no red sphere	Green sphere and red sphere exist	Neither red sphere nor green sphere exists

A rational agent assigns probabilities to each possible world. Updating on a piece of evidence will eliminate all possibilities incompatible with the evidence. By construction, for each column, it either eliminates all the possibilities therein or eliminates none of them. For example, if in our toy model Sally received, as her total evidence, that a red sphere exists, she would eliminate exactly the worlds in the shaded columns:

	Red sphere exists but no green sphere	Green sphere exists but no red sphere	Green sphere and red sphere exist	Neither red sphere nor green sphere exists

On the Bayesian story, the probability in worlds in the greyed-out columns is reduced to zero, and the probability of worlds in the remaining columns is increased so that overall it sums to 1, while preserving the relative probability of the uneliminated worlds (if an uneliminated world is twice as likely as another prior to the evidence, it is twice as likely afterwards).

The relative likelihood of worlds in distinct columns can be changed, according to this story—one can be eliminated, while the other increases. But the relative likelihood of worlds in a single column is constant throughout the epistemic career of a rational agent.

---

[13] Technically, the columns are cells in the coarsest-grain partition which refines the set of propositions corresponding to total courses of evidence.

Each row is labelled by distinctions between possibilities implicit in the actions our agent could make. Just as before, courses of action may overlap. Sally can raise her arm, or kick her leg. But she can also do both or neither. So what we get is something like:

	Red sphere exists but no green sphere	Green sphere exists but no red sphere	Green sphere and red sphere exist	Neither red sphere nor green sphere exists
Raises arm, leg still				
Arm still, kicks leg				
Raises arm and kicks leg				
Arm still, leg still				

By construction, each possible world has a home in exactly one row (we include a 'null' row for those worlds where the agent doesn't exist, etc.). As it also can be located in a column, the upshot is that each possible world can be located in a single cell of the grid. Relative probabilities will never alter between worlds in a column under the impact of evidence, so a fortiori they do not shift between worlds in a cell.

Agents can suppose they perform an action by eliminating all those worlds where the action is not performed. For example, if Sally supposes she raises her arm, she eliminates the worlds where her arm remains still:

	Red sphere exists but no green sphere	Green sphere exists but no red sphere	Green sphere and red sphere exist	Neither red sphere nor green sphere exists
Raises arm, leg still				
Arm still, kicks leg				
Raises arm and kicks leg				
Arm still, leg still				

Just like receiving evidence, supposing you have acted a certain way gives rise to a new probability assignment, and on the Jeffrey-style Bayesian story, the probability of the eliminated worlds is set to zero, and the probability of others increased (while preserving relative probability). The relative probability of worlds within a single cell, being confined to both to a single row and single column, are unchanged by both the impact of evidence and the supposition that an action is performed.

If all we knew of Sally were her probabilities for each cell, we would have enough to predict her cell-probabilities under all relevant updates—whether by evidence or as part of supposing that an action is performed. Unless it is eliminated by the evidence/supposition, all the worlds within a given cell receive the same ratio-preserving boost, meaning the cell as a whole receives that boost. The evolution of cell-probabilities would not be autonomous in this way if evidence/supposition cross-cut a cell, eliminating some of its worlds and leaving others. But by construction that never happens.

That's all we need to know about probabilities. Consider now desirabilities. Each world has a desirability, and the desirability of a set of worlds must match the weighted average of the desirabilities of those worlds, where the weights are given by relative probabilities of each world in the set. We saw above that the relative probabilities of worlds within a cell of our grid are forever fixed, for our rational agent. So assuming that the desirability of each world is also forever fixed, the desirability of each cell is forever fixed.

If you want to know the desirability of an act—for example, to predict what a desirability-maximizing agent will do when faced with a choice—it will suffice to know what those forever-fixed cell-desirabilities are, and what the current cell-probabilities are. The reader may verify that the desirability of the action will match the weighted average of cell-desirabilities (weights being cell probabilities) of the cells where the act is performed.

The upshot of all this is the following. If two agents assign the same probability and desirability to cells, then they agree on the desirability of each act. If they choose to act to maximize desirability, they act in exactly the same way. Further, this match persists under any possible course of experience, since the cell probabilities and cell desirabilities will continue to match each other.

Now consider Sally, in the context of Structural Radical Interpretation (Bayes-style). The correct interpretation of her, *ex hypothesi*, is that one which makes her structurally rational, granted her dispositions to act and the evidence available to her. But we have just seen that these criteria will at best determine her attitudes at the level of cells of the grid. Interpretations which attribute different probability/desirability assignments to the worlds within a cell, but give the same cell-level upshot, will rationalize Sally's actions/evidence just as well as each other.

What we have just seen is the schematic version of the bubble puzzle. Remember that the bubble was to include the entirety of the observable and manipulable world around Sally. Worlds which coincided on how things go within the four-dimensional bubble will have the agent perform exactly the same actions over time, and receive exactly the same evidence. They lie within the same cell of the grid, no matter how they differ on extra-bubbular matters. So although Original, Paranoid, and Deviant are interpretations attributed very different beliefs about the way the world is, they agree on how things are within the local bubble (or on what credence should be assigned to different ways the local bubble might be). They do not differ on how likely each cell of the grid is, only over how that likelihood is divided between the worlds within the cell. Likewise, they do not differ on how desirable each cell of the grid is, though they do differ markedly on the desirability of the individual worlds within the cell. They are all structurally rational interpretations of Sally.

The argument of this section has been given against the background of a specific Bayesian interpretation of structural rationality. There are variations we might want to consider—for example, even within the Bayesian tradition, we might want to extend the argument to updates on evidence that is less-than-certain, or to accounts of desirability other than Jeffrey's. That's where formalization can help, since we can pin down the arguments given above precisely and explore variations. Williams (2016d) shows that the argument just given is robust under such perturbations.

Central to all this are assumptions that the canonical description of experience and action—the basic data that Radical Interpretation has to work with—are restricted to the local bubble. But this is not a problem for the argument. Throughout, I have been silent on how 'local' the local bubble is. At one extreme, one might think that the canonical descriptions of experiences are patterns of sense-data, and canonical acts are internal volitions. The argument will then proceed with a 'local bubble' consisting of a trajectory of sense-data and strivings. At the other extreme, one might be very externalist, and even allow descriptions in terms of distal causes of experiences and remote goals of action. But if one goes that way, the bubble constructor should just set the boundaries of the bubble extremely wide, to include anything that turns up in such descriptions. As Sally sits on the train heading south, I take it that her perceptible and manipulable environment does not extend as far as a house in a city a hundred miles away.[14]

This is all pretty terrible for Structural Radical Interpretation. Its analysis of 'correct belief/desire interpretation' was that such an interpretation structurally rationalizes dispositions to act in the light of experience. And if the above is right, then Paranoid and Deviant are just as correct as Original. But they aren't! Sally could be you or me—she's just an ordinary person, acting and experiencing in ordinary ways. Sally is a person who believes that the world is uniform, and who rejects the bubble-and-void scenario. Structural Radical Interpretation cannot capture this, and so must be amended or replaced.

1.5 Substantive Radical Interpretation Needs a Story about Substantive Rationality

We've just seen that it is possible to construct an interpretation on which an agent is agnostic and indifferent to the character of the world outside her local bubble (the part of the world she can directly perceive and manipulate). This can be done in a way that still makes her 'structurally' rational— formally and means-end consistent, updating coherently in the light of experience, and so forth. That is trouble for Structural Radical Interpretation, which said that what it was for an interpretation of Sally to be correct

---

[14] If modern communications technology makes you doubt this, then place Sally in Victorian times and rerun the dialectic. Another way in which we might 'extend' this bubble would be to make a case that the content of our perception (e.g. of a tree, or a house) is *incompatible* with the item perceived blinking out of existence when it leaves our local bubble. Now, there are some very interesting issues surrounding perceptual mechanisms in cases of *object permanence*, as when a ball passes behind a barrier and another similar ball emerges from the other side. Perhaps there is here perceptual content that *it was the same ball* that emerged. However, (i) this claim does not entail that perception represents the ball as continuing to exist behind the barrier—it is compatible with one and the same ball blinking out of existence when it goes behind the barrier, and coming back into existence as it emerges; (ii) even if object-permanence gave us reason to extend the bubble behind visible barriers, it would be a quite different thing to say that *perceptual* experience reidentifies my house over gaps of days or weeks; (iii) if perceptual experience does reidentify a house or tree as same-again, this is presumably a paradigm of cognitive penetration of perceptions by beliefs, and I argue only a more primitive layer of perceptual content will be a legitimate resource for Radical Interpretation (this will be discussed, in the context of my own positive theory, in later chapters). Finally, to the extent that object-permanent and associated externalist content allows for perceptual content itself to be inaccurate (and so illusory in a strong sense), one can construct versions of the bubble puzzle on which the paranoid beliefs support a world-view on which perceptual content is in these respects inaccurate (e.g. because a demon is carefully setting things up to generate an illusion of permanence).

was for it to rationalize her dispositions to act in light of her course of experience. But we've seen that structurally rationality alone can't rule out obviously incorrect interpretations on which Sally is agnostic about extra-bubbular matters, or even takes the world outside her bubble to be void.

The bubble puzzle refutes Structural Radical Interpretation. But it is only a problem because of the unforced error in building Radical Interpretation atop structural rather than substantive rationality. Recall: there's nothing structurally irrational about future Tuesday indifference or a basic desire for a saucer of mud, and we can now add: nothing structurally irrational with taking one's local bubble to be radically different in character from the world outside that local bubble. But forming such beliefs or desires is nevertheless not a reasonable place to end up, given standard, mundane courses of experiences. Such beliefs and desires are irrational (given the available evidence) in an ordinary, non-technical sense, and it is only when we refine the notion to focus on attitudes whose badness is distinctively 'formal' that we generate these difficulties. Structural rationality is an important norma-tive notion. But it is not the right tool for this job.

The trouble is that the ordinary, broader notion of rationality is at this point inchoate. In the case of structural rationality, we have many ideas about what sorts of things are in the offing to be rational constraints, and we have a century of development of formal articulations of these constraints to model the account being proposed. This level of detail makes Structural Radical Interpretation a predictive theory, since we can apply our existing theory of structural rationality to patterns of acts and experiences, and see what interpretations pass the test. If it weren't predictive, we wouldn't get the kind of nasty surprises we've just been worrying about!

If Substantive Radical Interpretation is to be a credible option, we need something similar. We need some body of theory about substantive rationality that we can bring to candidate interpretations of an agent, which we can use to see what the theory predicts. The bubble puzzle makes this a pressing concern. Do the Deviant and Paranoid interpretations make Sally substantively irrational, or at least less substantively rational than the Original interpretation does? On what basis shall we adjudicate such questions?

In what follows, I add content to this theory in a number of ways, by:

1) endorsing specific assumptions about what a substantively rational agent is like;

2) endorsing more general, but restricted identifications between substantive rationality and other normative rankings; and

3) giving general theoretical glosses on the notion of substantive rationality.

In the chapters to come, strategy 1—specific assumptions—will be centre-stage. Any reading of substantive rationality on which those specific assumptions hold true will work for the applications and predictions I derive in those chapters. But specific assumptions may look ad hoc without the wider theoretical context provided by (2) and (3). The second and third approaches will link substantive rationality to existing normative notions and theories, and will tend to involve some contentious choices. Accordingly, I will now spend some time talking about substantive rationality in this spirit.

As regards (2), I'll give two examples. More such constraints could be added, further fleshing out substantive rationality. First, I will take it that a (perfectly) substantively rational agent is one whose every belief (disbelief, suspension of belief) is justified. Further, I assume that subjects are, all else equal, more substantively rational the more their beliefs are justified by the evidence they possess. Substantive Radical Interpretation tells us, therefore, that *ceteris paribus*, the correct interpretation of Sally is a justification-maximizing one. Second, I take it that a (perfectly) substantively rational agent is moral, and that agents all else equal are more substantively rational the more their actions are ethically correct given their beliefs/desires. Substantive Radical Interpretation tells us, therefore, that *ceteris paribus*, the correct interpretation of Sally is a morality-maximizing one.

The latter claim, I have been told, sounds controversial. But remember that this is not the far more controversial claim that *structural rationality* requires morality—it's not the Kantian claim that as a matter of *form* we need to be moral. What one needs, in order to discern whether or not this claim is contentious, is a type-3 gloss on substantive rationality.

As regards (3), the conception with which I work is the following: that a substantively rational agent believes as they ought (or as is permissible), given their evidence, and that an ideally substantively rational agent acts they as they ought (or as is permissible), given their options and beliefs. Another way of putting it: substantive rationality is a matter of reason-responsiveness, where these may be epistemic reasons for belief, or practical reasons for action. The claim that among our practical reasons are *moral* reasons, and so that a substantively rational (i.e. reason-responsive) agent is all else equal a moral one, should now seem much more familiar.

Some further clarifications on how I intend this gloss to be read:[15]

- The 'oughts' in question factor in the agent's limited perspective. (Consider a bomb-disposal expert who is perfectly justified in believing that cutting the green wire will defuse the bomb, while this will in fact detonate it. In some sense, perhaps, they ought not cut the wire—it would result in an explosion. But in the relevant sense, cutting the wire is The Thing To Do, given their evidence.)
- The ought is 'all things considered'. On the practical side, it aggregates moral, prudential (etc.) considerations with the agent's subjective preferences (tastes, context) in whatever way is appropriate.[16] On the theoretical side, it aggregates different kinds of evidence from different sources, and if there are other constraints on belief (e.g. moral ones), it aggregates those too.
- In general, there will be many things it is all-things-considered okay to do in decision situations, and there may be more than one attitude it is okay to adopt in a particular context. In the case of acts, for example, we can have ties, incommensurabilities, supererogatory options, or individual differences in taste, etc., generating normative non-uniqueness. The permissibility gloss allows for this—so long as an agent isn't acting (or believing) in a way that's all-things-considered wrong, they will count as substantively rational. For ease of exposition,

---

[15] See van Roojen (2018) for a discussion and defence of a similar notion of rationality, including its role in Radical Interpretation. His reconstruction of a notion of reasons on this basis—as true propositions that would or do rationalize belief or action—is something that I can also endorse, and one can then regloss the notion of rationality as being reason-responsive, which at times below I do when it is helpful to distinguish it rhetorically from structural rationality.

[16] What if there's no such thing as the 'all things considered ought'? I would be happy simply to list the assumption that there *is* such a notion as a presupposition of my argument. While there may well be incomparabilities, indeterminacy, and uncertainty about what is all things considered better than what, I find it hard not to think that, all things considered, it's *impermissible* to steal from orphans in order to get a third helping of pudding. It's technically possible, I guess, to shift the aggregation assumption from normative theory to theoretical evaluation, by saying that the best interpretation is the one that aggregates scores on the individual normative dimensions (justification, morality, prudence, etc.), but I don't see much dialectical advantage in doing so. I agree it's very hard to theorize about the details of the aggregation of oughts, but in general the obscurity of aggregation doesn't engender scepticism about the aggregated virtue, and in particular is no easier for the case of aggregating theoretical virtues. See also Chang (2002, 2005).

I'll drop the caveat here, and only reintroduce it where non-uniqueness is particularly salient.[17]

Characterizations of substantive rationality that favour justification-maximization fit this overarching gloss. Principles that favour truth-maximization do not (even if on some reading or other, one ought to believe what's true). That's significant: maximizing justification points us in a very different direction when it comes to selecting interpretations than does maximizing truth. Principles that favour morality-maximization fit this overarching gloss so long as the moral ought in question factors in the agent's factual uncertainty.

So when it comes to determining the correct interpretation, we should ideally find an interlocking hierarchy. Specific normative principles explain why *this* interpretation is favoured over *that* one. The specific normative principle is backed up by some general first-order normative theory (e.g. the theory of justification, the theory of morality), which is a determinant of substantive rationality via the kind of 'restricted identifications' recently illustrated. And those restricted identifications need to be defensible as determinants of what the agent ought to believe and ought to do, on an appropriately information/evidence-sensitive reading of 'ought'.

Turning back to our earlier examples of specific constraints of substantive rationality, we can set them in context. Counterinductive belief formation is structurally rational, but doesn't lead to epistemically justified beliefs. What you ought to believe is determined (at least in part) by what you're epistemically justified in believing. So counterinductive beliefs are not substantively rational, and interpretations that attribute them are disfavoured. Being indifferent to what happens on future Tuesdays is structurally rational, but leads to imprudence—a failure to properly respect your own future interests. What you ought to do is determined (at least in part) by what it is prudent to do. So such desires are not substantively rational, and interpretations that attribute them are disfavoured. What about basic desires for saucers of mud? The underlying idea here, I take it, is that even idiosyncratic desires need to be for something valuable, and so substantively rational agents, though they may differ in their preferences, would always lock onto goals that are of value. Personally, I don't know if I accept this piece of normative theory—or if it is a constraint on what the agent all things considered ought to do, in the

---

[17] For normative incommensurability and its relation to normative indeterminacy, see Williams (2016b, 2017) and the references therein.

appropriate sense. So I'm agnostic, at this point, about whether this really is an example of something that would make an interpretation disfavoured. That shows that the framework I've introduced has teeth, and that we are no longer just dealing with an ad hoc list of psychological features that strike us as odd. To figure out whether desires for saucers of mud are disfavoured in interpretation, we must figure whether they areto count as substantively irrational, and that can be resolved within first-order normative theory.

We have enough here to flesh out our understanding of what substantive rationality is, and how we can sensibly propose and defend specific constraints of substantive rationality. Accordingly, Substantive Radical Interpretation has content. So let's turn back to the bubble puzzle, and see what happens.

1.6 Substantive Radical Interpretation Pops the Bubble Puzzle

To recap: I distinguished two forms of Radical Interpretation: structural and substantive, based on a distinction between two corresponding readings of 'rationalization'. Structural Radical Interpretation has a counterexample in the bubble puzzle: obviously wrong interpretations of an agent can structurally rationalize her actions, given her course of experience, perfectly. Attention turns then to Substantive Radical Interpretation. That's not going to be any good if all we have to offer by way of fleshing out 'substantive rationality' is an ad hoc laundry list of odd-seeming psychological states. But I've set out a principled framework which we use to explain and predict which interpretations will be counted as substantively rational, and which will not. In this section, I turn back to the bubble puzzle, and show why it isn't a problem for Substantive Radical Interpretation.

What the bubble construction provides us with are (structurally-rational) candidate interpretations Deviant and Paranoid. These were a counterexample to Structural Radical Interpretation, but because we deny that all structurally rational interpretations are substantively rational, they are not (at this point) a counterexample to Substantive Radical Interpretation. They still generate a challenge: to pin down the constraints of substantive rationality they violate.

Consider the case of a character to whom Deviant would truly apply, who really is agnostic and indifferent about matters outside her local bubble. You might think of her—at least as far as her beliefs are concerned—as someone who read too many classic Cartesian and Humean sceptical arguments and, convinced, ends up suspending judgement on the character of the wider world beyond her local surroundings.

This suggests a recipe for identifying what's wrong with Deviant. Take your favourite anti-sceptical story about how and why agents are justified in their (standard) beliefs about the world around them, given their evidence. Cite the anti-sceptical story to defend the view that the beliefs attributed by the interpretation to Original are justified by the agent's course of experience, but suspending belief or having paranoid beliefs is not. Then (via a restricted identification of kind (2) above, e.g. that substantive rationality of beliefs coincides with justification) we explain on this basis why Original is more substantively rational than Deviant or Paranoid (all else equal).

To illustrate, suppose the local bubble around an agent encompasses a region of space-time varying from a few metres to a several miles (perhaps on occasion, when gazing at the stars, it is much more extensive). We believe that the world outside that bubble—in the region now behind the wall that blocks my view, in the years before I was born and after my death, in the areas of space outside my light cone—is similar in character to the world in my bubble. That belief in the spatiotemporal uniformity of nature, across the boundaries of the bubble of my experience and action, is a presupposition of my reasons for holding more specific beliefs, e.g. that the hose I left in the yard yesterday is still there now, that there was some decent popular music recorded in the 1960s, and that pouring chemicals in the local streams will cause environmental damage that will last centuries. What justification we have for believing that nature is uniform in this way is a familiar Humean question, to which first-order epistemology owes us an answer. Perhaps it is this: a belief in the uniformity of nature is the best, simplest explanation of the uniformity that we do see within our local bubble. Add to this the claim that we are justified in believing the best explanation of the phenomena we observe, rather than suspending judgement, or believing something that offers a worse explanation of observed phenomena, and we have an epistemic principle we can wield in defence of Substantive Radical Interpretation.

Suppose that the local bubble is more 'Cartesian', including only the agent's pattern of sense-data and inner volitions—this on the basis that sense-data constitute the sphere of experiential evidence and volitions the sphere of basic action. In that context, we will need to look to epistemology to tell us what justifies ordinary beliefs about the material world around us (insofar as that world is not an idealist construct out of sense-data and volitions). We need an answer to what justifies the agent in thinking that there is a solid material chair in which she is sitting, given that her evidence consists of a mosaic of colour patches in visual space, pressure patches in bodily space, etc. Given the starting assumption about the character of basic experiential evidence, unless the sceptic is going to win, there must be some good answer to that question. Perhaps inference to the best explanation is again the key.[18] Or perhaps there are simply a priori justified 'dogmatic' conditionals, that experience as of a material object so-shaped justifies the belief that there is a material object so-shaped. Having got to the material contents of the local space-time region, we are at the starting blocks of the Humean puzzle just discussed, and by chaining the stories together, our first-order anti-sceptical epistemology again is the source of the detailed story about why the bubble puzzle is answered.

It is characteristic of the approach that the necessary first-order epistemology will be a matter of controversy. It is not uncontroversial that justifying a belief in the uniformity of nature proceeds by inference to the best explanation. It is not uncontroversial that suspending judgement in the uniformity of nature is unjustified. And even once the operative principles are accepted, there is of course a lot of work to be done in understanding the most foundational epistemic principles on which the epistemic principle operative here—inference to the best explanation—is based. Substantive Radical Interpretation, for better or worse, simply doesn't offer many autonomous predictions, independent of the details of first-order epistemic or practical normative theory (though as we'll shortly see, it generates a rich set of *conditional* predictions). But the case of the bubble puzzle is special, exactly because it's linked to familiar sceptical scenarios. In this case, we are entitled to assume that some anti-sceptical story or other will be forthcoming, and however this plays out, the bubble puzzle will have an answer.

One caveat to the above. An anti-sceptical epistemology is not quite enough. We need an intolerant anti-sceptical epistemology, that is, one that doesn't simply say that it's okay (epistemically permissible) to believe in the material world around you and the uniformity of nature, given a standard course of experience, but that such beliefs are epistemically obligatory.[19] Subjective Bayesianism as an epistemic theory is tolerant rather than

---

[18] See Russell (1912), and Vogel (1990) for a more recent examination of the view and a list of advocates.

[19] I think it's pretty clear that Russell (1912) and Vogel (1990) are intolerant anti-sceptics. A satisfying defence of intolerance would articulate what it is about the basic belief-forming

intolerant. Subjective Bayesians are not classic sceptics, and might even endorse the letter of inference to the best explanation. But for them, having prior probabilities that favour explanations with such-and-such character in response to a standard course of experience is simply one rational option among many. Sure, your and my prior probabilities have this character, and perhaps there's a good, non-rational, evolutionary explanation about how we come to be disposed to react to evidence like this. But on this view, there'd be no normative defect in having very deviant priors that favour more complex explanations over simpler ones, and priors that favour e.g. the beliefs attributed by Paranoid over those attributed by Original. Subjective Bayesians, at least as I'm understanding them here, essentially deny there's a category of 'substantive rationality' in epistemology that can't be analysed as the joint upshot of structural rationality constraints plus facts about the priors that are typically shared among creatures like us, priors which have no special normative privilege. It is not immediate that the subjective Bayesian reduction of 'substantive' rationality would reinstitute the bubble puzzle, since Paranoid and Deviant attribute paranoid and deviant desires as well as beliefs, and one might combine the subjectivist epistemology with a more objectivist account of practical normativity. But I think that's a faint hope, and we should simply insist that a demanding anti-sceptical epistemology, as opposed to be the permissive one just sketched, is a presupposition of the project.

1.7 Conclusion

So this is Substantive Radical Interpretation, the account of how second-layer facts about representation—concerning what an agent believes and desires—are grounded. As promised, I've concentrated on the selectional story: the role of rationalization. In the next few chapters, I want to extract more mileage out of the story of belief and desire, and show how this foundational story can predict and explain aspects of particular kinds of representational states in a detailed and nuanced way. They show how we can use Substantive Radical Interpretation to explain patterns in representation facts: the way that we think about the logically complex and the

---

methods we deploy that makes them special—not just one set of priors among many. For an intriguing attempt to address this question, see Enoch and Schechter (2008).

unrestrictedly general, about individual objects, and about the normative and categorical features of such things.

Coda: States and Stages

Lewis and Stalnaker ran a metaphysics of representation that (at least in the first instance) takes belief to be a relation between a time-slice of an agent and a proposition. It is Sally, after all, who today believes that emeralds are green. An alternative is to think of belief as in the first instance a state that an agent is in: for Sally to believe that emeralds are green is for her to be in some state s, where that state counts as a belief state and has the representational content *that emeralds are green* (cf. Field 1978).

In the chapter above, I formulated Radical Interpretation in a way that is neutral between these two approaches. But ultimately I think it is the second that has to be correct, based on the following argument due to Block (1978).[20] Consider 'Smartypants': a possible intelligent creature, who has the capacity to realize only finitely many action-types, and register only finitely many sensation-types. Smartypants' inner processing, upon empirical investigation, looks similar to how ours must be: a complex array of inner processing. Let the Smartypants function map the finitely many possible sequences of stimuli that could affect Smartypants, to one of her possible outputs—the one that should would perform under that history of sensation. A large finite lookup table describes this function.

Now consider 'Blockhead'. Blockhead looks outwardly just like Smartypants, but has different internal engineering. Inside Blockhead is a copy of a table that lays out the Smartypants function. Blockhead proceeds by faultlessly recording all stimuli, matching the description of the stimuli to an appropriate entry in column 1 of the table, reading off the corresponding entry in column 2, and then transducing the resulting action-description to relay instructions to Blockhead's motor systems.

The critical observation here is that Smartypants and Blockhead will have exactly the same input-output dispositions: they will move in the same ways under the same history of sensation.

Ned Block originally used the case to argue against a specific thesis concerning the metaphysical grounds of *being intelligent*. His argument

---

[20] Thanks to Daniel Stoljar for pressing me on this.

was this: *Smartypants is intelligent, Blockhead is not. But they have the same (sensory) input/behavioural(output) dispositions. So intelligence does not supervene on input-output-dispositions.* The argument is compelling and can be extended to any other property that Smartypants has and Blockhead lacks.

There is a prima facie threat to Radical Interpretation here. For the best (structural or substantive) rationalization of dispositions to act in the light of experience looks like it will be the same for both Smartypants and Blockhead. Psychological properties of an individual—their beliefs and desires in particular—supervene on their input-output dispositions. But now we deploy an instance of the Blockhead argument: Blockhead and Smartypants have the *same* dispositions to act in the light of experience, and yet differ in psychological properties.[21]

The reaction of a time-slice-based radical interpreter could either be to embrace equality between Smartypants and Blockhead (I think utterly implausibly) or to find some difference. But the differences between the two are differences of inner structure, so one way or another, that has to be made to matter in the account.

One way to do this is to claim that although beliefs and desires are properties of individuals, not of their inner states, whether those beliefs and desires rationalize action in the light of experience nevertheless depends on having the right inner structure. I do not know how to spell out this option further, so I'll leave it aside.

The other thing to do is give up on time-slice version of Radical Interpretation, and move to the state-based formulation. If what interpretations do is map states to contents, then Blockhead simply could not have the same interpretation as Smartypants, since they differ in inner architecture. The interpretation that correctly describes Smartypants maps each of her many inner state-types to contents. That interpretation can't be the one that is true for Blockhead, because Blockhead is not in the same or even isomorphic states. So the response to Block on behalf of this kind of Radical Interpretation is to agree that psychological states do not supervene on input/output dispositions alone: they supervene on input/output dispositions *together with an appropriately rich mediating structure of states.* Further, that

---

[21] There is wriggle room here: the Blockhead argument is framed in terms of sensation and movement as input and outputs, whereas the envisaged account is framed in terms of (intentional) experience and action. One might argue that Blockhead, unlike Smartypants, is incapable of experience and action, and so evade the argument. Given the way that I wish to reduce the intentionality of experience and action, this loophole is not easily available to me—see part III.

mediating structure is not normatively idle. Whether or not an agent is substantively rational in her beliefs and acts depends on which other psychological states those beliefs and acts are causally based upon.

In the coming chapters, I consider hypotheses about the inner architecture of creatures. The details of the inner architecture—whether states have language-like structure, what sorts of inferential and other relations link the states together—are very much up for grabs. But that there is an inner architecture whose details matter for Radical Interpretation is something for which the Blockhead case forms a convincing a priori argument.

2

Radical Interpretation and the Logical Form of Thoughts

Radical Interpretation tells us how the facts about what agents believe and desire are grounded. What it is for Sally to believe (to degree d) that Leeds is a city in the UK or desire (with a certain strength) that she drink coffee right now, is for the correct belief-desire interpretation of Sally to attribute such beliefs and desires to her. What makes that interpretation correct is that it best rationalizes the way Sally is disposed to act given her course of experience. A story about the latter, 'first layer' of representation remains on the to-do list. I presented a challenge to this story—the bubble puzzle—and noted that so long as the rationalization to which Radical Interpretation appeals includes more than mere structural rationality—as long as it requires we make Sally, so far as possible, believe things for good reasons and act for good reasons—an anti-sceptical epistemology will undercut the challenge.

It's not much of a defence of a theory to say that it survives refutation, but it's a start. The real selling point of a theory of representation, however, should be whether it predicts and explains the patterns we find in representation. This chapter begins to make the case for that, by connecting Radical Interpretation to a broadly 'inferentialist' accounts of the nature of logical concepts.

For a long time I was confused about this. I thought of the work that went under the title 'theory of reference' as a kind of *competitor* to Radical Interpretation. There was the literature on inferentialist treatments of conjunction, quantification, negation.[1] In the same way, there were causal theories of names and demonstratives, and related accounts of natural kind terms or concepts.[2] It felt like this was part of the project that Davidson (1977) mocked

---

[1] The literature on inferentialism goes back a long way and seems to be the focus of much attention, but the versions that have been particular significant in shaping my own thinking are Peacocke (1987,1992), Field (1977), and Restall (2015).

[2] I'm thinking in particular of causal theories of reference for names in Kripke (1980) and Evans (1973). Dickie (2015) is an excellent recent account of singular thought that helped me

The Metaphysics of Representation. J. Robert G. Williams, Oxford University Press (2019).
© J. Robert G. Williams.
DOI: 10.1093/oso/9780198850205.001.0001

as the 'building block' account of reference: an approach to the metaphysics of reference by painstakingly dividing all possible concepts into categories and then laying out for each in turn how reference *for concepts in that category* is grounded (for advocacy of exactly this approach, see Field 1972). This didn't seem like a very promising project. While progress had been made on the handful of cases that had been intensively studied (normally because they were independently of philosophical interest), if even one philosophically boring concept lacked a convincing metaphysics of reference the edifice would collapse. I thought the best way to run this sort of account was to add to it some kind of catch-all theory of reference that would cover all the other concepts for which we had no particularly good ideas about a local theory of reference (anyone got any good ideas about a local theory of reference for the concept *very*?). So the best I could make of the programme was an unlovely hybrid: Radical Interpretation as a catch-all supplemented with ad hoc side-constraints in the form of the local theories of singular concepts, natural kind terms, and the like. In the very best case scenario, the overall theory of reference that would emerge would be massively disjunctive.

But this was to misunderstand the relation between a foundational metaphysics of reference and the kind of illuminating generalizations that these local theories of reference are latching on to.[3] If you want a story about how reference is grounded, Radical Interpretation is the thing to go for (say I). But that's perfectly consistent with the local theories of reference being *true generalizations* about the resulting patterns of reference. It might be true, and illuminating, to note that when a certain object is the dominant causal source of information involving a name-like concept *c*, then *c* refers to that object. Those sorts of generalizations aren't part of the reduction of reference, so there's no reason to demand they be stated in some austere vocabulary free of representational ideology. And we needn't assume that there's something interesting and illuminating to say about every concept: the focus on the most philosophical interesting concepts seems perfectly in order.

If you think of the relation between local patterns of reference and foundational metaphysics of representation in this way, then not only are

---

see the connections between this literature and my own interests. On natural kinds (and social kinds) key texts are the classical arguments for externalism of Putnam (1975) and Burge (1979).

[3] There are definitely those committed to the building-block theory! I cited Field above; but Fodor (1987) is perhaps the most explicit proponent, and so I still raise a sceptical eyebrow at those engaged in the piecemeal project of reductive causal theories of reference, Fodor-style.

the two projects compatible, they can be mutually supportive. We can use observations about local patterns in reference to test and evaluate the foundational theory—not by asking whether it survives refutation via underdetermination challenges like the bubble puzzle of chapter 1, but by seeing whether it can predict and explain the local patterns. This is the project of the current chapter.

The patterns of reference involving logical concepts have been some of the most intensively studied, and the three that I discuss below (which are together expressively complete for a first-order language) represent three interestingly different cases. I first discuss conjunction, which is perhaps the cleanest, simplest case for an inferentialist to articulate. Next I discuss negation, which is treated in very different ways in different logics. And finally I discuss unrestricted universal quantification—a notion that brings us back to underdetermination arguments, since there are powerful arguments that suggest that we might not be able to express truly *unrestricted* generality at all. I show that Substantive Radical Interpretation can respond to that challenge.

2.1 How Conjunction Gets Its Meaning

I start right now with the simplest example I know which illustrates the moving parts at work in what follows. This is the case of the propositional logical connective concept *and*. My focus is not on the word 'and' in a natural or artificial language. I am assuming that there is a logical concept *and* as it appears in thought, and it is the denotation of this concept that is my target.[4] ('Concept' as I'll be using it is a term for a presumed vehicle of mental content, the mental analogue of a word. It should not be confused with another possible use of the term 'concept' to pick out a layer of meaning

---

[4] For uniformity of presentation, I will presuppose a style of meaning theory that assigns denotations to concepts/terms of any syntactic category, including logical concepts, and so my question is: in virtue of what does 'and' denote the truth function *conjunction*. Some might prefer a style of meaning theory that does not assign logical concepts a denotation at all, but writes in an axiom that fixes the truth value/conditions of a sentence in which 'and' is the main connectives in terms of the truth value/conditions of its subsentences. In that case, the analogue to my question would be: in virtue of what is the conjunction-axiom the correct element of a meaning-theory? Similar issues will appear when we consider predicate-meaning—I will talk in a way that presupposes a mild Platonism for simplicity's sake, leaving the nominalist rephrasing as an exercise for the reader.

at the level of Fregean sense. If our thoughts have sense as well as reference, then on my use of the term it is concepts that *have* sense and reference).

Let me remind readers of a familiar inferentialist story about how this concept gets its meaning.

Suppose that Sally's cognitive economy contains a connective-concept c that is associated with the following inferential patterns:

from A, B *derive* AcB
from AcB *derive* A
from AcB *derive* B

The crucial claim is that what makes it the case that the connective concept c denotes the truth-function conjunction is the fact that it is associated with the rules just mentioned.

Different versions of this idea will fill in the two steps in more detail: saying more about the nature of the 'association' between concept and the patterns expressed above with 'derives', and saying more about the recipe for getting from such patterns to denotation. On the first point, for example, Peacocke (1992) held that each concept figured in patterns of belief formation that were 'primitively compelling': that the derivations seem obvious to the agent, and that this seeming obviousness is not the result of their relation to other patterns of belief formation. The above rules are associated with the concept, for Peacocke, because they are the set of all the primitively compelling rules whose specification involves c. Peacocke further held that for a concept like c to denote the truth function f was for f to make valid the primitive compelling inferences essentially involving c.[5]

---

[5] Kurt Ludwig, in a review of Peacocke, summarizes his view thus (where possession conditions are the properties a subject must have in order to count as understanding a concept): 'Thus, for any concept [Fregean sense], given its semantic value, its possession conditions will be determined to be the set of practices involving contents with that concept that are required for the thinker who employs such contents to be rational. This has been a familiar theme in the philosophy of mind in the latter half of this century, though its presentation in Peacocke obscures a bit its relation to its antecedents' (Ludwig 1994, p.477). Notice the way that Ludwig (a Davidson scholar) alludes to the role of rationality in reference-determination—this is exactly the connection I am exploring, except that I substitute empirical hypotheses about cognitive architecture involving a vehicle of content for the presupposition that there is Fregean sense characterized in terms of 'possession conditions'. Peacocke himself, when he discusses radical interpretation (1992), construes it as a possible rival to his account of possession conditions, and criticises it on those grounds (though he admits it might still be a true thing to say). My version of it is a rival—or better, subsuming account—of what he calls 'determination theories'.

My interest lies in the second step, so I'll pass over the first without minimal comment. There is a core commitment here, but beyond that, a lot of flexibility. The core commitment is that our interpretee's deductive reasoning gives a special role to certain 'basic' rules involving the target concepts. The flexibility comes in spelling out what it takes for a rule to be basic. Peacocke's gloss appeals to dependencies among what is *obvious* to the subject. A natural alternative is to appeal to mereological structure within a subject's cognitive processes—concrete chains of reasoning being literally built up of tokens of a set of basic rule-types, just as a valid natural deduction proof laid out on a page is literally built up of tokens of the relevant rule-types. That deductive reasoning takes this natural-deduction-like form is an empirical hypothesis about how our subject's mind works, but none the worse for that for my purposes.[6] I'll use Peacocke's evocative label in what follows, but this is just a placeholder.

My aim in this section is to capture what's right about this inferentialist idea within the overarching theory of Radical Interpretation. Radical Interpretation unaided won't get us there. Here (and in following sections) I'll be adding two kinds of auxiliary assumptions to the set-up. These will comprise, first, assumptions about the specific cognitive architectures that our subject—Sally—possesses, and second, normative assumptions (epistemic or practical) involving specific kinds of content.

The first and most basic architectural assumption (one crucial to securing our subject-matter) will be that Sally's thinking consists in tokening state-types which have a language-like structure, within which we find analogues to the logical connectives 'and', 'or', 'not' etc.[7]

Second, I'll be assuming also that the syntactical properties of the structured states in question, and the attitude-types they token e.g. flat-out-belief, supposition, degree of belief, degree of desire), are grounded prior to and independently of the determination of content that they are paired with. The job of the correct interpretation is purely to assign content, which it does in a

---

[6] For empirical work defending the claim that human deductive reasoning works like this, see Rips (2008). Rips uses empirical data about the pattern of deductive fallacies to which humans are prone to identify a set of rules, paired with weights reflecting their probabilities-of-being-applied-in-triggering-conditions. According to Rips, the way these probabilities of application accumulate in complex chains explains the observed fallacies. For a contrasting hypothesis, see Johnson-Laird's mental models theory, which posits a very different kind of mental architecture underlying human deductive reasoning.

[7] The locus classicus for this type of view is Fodor (1975).

'compositional' way via assigning content to the atomic elements and specifying compositional rules.[8]

Third, I make the assumption that we can identify, prior to content-determination, which inferential rules involving c Sally finds primitively compelling.

The fourth and final architectural assumption is that such associated entailments for the case of c turn out to be those given above and repeated here:

from A, B *derive* AcB.
from AcB *derive* A
from AcB *derive* B

In the case of a fictional character like Sally, we can make these four assumptions true by stipulation. But to hypothesize that actual flesh and blood thinkers are like Sally in these respects would be a theoretical posit about our cognitive architecture, not something that is a priori or analytically obvious. To emphasize: such assumptions are not essential to Radical Interpretation as such. But Radical Interpretation will have something to say about who do possess this particularly clean sort of architecture—which for all we know from the armchair, includes us. We want it to say plausible and attractive things about creatures with such an architecture—we can evaluate a theory by its conditional predictions as much as by its categorical predictions. Let's see how it fares.

Radical Interpretation tells us that the correct interpretation of mental states is one that maximizes the rationality of the individual concerned—where rationality in the relevant sense means that as far as possible the subject believes as they ought to, given their evidence, and acts as they ought to, given their beliefs and desires. All else equal, an interpretation will score

---

[8] In my previous terminology (see section 1.1), these first two assumptions concern the 'framing' of the space of interpretations, and in particular, the kind of entities that are in the domain of any abstract interpretation in that space. There is a tradition of appealing to functional role both to individuate the syntax of mentalese and word-types. In Fodor (1987), for example, such assumptions are preliminaries to giving a causal metasemantics to pin down the content of the attitudes. That would be a suitable backdrop for this discussion, though of course, the metasemantics I explore is a rival to Fodor's. If one thought that interpretations should do all these jobs holistically, then you can read what is to follow as a story about what, in Substantive Radical Interpretation, favours one interpretation over others among all those agreed on syntax and attitude-type, and there will be further discussion about how such local rankings interact with factors that fix the attitude-types.

well on that measure to the extent that it makes the most basic patterns of belief formation ones that preserve justification (we don't want leaky pipes!). And so, given the assumptions about cognitive architecture, we need our interpretation of the concept c to make rational our practice of treating the given rules as primitively compelling (inter alia, being willing to reason in accordance with them).

We can already see this desideratum has teeth. Interpreting c as disjunction, for example, makes a nonsense of the fact that Sally associates with it the rule that A is entailed by AcB. Having a basic disposition to infer A from A or B would be irrational! This is representative, and what we need to do is add more auxiliary assumptions, this time about what a rational agent could or could not be like—in order to derive specific predictions about what c denotes.

The following auxiliary normative assumptions will suffice to generate the prediction that c denotes conjunction:

- A substantively rational agent would be such that they find primitively compelling the inference from A and B to A, they find primitively compelling the inference from A and B to B, and they find primitively compelling the inference from A, B jointly to A and B.
- For no content X other than conjunction would a substantively rational agent be such that they find primitively compelling the inference from AXB to A, they find primitively compelling the inference from AXB to B, and they find primitively compelling the inference from A, B jointly to AXB.

Notice here we *use* rather than mention the concept of conjunction in formulating the normative claims. The first normative assumption identifies a content that *does* make these practices rational: conjunction.[9] The second is a uniqueness assumption: that *only* conjunction does this. This pair is characteristic, and typically, the normative uniqueness assumptions are far

---

[9] If we had started with bizarre cognitive architectures, such as a subject who found the introduction and elimination rules of Prior's *tonk* compelling, then the parallel story would break down at this point. No substantively rational agent would find those rules primitively compelling, no matter what connective property it denoted. What the *most* substantively rational interpretation would do with such recherché cases is an open question: it might be that assigning it conjunction, disjunction or treating is as denotationless are all in the running. In general, drastic, unsalvageable irrationality will often lead to indeterminacy in interpretation.

more problematic than the identification assumptions—but in the present case, I hope the reader will agree both are very plausible.[10]

The argument to the conclusion that Sally's connective concept c denotes conjunction is as follows.

First, we have the a posteriori assumption that c plays a distinctive cognitive role in Sally's cognitive architecture, captured by the given rules. Second, we have Substantive Radical Interpretation, which tells us that the correct interpretation of c is one that maximizes (substantive) rationality of the agent. We now need, third, a 'localizing' assumption, *inferential role determinism for* c, which says that the interpretation on which Sally is most rational overall is one on which Sally's inferential practices concerning c (the ones specified earlier) are rational. Putting these three together, we have the following: the correct interpretation of Sally is one that makes the inferential role associated with c most rational.

The final element to add to this is the pair of normative premises introduced above, which tell us that conjunction is the thing that (uniquely) makes those particular inferences rational. With that added, we can derive that Sally's connective concept c denotes conjunction.

I finish by emphasizing a few things in this derivation. First, the assumptions about cognitive architecture are sufficient (given the other premises) to derive the metasemantic result that c denotes conjunction. There's no suggestion here that they're necessary, in order for c to denote conjunction. Remember—the aim was to show what Radical Interpretation predicts for a certain possible, contingent architecture, not about what is required in order to think conjunctive thoughts per se.

Second, the localizing assumption that I flagged up plays a very significant role. The most rationalizing global interpretation of an agent can in principle attribute local irrationalities—there could be other inferences Sally makes that involve c, which are irrational by the lights of the interpretation of c as conjunction. For example, the stated rules are silent about the way that conjunction figures in desires, and if it figured in desires in a way that would be best rationalized by interpreting c as disjunction, then there would

---

[10] Thomas Brouwer suggests the concepts *and* and *but* as a potential problem case. But I think that on reflection, it is no counterexample. Either the distinctive contrast associated with the *word* 'but' is a linguistic phenomenon, with the *thought expressed* by 'A but B' being *A and B*, but with an additional contrastive thought implicated. Then the best deserver for the label 'the concept *but*' is the concept conjunction. Alternatively, there is a single fused contrastive-conjunctive *thought A but B*. In that case, one should not move from A, B alone to the contrastive-conjunctive thought *A but B*.

be an interpretative tension, and it is not at all clear that a plausible theory would predict that *c* picks out conjunction. Inferential role determinism assures us that we're dealing a case where 'all else is equal', where such pressures are absent.

Third, the normative assumptions themselves, even if accepted as true, are the sort of things we would expect to be backed by more detailed first-order normative(/epistemological) theory. The need for that kind of principled backing is something that I emphasized in chapter 1. Why is it that it's rational to perform, and find primitively compelling, the inferences involving conjunction? Surely the full story has something to do with the fact that those inferences are guaranteed to be truth-preserving, since they are valid. Why is it that no other connective content will do the job? Presumably this will be defended on the grounds that conjunction uniquely has the property of making the inferences in question valid. But why is validity required to rationalize those rules?[11] Certain of the inferences we're disposed to perform—even those that are plausibly basic—are not guaranteed to be truth-preserving, so it's not clear why validity is required for rationalizing an inferential disposition. This is, essentially, to ask a first-order question about the epistemology of logic, about whether and why validity should be an epistemically significant relation. The normative uniqueness assumption I have used assumes, in effect, that it is especially significant. But we could spend a lot of time debating whether this is correct. For reasons of space, I won't enter into that here, but I want to highlight the delicate dialectical interplay here between the cognitive architecture and normative assumptions: to explain in the way I have indicated why a concept means what it does, we need to draw on substantive theses in epistemology or practical reason, and potentially refine our assumptions about cognitive architecture to reflect what we learn about the way that a concept should be deployed, if it is to play that normative role.

2.2 How Negation Gets Its Meaning

The previous section showed how a familiar idea about how the reference of *and* is fixed may be derived from Radical Interpretation. But conjunction is

---

[11] This is the point where explanations end, for Peacocke: His 'general form' of determination theories (theories that fix reference) simply stipulate that the rules are to be made valid. On the present theory, validity gets into the act only if we can defend its epistemological significance.

in many ways the simplest case. One with far more intricacy is the concept of negation. One reason the case is more complex is that there is real disagreement about what inferences are valid for negation, and what sort of semantic value it should be given. Classical logicians say one thing, intuitionists, paraconsistency theorists and others say something else. The sort of debate about the epistemology of logic I highlighted at the end of the last section is about how to pin down the epistemic significance of agreed-on rules of conjunction introduction and elimination. In the case of negation, the rules are not agreed-on. We will need to keep track of this potential variation both at the level of the agent's architecture (what rules they in fact find primitively compelling) and at the level of normative theory (what rules are in fact valid).

The first three framing assumptions about this set-up are as in the previous section: Sally's mental content is carried by individual states, which can be typed as beliefs, desires, etc., prior to and independently of interpretation.

The fourth assumption for conjunction consisted in some *inferential rules* which Sally found primitively compelling. I switch the focus in the present case from patterns of belief formation, to other aspects of the way she manages attitudes. For example, as well as believing some things, Sally also disbelieves others. Sally never flat-out believes and disbelieves the same proposition (this is part of the functional role that allows us to identify her belief states and disbelief states as such, irrespective of their content). Further, both belief and disbelief come in degrees, and the fact about flat-out belief is subsumed in this generalization: her degree of belief and of disbelief in a single proposition A sum to 1.[12] When she finds a derivation-relation primitively compelling, such as the one from AcB to A, she sees to it that her degree of belief in AcB doesn't exceed her degree of belief in A (or equivalently, that her degree of disbelief in AcB is at least as high as that which she has in A). That goes also for derivations that she finds derivatively compelling, in virtue of chaining together primitively compelling derivations. I see these patterns as subsuming and generalizing those cited in the previous section.

I am taking Sally to be classically minded, and so for her, here is a way in which beliefs and disbeliefs relate:

---

[12] This is an assumption about the structure of Sally's attitudes, formulable independently of the particular contents involved (even *logical* contents). It's a good candidate to be a constraint of *structural* rationality even in the ultra-thin sense that I defend in Williams (2017).

Sally's degree of belief in nA is equal to her degree of disbelief in A.[13]

This pattern in Sally's attitudes is 'primitively compelling' in the same way as the belief-to-belief transitions of the previous sections were.

We can use these facts to draw out other features of Sally's cognitive economy involving the concept n. For example, if Sally were to flat-out believe A and flat-out believe nA, then she will end up believing and disbelieving A. But as remarked above, Sally avoids that combination of attitudes, so she will avoid believing both A and nA. We can expect a version of reductio: if she thinks that A and nA follows from X, then since she's committed to disbelieving A and nA, she's committed to disbelieving X, and so to believing nX.

At this point, the story rolls on as it did for conjunction, *mutatis mutandis*. Again, normative assumptions will play a big role, and we can expect them also to be committal. Here they are:

- A substantively rational agent will find primitively compelling an equality between their degree of belief in not-A and their degree of disbelief in A.
- For no content X other than negation would a substantively rational agent find primitively compelling an equality between their degree of belief in X-A and their degree of disbelief in A.

Again, the first identifies a content that makes rational sense of the way Sally deploys n. The second claims that the content is unique in doing this.

From this point, we derive that n denotes negation just as before. First, we have the a posteriori assumption that n plays the mentioned cognitive role in Sally's cognitive architecture, captured by the given rules. Second, we have Substantive Radical Interpretation, which tells us that the correct interpretation of n is one that maximizes (substantive) rationality of the agent. Third, there is the 'localizing' assumption, *inferential role determinism for n*, which

---

[13] For a systematic discussion of probability and nonclassical logics, see Williams (2016a), which covers both intuitionistic and paraconsistent probabilities as generalizations of the classical case. In theorizing about nonclassical probabilities, it may be helpful to appeal to an attitude of *conditional disbelief*, which measures how much we reject one thing conditionally on rejecting another. This allows a generalized formulation of the above: the conditional degree of disbelief in C on A is equal to the conditional degree of belief in nC on nA. Conditional disbelief allows us to formulate a logic-free version of proof by cases: $B(C)=1$ when $B(C|A)=1$ and $D(C|A)=0$. This turns into a more familiar (probabilistic) formulation of proof by cases when reformulated in terms of n.

says that the interpretation on which Sally is most rational overall is one on which Sally's inferential practices concerning n (the ones specified earlier) are rational. Putting these three together, we have the following: the correct interpretation of Sally is one that makes the inferential role associated with n most rational. The normative premise then tells us that negation is the thing that (uniquely) makes those particular inferences rational. Upshot: Sally's n denotes negation.

Since the derivation is just as before, the same structural caveats and vulnerabilities affect it—we can again expect an interplay between first-order epistemology of logic and the assumptions about cognitive architecture.

A new issue with negation, however, is that revisionary logicians will certainly deny the normative premises. On a paraconsistent treatment of negation one should sometimes believe both A and not-A—e.g. when A is a paradoxical proposition like the Liar. In general, the paraconsistentist urges that degree of belief in not-A can and should sometimes exceed degree of disbelief in A. An intuitionist urges that degree of belief in not-A can and should sometimes be less than degree of disbelief in A. If Patchy is a borderline red/orange colour patch, one might reject both the proposition that Patchy is red and the proposition that Patchy is not red, without believing either.

The dispute about normative principles is reflected in a point about the assumed cognitive architecture. If Sally is as described, then she has internalized classical assumptions. Someone who has internalized paraconsistent or intuitionist logic would not have the kind of cognitive architecture just described.

If Sally has internalized classical logic, and classical logic is the right logic, then the derivation works as stated. A second case to consider is where intuitionistic logic is correct, but a match is maintained since Sally has internalized intuitionistic deployments of n, not classical ones. The derivation above needs to be adjusted as regards both cognitive architecture and normative assumptions. In this setting, there is an 'intuitionistic negation' to be meant, which will make sense of Sally's deployments of n, and the only challenge is to describe them in enough detail that a normative uniqueness assumption is plausible.[14]

---

[14] See Harris (1982). Let me flag one issue here. Standard intuitionistic proof rules are all classically valid, and so *classical* negation is prima facie a candidate interpretation that would make sense of intuitionistic-Sally's cognition. To this, let me note that intuitionistically structured degrees of belief involve patterns that are not rational by the lights of classical logic—e.g. zero degree of belief in both A and in not-A. So for the sort of cognition I was just appealing to,

Let us consider then the case where cognition and normative require-ments do not match. Suppose that intuitionist logic is the right logic, but Sally has internalised classical rules—in that setting, I think the result we would want is that her concept n denotes intuitionistic negation, but the rules that Sally finds primitively compelling for negation are *mistaken*. But the question will arise about why *that* would count as the correct interpret-ation. In the Radical Interpretation framework, the answer must be that doing so *best* rationalizes her cognitive economy. That is perfectly plausible: the intuitionist should say that there is no way of making Sally perfectly rational, but the claim would be that interpreting her as speaking about intuitionistic negation scores best. It depicts her as following mistaken rules, but modulo that important mistake, her mental economy makes perfect sense.[15]

The obvious challenge is: why shouldn't we interpret Sally as talking about *classical* negation? This, it might be thought, would preserve a perfect rationalization of the way she deploys negation. To this, the appropriate response is that if intuitionism is correct, there is no such thing as classical negation. If there were a 'classical negation', for which unrestricted classical introduction and elimination rules were valid, as well as an 'intuitionistic negation' for which unrestricted classical introduction and elimination were valid, then we can prove that the classical rules are also valid for the so-called 'intuitionistic negation' (Harris (1982)). So part of assuming intuitionistic logic is correct is assuming that there's no classical competitor.[16]

---

classical logic would prima facie be a bad candidate. The point, to be discussed further below, about whether there is such a thing as *classical negation* if intuitionism is true or vice versa, is also pertinent.

[15] In my 2017, I argue for a model on which *structural* rationality does not commit an agent to endorsing any particular logic. On that view, the interpretations that attributes to the subject thoughts involving classical negation, despite patterns of partial belief which are characteristic of paraconsistency or intuitionism, can still make her structurally rational. And of course, if one has been taught that such-and-such is the right way to handle negation, then these facts may justify (at least pro tanto) one handling negation in those ways.

[16] We could consider interpreting Sally's n as denoting a connective for which restricted versions of classical negation rules are valid. But since Sally's classical presuppositions were not restricted in this way, this moves us back into the terrain of trade-offs, where we admit Sally is not perfectly rational, but argue about the most rationalizing of these not-perfectly-rational interpretations. I suspect that attributing Sally tacit (and perhaps not fully justified) beliefs that the law of excluded middle holds will be better than attributing to her some gerrymandered content with ad hoc restrictions to which she is insensitive. A relevant factor here will also be the pressure towards *shared* content that I later argue will arise if there is a linguistic expression of this concept—in that case, where Sally is in conversation with intuitionists who can be perfectly rationalized using intuitionistic negation, there are additional pressures towards attributing to her the intuitionistic content.

The fourth case is where the match breaks down in the opposite direction. Sally has internalized intuitionistic rules, but classical logic is the right logic. Here, I think the best rationalization would be that her concept denotes classical negation. It is again true that some of her deployments are mistaken—she won't draw inferences that she should do, and she will assign degrees of belief to negated propositions in ways she ought not to. But the claim would be that the interpretation which scores best depicts her as speaking about classical negation, but holding some false beliefs about it.

In cases where there is a match between cognition and normative requirements, I anticipate derivations that n means *negation* being available, and so we can claim that Radical Interpretation (together with architectural and normative assumptions) predicts the denotation of that concept. I don't expect a neat prediction like this when there is a lack of match between the internalised logic and the true logic. In that case, the facts about content are fixed by the result of a trade-off between different ways of locating Sally's mistake, and I am content to claim that it's plausible that Radical Interpretation can accommodate such cases.

2.3 Skolemite Puzzles about Quantification

We can express thoughts that range over *everything* without restriction. Our ability to do so is, furthermore, significant to us. The philosophical thesis of physicalism is that absolutely everything is physical, not that everything-around-here is physical. Without the ability to talk about absolutely everything, such theses would be ineffable. The moral rule is that *all* people should be treated fairly, not that all people-who-meet-some-further-condition should be so treated. The 'all' still needs to be absolutely unrestricted in force in order to capture the intended thought, and this illustrates that even explicitly restricted quantification ('all people') presupposes that we are not missing out on absolutely anything in the underlying domain from which the restricted class is selected.

But against this, there are formal results that show there are 'skolemite', restricted interpretations of the generality of 'everything' and 'all' on which our interpretee Sally doesn't quantify over absolutely everything—and which are otherwise very similar to the correct interpretation.[17] It has

---

[17] Skolem (1920), Putnam (1980).

proved to be a headache for metasemantics to explain how the unrestricted, rather than skolemite, interpretation is selected. The current section describes these skolemite interpretations. The next section puts forward an account of how quantification gets its unrestricted meaning. The reader who wants to black-box some of the background may skip ahead now.

Take Sally's language of thought, and let us suppose that we know what objects her singular concepts denote, what properties the general concepts pick out, what concepts pick out conjunction, negation, existential and universal quantification for her. We'll be assuming that Sally's language of thought doesn't have expressive resources beyond these 'first-order' ones. That's a restriction on the argument, but if unrestricted quantification is possible, it's surely possible for a thinker with only these resources, so we have no need of extra generality to set up our puzzle. In sum: everything about the interpretation Sally's first-order conceptual repertoire is fixed, other than the things that her quantifiers range over—the domain.

Here's the standard skolemite result:

Let (first-order) language L have an intended interpretation, I, with (infinite) domain D. Then there is an interpretation I* with domain D*, D* a subset of D, which makes exactly the same sentences of L true, where I* is chosen so that D* is countable, and so that I and I* will coincide on the extensions assigned to names, predicates and function-symbols, modulo the cut-down domain.[18]   (The interpretations give the standard meanings to connectives and quantifiers.)

Now take D to be the correct, unrestricted interpretation (if you're worried about whether there can be a 'domain' of absolutely everything, I have a footnote[19] for you). D is hugely infinitary, containing uncountably many

---

[18] The standard result is stronger than this: it is that every open sentence of L satisfied by a tuple of objects drawn from D* according to I* iff it is satisfied by the tuple according to I. The condition stated in the text is 'elementary equivalence' whereas the full condition is 'elementary substructure'. This matters a great deal to model-theorists, but won't matter for our purposes here, except that it shows one could also throw in the constraint that the properties assigned to multi-placed as well as one-place predicates be held fixed, and the construction would go through.

[19] There are several ways to get worried about a domain of absolutely everything, from the metaphysical (the idea of 'indefinite extensible' kinds of objects) to the technical (that there is no set of everything). In both cases, an analogous skolem puzzle can be set up so long as there is some uncountable set of things (e.g. real numbers, regions of space time) that we think that Sally definitely can quantify over. To recover the challenge for truly unrestricted quantification, there are various options, but the one that fits best with the presuppositions of this book is to insist

regions of space time, possible people, and sets. But D^* can only contain countably many such things. It must leave out most of the things we quantify over. Yet any book of information we might write down to capture the truths will be true also on this restricted interpretation.

The restricted interpretation also doesn't disrupt any aspect of the correct interpretation *other* than the domain. The denotations of individual concepts are the same, for example. The same goes for the denotations of general concepts—not everything that satisfies that property will be in the extension of the concept according to the new interpretation, admittedly, but the following condition is satisfied: that the extension of a concept that denotes P is the set of all things in the domain that instantiate P. This is what makes the challenge strong and distinctive: many philosophers have proposed constraints on the interpretation of predicates/general concepts that would rule out deviant interpretations of predicates/general concepts. In the next chapter, I'll be discussing such constraints myself. But the skolemite challenge as I construe it simply sidesteps all such constraints by holding the interpretation of everything but the quantifier constant.

I want to extract from this a result not about the truth values of sentences of Sally's language of thought, but truth conditions: the truth-value distribution across worlds. To do this, we need to work not with interpretations that assign only extensions to Sally's concepts and thoughts, but intensions: functions from worlds to extensions.

Extended skolem   Let L be a first-order language with an intended interpretation, I, which at world w has (infinite) domain D_w. Then there is an interpretation I^* with domain D^*_w at w, D^*_w a subset of D_w, which makes exactly the same set of sentences of L true at each w (i.e. assigns the same truth conditions to L-sentences as I does). Furthermore, I^* can be chosen so that D^*_w is countable for each w, and so that I and I^* will coincide on the extensions at each world assigned to names, predicates and function-symbols (modulo the cut-down domain in each case).

You get this extended result just by 'walking around' from world to world and apply the standard skolem result at each one, and gluing the pieces together. We can push this yet further. Perhaps the correct interpretation for

---

that 'interpretations' are higher-order entities, and in particular domains are values of higher order variables, not sets. I continue to talk about them mostly as if they are sets, for convenience, but I trust that the reader can reconstruct the type-theoretic official versions if required.

Sally's language of thought determines not truth conditions for her thoughts, but a rule that determines the truth conditions for those thoughts as tokened in this or that context. Again, by making the domain relative to a context-world pair, and walking around and applying the skolem result, we can get a doubly extended skolem result.

We can extend the skolem result again, in exactly parallel fashion, if we want to construct a deviant restricted interpretation.

So what we have here is an obviously deviant, restricted interpretation of Sally's language of thought. But it assigns exactly the same coarse-grained content to her thoughts as the correct interpretation (in the case of indexical thoughts, it matches the assignment of truth conditions at contexts). There is no difference in which patterns of inference are valid or invalid, since all the logical aspects of the interpretation are held fixed. And no constraints on the interpretation of singular or general concepts in the language are going to explain what rules out the deviant interpretation in this case, since they're held fixed. What on earth could explain how Sally manages to quantify unrestrictedly, then?

2.4 How Quantification Gets Its Meaning

To recap: we can find a deviant interpretation that agrees with the correct, unrestricted, interpretation of Sally on the truth value of every thought she can think. We can choose the interpretation so it agrees with the distribution of truth values over thoughts not just in the actual world, but at every possible situation. Indeed, we can choose an interpretation of an indexical thought so it coincides with the correct interpretation on the truth conditions assigned at every context. And here's the rub: such deviant interpretations diverge from the correct interpretation only on the domain of the quantifiers. So they assign the same denotation to singular concepts, predicative concepts[20] and the propositional connectives.[21]

---

[20] Technically, the extension of predicates/general concepts is the intersection of their 'original' interpretation with the new domain. But that's just a technical detail: we could imagine assigning the properties as denotations, constant no matter what the domain is, and their 'extension', in a given context, is then to be the things within the contextual domain that have that property. So we can't dismiss the restricted interpretations on the Lewisian grounds that they assign less natural properties to predicates, since they do not do so.

[21] Lewis (1984) puzzled why Putnam (1980) used the rather involved apparatus of Skolem's result in his arguments, rather than the technically simpler underdetermination-by-permutation that is the focus in Putnam (1981). One good answer to this (though maybe not Putnam's!)

Because of the match with truth values/truth conditions, you won't be able to rule out the deviant interpretation of Sally on the grounds that it makes her thoughts any less reliable than the original interpretation. Because of the way the interpretations on everything-except-quantifiers work, side-constraints on the interpretation of singular terms and the like won't help at all. The challenge for us is to explain how, despite the existence of such 'skolemite' interpretations, Sally manages to generalize unrestrictedly, in the way that philosophy and morality presupposes she can.

Following the pattern of the previous two sections, I will make some architectural assumptions about the way that quantificational thoughts figure in our psychology, and explore what Radical Interpretation will predict under those assumptions. The first three architectural assumptions I will make are just as before—that belief states are structured, that facts about syntax are grounded prior to questions of content arising, and that we can pick out inferential dispositions interrelating belief-types, again prior to questions of content being determined. I will continue to use the Peacockian idea that certain core inferences are treated as primitively compelling.[22]

The fourth architectural assumption is about the character of the inferential role associated with the quantifier concept *everything* which I write as q. I'll concentrate on just one of these rules:

- *From* qx:Fx *derive* Fa

is that the Skolem construction, though clearly an unintended interpretation, holds fixed so much of subsentential structure that throwing in a causal theory of reference for singular terms would cut no ice, whereas that would be an effective gambit against permutation arguments. In the latter context, Putnam will be forced to deploy his notorious 'just more theory' manoeuvre against causal side-constraints, which Lewis 1984 very effectively debunks. So many theories—perhaps even Lewis's own—don't have a very effective response to the original 1980 underdetermination argument.

[22] One thing that's often noted is a restriction to first-order languages, since the technical results don't go through given 'full' second-order quantifiers. That restriction will cut ice only if we had reason to interpret these higher order quantifiers with 'full' as opposed to 'Henkin' interpretations (see Shapiro 1991 for the generalization of skolem to the second-order setting with Henkin semantics). More interesting is the presence of quantified modal resources. However, I don't find it at all credible that our ability to quantify restrictedly depends on our ability to think thoughts whose logical form goes beyond that of the first-order extensional calculus, so even if there was a failure to generalize, the original problem would be pressing. So I'm happy setting these aside.

Let me also highlight the point just made that skolemite interpretations aren't ruled out by metasemantic constraints on the denotation of singular or predicative concepts or propositional connectives. That's one reason why the skolemite challenge is so interesting—you can fix determinate reference for everything else, and the puzzle over what fixes the domain of quantification remains.

Our interpretee, Sally, endorses an instance of this for every individual concept a that she possesses. We'll come back in a moment to the question of whether this is all of the relevant facts relating Sally to tokens of this inference-type.

If the story rolled on from this point as it did for conjunction, we might expect that we'd find Radical Interpretation predicting something along the same lines as the Peacockian 'determination theory' for conjunction, that is, the semantic value for q will be the quantifier, whatever it is, that make all instances of the above instances of a valid type. Just as before, Radical Interpretation will approximate an interpretative constraint of this kind. Maximising Sally's rationality includes maximizing her justified beliefs, which *ceteris paribus* includes interpreting q so as to make the inferences justification-preserving. Making them valid looks just the ticket.

If that was all we could extract from the story, we'd be in trouble. There are so many ways of choosing restricted quantifiers as an interpretation of q to make all instances of the above truth-preserving. The ones that are constructed by the skolem procedure are among them, since the skolemite interpretation's restricted domain includes every object for which the subject has an individual concept a.

In some special restricted cases, we have devices that allow us to construct concepts for every member of a restricted domain (as in our procedure for constructing numerals for natural numbers). But that's not so in the general case. It's not even so in very large restricted domains, for example for quantifiers over the real numbers, over space-time points, or sets.[23]

Radical Interpretation can explain how finding tokens of the elimination rule above primitively compelling can fix a truly unrestricted interpretation of

---

[23] One reaction in the literature has been to double down on the idea of making instances of the above scheme valid, and argue that more 'instances' are relevant than one might at first think. Thus, one might argue that Sally is disposed to find compelling not just instances of the above scheme for singular concepts she currently has available, but also for potential singular terms not currently within her ken (this is how I read McGee 2000). I think, though, that this is ultimately not a productive approach. Although the general idea that Sally's endorsement of the inference pattern above is 'open-ended' when she's using an absolutely unrestricted quantifier is a good one, I do not think that this is best factored into the theory of how denotation is fixed by an insistence that those extra token inferences be interpreted so as to be instances of a valid type. Briefly, the problem is that consistently with this constraint, one can interpret the agent as deploying a contingent and contextually flexible restricted quantifier whose domain 'expands and contracts' in sync with the agent's available singular conceptual resources. In a slogan: using counterfactual pegs to fix quantifier domains only end up constraining the counterfactual domains.

our quantificational concepts. It can do so by appeal to the epistemological character of even a single token instance of the inference-type.

Take an interpretation where Sally uses a quantifier tacitly restricted to some skolemite domain S, and see what we think of the epistemological status:

- *From* Everything (psst... in S) is beautiful, *derive* Toby is beautiful.

Now, Toby is among the items in the skolemite domain S, we may assume. So the inference preserves truth, on the suggested interpretation. But what's striking is that Sally is not interpreted as having or utilizing any information either way about this fact. To state the obvious: that's not the usual way we would think of restricted quantification as going. For example, in order to justify my belief that 'Toby should be treated fairly' by inference from my (justified) belief that 'All people should be treated fairly', I surely also need to have the justified belief that Toby is a person. After all, if I wasn't justified in thinking that Toby was a person—if my evidence was that he's my neighbour's cat—then the justification for the derived claim would be undercut. The same goes for ordinary, tacitly restricted quantification. From 'everyone has some marking to do' (contextually restricted to faculty members) I can't be justified in believing 'Toby has some marking to do' unless I have some justification for believing that Toby is a member of faculty. What's striking and central about Sally's deployment of an unrestricted quantifier is that her inference is not enthymematic in this way. She doesn't pause to check whether or not Toby has this or that feature before inferring that he's beautiful.

In sum: Sally's justification for the belief that *everything is beautiful* transfers to *Toby is beautiful* without mediation. The lack of mediation explains why her acceptance of the inference rule is 'open ended', as theorists like McGee (2000) have emphasized. But what matters for grounding quantifier-meaning is not the way this open-endedness manifests in the piling up of accepted instances of the inference across endless counterfactual scenarios, but the lack of mediation in the epistemological structure of the inference, a feature that is already present in the actual cases.

I propose the following piece of epistemology. Consider an elimination rule for a *restricted* quantifier—whether restricted explicitly (all people) or restrictedly tacitly (either by contextual mechanisms or in the way proposed by the skolemite construction). If deployments of that rule are to transfer justification, then that rule will have to include a side-premise, to the effect that the object in question has the feature that defines the restriction. That side-premise is unnecessary to transfer justification for an *unrestricted* quantifier.[24]

This piece of epistemology then tells us why we wouldn't be interpreting Sally as substantively rational if we interpreted her as using a skolemite quantifier—we'd be representing her as constantly engaging in inferences that would require enthymematic premises for which she has no justification.[25]

This story is my proposed resolution of long-standing skolemite puzzles about what grounds our ability to quantify unrestrictedly.[26] Methodologically, it illustrates the virtue of thinking through what Radical Interpretation requires in detail—in the case of conjunction, we only needed to make the primitively compelling inferences valid in order to pin down the denotation. That is insufficient here, since making valid the elimination rule (and indeed, the analogous introduction rule) wouldn't eliminate the deviant interpretations.

---

[24] Anandi Hattiangadi raised the following query. What if the restricted domain turned out to be something like: all cognitively accessible things. Then, it might be thought, even without side-premises the inference from 'Everything cognitively accessible is F' to 'A is F' is justified without additional assumptions, since the very fact of naming A ensures that it is within the domain. The success of my defence against the skolemite in this sort of case would rest on recherché question of epistemology: does the justification of the instance depend on the (self-verifying) side-premise that 'A is cognitively accessible', or does the very automaticity of this side-premise mean that it can be cut out of the justificatory story altogether? Considerations of uniformity in epistemological theory support the first option, I think. Side-premises are needed in almost every restricted quantifier, and there's no obvious reason to make these recherché cases exceptions. So I think the rebuttal offered in the main text would extend to this case, if necessary. It should be noted, too, that there's no guarantee at all that skolemite constructions would produce domains as well-behaved as the interesting one that Hattigiangadi flags up—consider the problem of finding a witness for 'there are things that are not cognitively accessible' in worlds where that thought is true.

[25] Jason Turner raised the following query. Suppose—plausibly enough—that some of the mental names in Sally's head lack denotation. In such a situation, even unrestricted quantifier rules would need side-premises. E.g. in a simple negative free logic, if everything is beautiful, it follows that Pegasus is beautiful only if we assume that Pegasus exists. Once we add that side-premise, then the skolemite might suggest reinterpreting the *existence* concept as *within the skolemite domain* and the dialectic restarts. However, in that negative free setting, the existential generalization rule (on atomic concepts) will not need side-premises: we can infer unrestrictedly from Pegasus being beautiful to something being beautiful, since ex hypothesi empty names don't figure in true atomics.

[26] It also undercuts one of the arguments in Sider (2009, 2011) for positing that 'naturalness' (or his generalized notion of a 'structural' entity) applies to quantifiers—since a key selling point of that is that when married to the kind of reference-magnetism, it could explain how we manage to quantify absolutely unrestrictedly. If the above is correct, this is fixed independently of considerations of naturalness.

I finish by running through the derivation of Sally's q denoting the unrestrictedly general universal quantifier. First, we have the a posteriori assumption that c plays a distinctive cognitive role in Sally's cognitive architecture, captured by the unmediated elimination rule. Second, we have Substantive Radical Interpretation, which tells us that the correct interpretation of q is one that maximizes (substantive) rationality of the agent. We add the 'localizing' assumption, inferential role determinism for q, which says that the interpretation on which Sally is most rational overall is one on which the particular inferential dispositions captured by the rules just given for q are rational. Putting these three together, we have the following: the correct interpretation of Sally is one that makes the inferential role associated with q most rational. And now we add the conclusion of the discussion we've just been having: that the way to make the inferential role that consists in the elimination rule without side-premises most rational (especially to make it most justification-preserving) is to make it denote the unrestricted quantifier.

2.5 Conclusion

This chapter has outlined three conditional predictions of Radical Interpretation. Assuming a suitable architecture, and granted suitable normative assumptions, we can explain in virtue of what agents' concepts have the contents of conjunction, negation, and universal quantification. Unlike some inferentialists, I do not claim that this is the only way to have concepts with those contents. Nor do I even claim that this is the right metasemantics for us—I see the questions about cognitive architecture as answerable to empirical facts, which I have not surveyed here (questions of the extent to which we each internalize, say, classical logic I think are particularly tricky, and the whole issue of the format in which human reasoning is carried out is an open psychological question). I do think that the broad *framework* of this account is representative, though our own case is likely to be much more holistic and messy. Fictional characters like Sally, with her neat inferential behaviour, are undoubtedly idealized. But just as with other idealizations, this allows us to isolate and study vector components that are active in our own case.

The three logical concepts in this chapter form a natural stopping point—particularly if we continue to assume classical logic as a background and that Sally has appropriately classical concepts. For negation and conjunction are expressively adequate for propositional connectives in general—disjunction, material conditionals and biconditionals and the like can all be characterized in terms of them. That means that, if the content of conjunction and negation are nailed down in the way described, it's very plausible that the content of other propositional connective concepts will be nailed down, if by nothing else, by their relations in Sally's cognitive economy to the ones already described. Of course, it's plausible that there will be primitively compelling transitions featuring, say, disjunction just as much as there are for conjunction and negation. Those will certainly matter to reference-fixing. But the fact that disjunction $A \vee B$ are (for a classicist like Sally) treated as equivalent to a negated conjunction $\sim[\sim Ac \sim B]$ will be an additional source of interpretative pressure that helps us explain why '$\vee$' has the content that it does. A similar story goes for the relation between the unrestricted existential quantifiers, which Sally will treat as equivalent to a combination of negations and the unrestricted universal. Unless the rest of Sally's cognitive architecture in dealing with such concepts is somehow *in tension* with these facts about what she treats-as-equivalent, then rationalization will indeed favour the obvious assignments of classical content to these concepts.

Moving forward, then, I will be taking as given the content of the first-order logical structure of Sally's thought. The question then becomes: what should we expect, given Radical Interpretation, to be the pattern of denotation for singular and general contents?

3

Radical Interpretation and Reference Magnetism

3.1 Reference Magnetism Would Explain the Denotation of Observational Concepts

Observable properties include textures, sizes, shapes, motions, colours, tastes, and sounds. Observable concepts such as *rough*, *large*, *round*, *in motion*, *red*, *sweet*, or *loud* denote observable properties, and for each of these concepts we have a disposition to treat certain kinds of characteristic experiences as good—even overriding—evidence for the presence of something satisfying the concept. It's easy to make a start on assumptions about cognitive architecture that would help explain why observable concepts denote what they do. Following the pattern of the last chapter, we set out a conceptual role for *green* or *in motion* just as we did for *and* or *all*, this time built around links to the canonical observational grounds for classifying something as green or in motion. However, a problem for generalizing that recipe is that there are plenty of properties that are reliably correlated with the cause of those experiences in us: whenever we see something in motion, the property *being in motion* is instantiated, but so is the disjunctive property of *being either in motion-and-visible or else in motion-and-invisible*. While we could plausibly argue that this observation-to-belief-forming practice was rationalized by the standard interpretation of our concepts, there are prima facie a multitude of competing candidates that would make the link between canonical observational grounds and deployment of the concept equally rational. In the last chapter, a critical part of deriving the prediction about why Sally's concepts denote what they do was a uniqueness assumption: only if they had such-and-such content would the way they're deployed be rational. This element of the story looks tricky to generalize.

There is a thesis about reference-fixing that would bridge that gap, if only we had the right to it. David Lewis famously claimed that all else equal, the

The Metaphysics of Representation. J. Robert G. Williams, Oxford University Press (2019).
© J. Robert G. Williams.
DOI: 10.1093/oso/9780198850205.001.0001

correct interpretation is that which attribute more *eligible* content.[1] Take the interpretation of predicates or general concepts, whose denotation will be a property. The *eligibility* of a property was a matter of its *degree of naturalness*, which in turn is measured by its 'distance' from the most basic, fundamental properties that (metaphysically) carve nature at its joints—the properties that Lewis would call perfectly natural. More disjunctive candidate properties are less natural. In Harold Hodes' now-familiar metaphor, natural properties are for Lewis 'reference magnets'.[2] On this story, patterns of deployment of a word or concept matter for fixing its reference, but the intrinsic nature of some properties matters too, and will in particular break a tie when two properties fit the deployment patterns equally well (the more natural ending up as the referent).

Given reference magnetism, a way forward becomes clear. If the conceptual role of these observational properties include not just the observation-link, but the fact that they are inductive concepts, then to predict that *green* denotes green or *in motion* denotes being in motion, we don't need to defend the view that greenness/being-in-motion is the unique way to rationalize our observational practice. Rather, we will only need to argue that among the candidates that would rationalize our observational practice, greenness or being in motion, etc., is the most natural. Reference magnetism will do the rest of the job. A role in generating good predictions about local patterns of reference for observational concepts is therefore one reason to like reference magnetism.

Another motivation—indeed the setting in which it was first introduced—is to rebut certain quite general underdetermination challenges. Start again from what we take to be the correct interpretation of Sally, which has her singular concepts (e.g. the perceptual demonstrative *that ball*) picking out objects in her local environment (a green ball she is in causal contact with) and her general concepts (e.g. *green*) picking out observable properties of the things around her. A permutation of the universe is a one-to-one, onto mapping f of the universe onto itself—the ball in Sally's environment is mapped, perhaps, to a small blue fuzzy creature in Alpha Centauri, and vice versa. Now consider a twisted interpretation defined up from this permutation. The twisted referent of a singular concept is just the image under f of the correct referent. If a general concept is correctly understood as denoting property P, it twistedly refers to the property that applies to something iff that thing is mapped by f onto something that has P. The small fuzzy

[1] Lewis (1983, 1984, 1992).   [2] Hodes (1984).

creature is in fact blue, so the property that 'green' picks out (accordingly to the correct interpretation) of course does not apply to it. But is the image under the permutation of something that is green, and so the property that 'green' picks out (according to the correct interpretation) does apply to it— and likewise though it is no ball, it satisfies the property that 'ball' picks out on the twisted interpretation. So 'that ball is green' is just as true under the twisted interpretation as it is under the original, even though now 'that ball' denotes a small blue creature rather than a green ball! The key is that the twisted interpretation puts in two twists into every such atomic thought— the twist in singular concept reference is cancelled out by a twist in general concept reference. The upshot is this: the twisted interpretation agrees with the in-fact correct one on the truth values of all thoughts, the truth conditions of whole thoughts, and the functions from contexts to truth conditions of indexical thoughts, despite the fact that the reference-scheme it embeds is entirely permuted.[3] So another challenge arises for the radical interpreter: what resources are there for declaring the twisted interpretation incorrect?

The suggestion of Lewis (1983, 1984) is that eligibility/degree of natural-ness saves the day. Even though the interpretation at the level of whole thoughts is invariant, the properties ascribed to predicates are less *natural* on the twisted interpretation than the original. The set of things green things are genuine similar in respect of colour. The set of things that green things map to under the permutation can be as dissimilar as you like, and in general our only fix on the property is by first characterizing what it is to be green, what the permutation is, and then putting the two pieces together. An eligibility constraint would help rebut the permutation argument.

Much hangs on the role of natural properties in interpretation in gener-ating positive predictions and rebutting objections. But it's unclear how they might enter into a Radical Interpretation story about mental content. For example, while Lewis endorsed both radical interpretation and reference magnetism, his explicit discussions focus on reference magnetism for the interpretation of natural language, not the interpretation of thought. He is clear in those discussions that natural properties will have some role or other in fixing mental content, but he never really discussed how. Even such a basic

---

[3] The origins of the argument go a long way back, but it is most associated with Quine (1960), Wallace (1977), and Putnam (1981). There are some delicate issues about how to generalize the argument, especially to languages allowing quantification over modal operators (see McGee 2005). The most general presentation I'm aware of, in which the results stated in the above text are proven and a response to McGee is given, is in Williams (2008b). I am here stating a version on interpreting thoughts rather than natural language.

question as the following is not clear: is the appeal to eligibility a factor which trades off against rationalizing the person's actions in the light of their experiences? Or is it something that arises out of rationalization? It is very unclear from a plain reading of the texts.[4] If naturalness is to play a role in Radical Interpretation as I've set it out, we can't leave such questions unsettled.

I will be arguing in this chapter that reference magnetism theses are generated by Radical Interpretation as I have been developing it. Magnetism is not a reference-determining factor that trades off against rationalization, but something predicted and explained by the latter, in a similar fashion to the results of the last chapter. Reference magnetism arises as a consequence of the combination of auxiliary assumptions about a subject's cognitive architecture and first-order normative (epistemological) assumptions.[5]

3.2 Explanatory Concepts Denote Potent Properties

We see a ball in motion, rolling from left to right. It vanishes behind a screen, and a few seconds later a ball emerges from the rightmost side. Given the observed motions, the best explanation is that one and the same ball persisted in constant motion while obscured by the screen. This is not just the best among bad alternatives, it is a *good* explanation and *much better* than rivals. Because of this, our observations justify our belief that the ball continued with constant velocity even while unobserved.

Abstracting from the details: we acquire data; we consider explanations of the data; among the explanations, if the best is sufficiently good and significantly better than the others, the data justifies our belief in the best explanation. This is a version of the normative, epistemological principle of inferring to the best explanation (IBE). I will be assuming that it is broadly correct.

(A terminological stipulation: henceforth 'best explanation' should be read as shorthand for explanations that are not just better than rivals, but also sufficiently good and significantly better.)

---

[4] No wonder many in the literature use the far-easier to understand discussion of how naturalness relates to linguistic interpretation in Lewis (1984), even though that toy model incorporates many assumptions of Lewis's dialectical opponent—even about natural language—that he himself rejects. That wouldn't matter too much if the toy model itself could be built up into a good metaphysics of content by factoring in naturalness—the aim isn't Lewis exegesis after all—but I have argued that the combination won't fly (Williams 2007).

[5] See Pautz (2013), Schwarz (2014), and especially Weatherson (2013) for the precursors to this combination of views.

In moving to a more precise formulation of IBE, one important choice point is this. In order to be IBE-justified in believing T on the basis of data D, must a subject (be justified in) believing that T is the best explanation of D? Or is that belief IBE-justified just in virtue of the fact that T is the best explanation of D? The former may fit highly sophisticated instances of theory-choice in science, but it would not apply to the ball-rolling case. Indeed, plausibly, the movement from observations to belief in that case is innate (Carey, 2009). The version of IBE I am interested in covers the ball-rolling case, so I assume that the principle takes the latter, more externalist form.

More specifically, the version of IBE I will work with is the following:[6]

IBE dogmatism (absolute version)
An agent is justified in believing T on the basis of data D if (a) T is the best explanation available; (b) the subject has no evidence to the contrary.

Life being what it is, subjects might not hit on the very best explanation of the data. But believing a pretty good explanation deserves more epistemic credit than believing a terrible one. More generally:

IBE dogmatism (comparative version)
An agent is more justified in believing T than she is in believing T* on the basis of data D if (a) T is a better theory than T*; (b) the subject has no evidence to the contrary.[7]

We now use this piece of epistemology to generate predictions about mental content.

---

[6] I am purposefully vague about what 'believing on the basis of data' amounts to. It may involve a real inference from one belief (whose content is the data) to another, or some more counterfactual dependence in which the data is one factor among several that sustain the belief. It may be pro tanto or all things considered justification. Alternatively, the agent's relation to the data may not be by believing it: perhaps perception of the relevant facts. It may be that in the relevant sense 'believing on the basis of data D' needs to be associated with a fairly rich functional role, whereby a proposition is not only believed, but treated *as an explanation* of D. In line with the generally externalist line, I do not think that it should involve having a belief with content: T is an explanation of D. But as illustrated, that is compatible with so many refinements, which I don't need to choose between for present purposes.

[7] Remember that 'best' explanation, as stipulatively understood here, involved more than just being better than all rivals: it has to be significantly better than them, and good enough. The comparative version entails that believing a theory that is better than all rivals is, in the absence of evidence, the belief that is *most* justified. That is compatible with it being *unjustified*, if no belief in any particular explanation is justified in the context in question (e.g. because the top explanations are clustered, or none is sufficiently good).

First, an assumption about cognitive architecture: Sally has some concepts that she is default disposed to deploy in explanations of her observations. These are her *explanatory* concepts. I will assume that items on the traditional list of observable concepts, both primary and secondary, work this way. In particular, Sally's concept M (*being in constant motion*), as well as being linked to observations of items visibly in constant motion, is for her an explanatory concept.

To supplement our normative assumption, IBE dogmatism, suppose also that some properties are such that explanations using them are ipso facto better—they are 'explanatorily potent' properties. Further: among these potent properties are smoothness, squareness, greenness, constant motion, and the rest of the familiar list of primary and secondary observable properties. Arbitrary disjunctions of potent properties are not potent.

Under these assumptions, Radical Interpretation entails that potent properties are reference-magnetic for explanatory concepts. Sally encounters balls rolling behind screens in period *t*, and the like, and believes on this basis *the ball is in M throughout t*. All else equal, we make Sally better justified (more reason-responsive) by interpreting *M* as denoting *in constant motion* rather than *visible and in constant motion or not visible and stationary*. This is because the first interpretation makes the content of her belief more potent, which all else equal makes it a better explanation of the data she has, which all else equal (by the comparative version of IBE dogmatism) makes her belief better justified, which all else equal makes her overall more substantively rational. And the most substantively rational interpretation is, according to Radical Interpretation, the correct one.

It's worth noting that this reference-magnetic role is restricted to concepts that feature in explanations. If a concept is not explanatory in an agent's cognitive economy (as the concept *grue* is not explanatory in my mental economy) then there is no argument that it will denote the most potent property possible. Potent properties are 'reference magnets' only for certain select concepts.

3.3 Natural Properties May Be Reference Magnets for Explanatory Concepts

Since 'potency' is just a label for any feature of properties that makes explanations better, the above argument is to this point schematic. We derive specific prediction about the reference-magnetism of *being in motion* against observationally equivalent rivals only by adding the extra assumption that *being in motion* is potent-whatever-that-may-amount-to, and its rivals are not.

The bare thesis that *the ball being in constant motion throughout t* (where *t* includes the period where it has vanished behind a screen) is a better explanation of the observed data than *the ball being in motion-while-visible and stationary-while-not-visible* might stand alone, independent of any analysis of 'potency'. A barrage of particular comparative evaluations like these, combined with Radical Interpretation, would explain some of our data, and if the same properties keep cropping up in them (including our list of primary and secondary observables), we might summarize the results by saying that smoothness, motion, greenness etc. are reference magnets, without having a grand theory of what it is about them that *makes* them feature in the better explanations. A particularist about potency would leave things there.

Non-particularists are those who offer an account of what it is about properties that makes explanations configuring them better (all else equal). For example: Ted Sider has argued that theories are better to the extent that they are couched in more natural terms, i.e. framed using concepts that denote more natural properties. In Sider's presentation, the naturalness of a theory is a basic explanatory virtue, to be set alongside simplicity, strength, and fit. Sider's thesis offers a swift and direct route to the conclusion (given Radical Interpretation and the background architectural and normative premises) that more natural properties are more reference-magnetic for explanatory concepts.

Sider's account is much more informative than that of the particularists, since it allows us to predict in advance which properties are reference-magnetic in this way, at least to the extent that we have an independent grip on relative naturalness. But many theorists will bump on the claim that the naturalness of a theory is a basic theoretical virtue, to be set alongside familiar basic virtues like simplicity, strength and fit with data.

Here is an alternative approach, which starts from those familiar theoretical virtues. In his work on laws of nature,[8] Lewis suggests we treat simplicity of an interpreted theory, which we can think of as a set of structured propositions, as a matter of what some call its elegance: how compactly expressible the theory is. Suppose, for example, one graphs a

---

[8] This is scattered through Lewis's writings, but his (1983) and (1994b) contain nice expositions.

finite array of data about the velocity of a falling ball (y-axis) against time (x-axis). There will always be some polynomial equation for y in terms of x that hits each data point exactly, though the curve it defines will in general wiggle this way and that between the points. Such a polynomial equation will typically take a long time to state, and use many parameters to specify. Despite fitting the data exactly, it is a bad theory. For example, as more data comes in, it will be extremely unlikely to lie on or even close to the wiggly polynomial curve that has been 'overfitted' to the existing data. The better theory posits a linear "curve": that the velocity is proportional to elapsed time. Unless the data has no noise in it whatsoever, this will have a *worse* fit to the data than the wiggly polynomial curve. But a simple linear equation, specified by a single parameter (the gravitational constant) is much more elegant than the complex polynomial that fits exactly. The wiggly theory is worse overall because a minor advantage in fit is outweighed by the linear theory's advantage in simplicity, understood here as measured by elegance (compact expressibility).[9]

A standing challenge to accounts of simplicity in terms of elegance so understood is that new expressive resources can radically change how compactly something can be stated. Here is Lewis's example of this: for an arbitrary theory T entailing the existence of at least one thing, let F be a new primitive predicate that applies to x iff T is true. Then 'there exists something which is F' is an ultra-compact formulation necessarily equivalent to T, entailing everything T entails, and fitting all the data T fits. Pull this trick for both the wiggly theory of the velocity-time data above and for the linear theory, and the result is two equally compact/elegant/simple theories, one that generates the wiggly curve, the other the straight line. The wiggly curve retains its advantage in fit, but is now as elegant as its rival. So the overfitted, wiggly theory (in its ultra-compact presentation) gets classified as best, and better than linear theory in either presentation. This is the wrong result.

To save the idea that simplicity is measured by elegance Lewis posited a 'canonical' language in which theories are to be expressed for the purposes of measuring their compactness. That canonical language won't contain trivializing predicates like F above—so the refutation is avoided.

Given a canonical language, we can then define a notion of simplicity for properties: simpler *properties* are those that are more compactly definable in the canonical language. The simplicity of an interpreted theory directly

---

[9] See Sober (2008, 2015) for overviews of the literature on model selection.

depends on the simplicity of the properties it invokes—the longer it takes to express the properties, the longer it takes to express the theory that ascribes them to things. For Lewis in his work on laws of nature, the canonical language was one that contained only broadly logical resources, plus predicates for every perfectly natural property and relation.[10] Since simpler properties are those that are more compactly definable in this language, simpler properties are those that are more compactly definable *in perfectly natural terms*. Lewis uses the term 'degree of naturalness' to measure the latter quantity, so the upshot is that more natural properties are thereby simpler.

Putting all this together, we get the following. Theories are better (all else equal) if they are simpler. They are simpler (all else equal) if they configure simpler properties, which is to say: if they configure more natural properties. So these theses entail that degree of naturalness is degree of potency.

What this means is that, given Radical Interpretation and the auxiliary architectural and normative assumptions, more natural properties are reference magnets. Lewis and Sider end up at the same place, though Lewis as I have reconstructed him took a longer route and from a more familiar list of the basic theoretical virtues.[11]

---

[10] Sider (2009, 2011) presses the following question: Lewis's perfectly natural properties and relations give a partial fix on a 'canonical' language, but what explains the rest of this language? Why unrestricted quantifiers rather than restricted ones, and which connectives does it contain? Will it contain mereological and set-theoretic terms, or will these be included only if they themselves are perfectly natural? Might the language contain modal or temporal operators? Sider's proposal for a principled fix is to extend the distinction between perfectly natural or 'structural' items and the rest beyond the case of properties and relations to which Lewis was committed, so that the only quantifiers that are included are the perfectly natural/structural ones. This is an interesting extension of the account, but I see no reason to think that it was Lewis's proposal. I think the Lewisian proposal is to list out a finite set of resources, and fill out the rest of the canonical language by appeal to the natural/non-natural distinction (in part because we lack the ability to keep on listing every natural predicate in a big long list). I don't want to take a stand between Siderian and Lewisian approaches here; it is less load-bearing, I think, on the current approach where magnetism is restricted to the inductive concepts, and what fixes e.g. the reference of our concept of unrestricted generality is the rationalization of inferential patterns of the last chapter, rather than the alleged magnetism of unrestricted generality itself.

[11] Take a theory T expressed in non-canonical vocabulary. Let D be a set of the shortest definitions of the non-canonical vocabulary in canonical terms. Then an equivalent to T in canonical terms $T^\wedge$ is obtained by conjoining D and T, replacing each non-canonical term by a variable, and closing under universal quantification. Relative to some way of measuring the elegance of strings of symbols, we can measure the elegance of T (in its own, non-canonical vocabulary). Define our non-canonical T's eligibility as the elegance of the quantifier block together with D. The elegance of $T^\wedge$ will be the sum of the elegance of T and the eligibility of T. Thus, non-canonical elegance plus eligibility is an upper bound to the canonical elegance of T. In cases where this $T^\wedge$ is the most compact way to translate T into the canonical language, Sider's approach will end up equivalent to Lewis's if we view the *simplicity* of a theory stated in arbitrary language L as measured by its elegance-in-L, but then appeal to the *eligibility* of a

3.4 Entrenched Properties May Be Reference Magnets for Explanatory Concepts

Notice that there are three theses involved in this derivation: that simplicity is a theoretical virtue, that simplicity is measured by compactness of expression in canonical language L; and that canonical language L contains primitive predicates only for natural properties. This defines a space of alternative potency theses. If the canonical language for measuring elegance/simplicity has predicates for properties other than the perfectly natural ones, those properties will be potent and hence magnetic. If the analysis of simplicity via elegance is wrong, but nevertheless part of what it is for a theory to be simple is for it to be framed in terms of a class of 'simple' properties, then these 'simple' properties will be potent and hence magnetic. One has to work quite hard *not* to get a reference-magnetic thesis for explanatory concepts from Radical Interpretation, given IBE-dogmatism, though the content of the magnetism thesis depends crucially on the fine details of the relation between explanations and the properties involved in them.

Here is an illustrative example. The conclusion that natural properties were reference-magnetic for explanatory concepts rested on identifying the canonical language (concision in which constitutes simplicity) with 'ontologese', a language with predicates for metaphysically fundamental properties. A radically different hypothesis, inspired by Goodman (1954), is that the canonical language contains all and only explanatorily *entrenched* vocabulary—properties that have a history of being used in successful explanations within the subject's community. The specification of the canonical language here involves representational facts—facts about the contents of past explanatory reasoning. The same metasemantic argument can be run, and its conclusion is a conditional magnetism: *Insofar as the property of being green features in past successful explanations in Sally's community and an observationally equivalent disjunctive property does not, then all else equal Sally's concept G will denote being green rather than the disjunctive property.* On this account of simplicity, the resulting magnetism of properties is a community-relative feature that is built up over time by layers of explanatory success. It predicts and explains the tendency of

theory as a theoretical virtue that trades off against simplicity. One way of motivating the idea that eligibility/naturalness is a basic theoretical virtue, is to insist (against Lewis) that simplicity is a language-immanent notion and introduce the language-transcendent notion of eligibility to avoid refutation to via the introduction of trivializing predicates.

concepts deployed within a single historical lineage to co-denote. It will not predict or explain any tendency of a privileged class of properties to be the denotations of concepts. This local referential stability is an interesting, non-trivial metasemantic result, but the community-wide question of why green rather than observationally equivalent disjunctions would not be directly addressed.[12] I will call this kind of metasemantic result co-magnetism, to distinguish it from the magnetism thesis previously discussed.

3.5 Natural Properties Aren't Magnetic for Inductive Concepts

Radical Interpretation predicts that potent properties are reference-magnetic for explanatory concepts. We bring this principle into sharper focus by saying more about which properties are potent, and which concepts are explanatory. Previous sections have looked at the former. This section turns to the latter.

One good set of candidates for concepts that we are default-disposed to use in explanations are the theoretical concepts introduced in actual explanatory scientific theoretizing—charge, atom, hydrogen, etc. Another good set of candidates are everyday concepts that have gained an explanatory role in those same theories—natural kind terms like water, as well as motion, location, and shape. Recall too that IBE need not involve an elaborate scientific theory. It also covers, I have assumed, ordinary hypotheses such as *that the motion of a ball is continuous,* which explain the perceptual appearances we encounter. The domain of application is therefore fairly large.

We could expand the scope greatly if could argue that any concept on which (by default) we were prepared to inductively generalize was an explanatory concept. The class of inductive concepts in this sense seems very wide indeed: we inductively generalize using normative concepts, using concepts of social categories, and much else. That would be a dramatic expansion of scope of my magnetism thesis. That there is a connection here is suggested by the familiar claim that induction is best seen as a special

---

[12] It is possible to derive a Goodmanian version of our IBE dogmatism, by taking the 'canonical language' for assessment of elegance/simplicity to be fixed via entrenchment, in this case a history of use in past successful theorizing. The same co-denotational version of magnetism would result.

case of IBE.[13] I will work through this idea under the assumption that explanatoriness requires elegance-in-ontologese, and the strategy will be to see if we can reconstruct instances of induction as IBE so understood.

Suppose Sally has noted a local regularity in the fundamental properties of her world—perhaps some pattern among the forces, masses, and motions of the objects around her. Let's suppose this takes the very simple form: *all observed Fs are Gs*, where F and G are perfectly natural. The best explanation of the local uniformity *all observed Fs are Gs* is plausibly its straight universal generalization: *all Fs are Gs*. It fits with and entails the relevant data, and there's no other hypothesis with these characteristics that can be stated more succinctly in ontologese, so by our current lights it is maximally simple. In this way, by applying IBE, Sally will be justified in extrapolating the local regularities among fundamental properties to global regularities among fundamental properties, absent some specific defeating considerations.[14]

The story just given vindicates one very special kind of inductive generalization—one involving only perfectly natural properties. The template is suggestive of more: the straight global generalization of any local regularity is always something that fits with and entails the local regularity. So it is a candidate for being the best explanation. It will, however, fail to be the best explanation if it conflicts with *other* data, or is outcompeted for simplicity by some rival hypothesis.

It's clear that outcompeting can happen. Let's say that something is grue iff it is green and first observed before the year 3000, or blue and not first observed before 3000. Modulo information about the present date, *all observed emeralds are grue* is equivalent to *all observed emeralds are green*, so if we have the first available as a premise we have the second also. The straight generalization of the local regularity *all observed emeralds are grue* is the proposition that *all emeralds are grue*—and the straight generalization as always fits with and entails the local regularity on which it is based, so is at least a candidate for being the best explanation. However, it's clearly not in fact the best explanation. It is less simple, in the relevant sense, than *all emeralds are green*. That is exactly because grue has a longer definition in

---

[13] Harman 1965.

[14] This kind of local-to-global inference, presented as a constraint on Bayesian prior conditional probabilities, is what Lewis saw as a main epistemological role for natural properties, according to Schwarz's (2014) exegesis of him. This should equally well with other cases, e.g. functional relationships between fundamental quantities. Schwarz attributes to Lewis a generalization of this idea to 'patterns' of fundamental properties, and I'm not sure how to reconstruct that on the sort of basis described above.

perfectly natural terms than green. IBE dogmatism doesn't vindicate grue-induction (which is a good thing).

The conjecture being explored is that induction is a special case of IBE. The reason we're exploring this is that if so, concepts that we're default-disposed to use in induction would be revealed as concepts that we're default-disposed to use in explanation, and the magnetism thesis would apply to them. We've had a couple of promising results so far: at least some good instances of induction (involving fundamental properties) can be reconstructed in this way, and it looks like paradigmatically bad instances of induction (involving grue) cannot. I will now argue that this idea runs into the buffers, and so we cannot hope to extend the scope of a magnetism thesis to all inductive concepts. In a restricted class of cases, there are prospects for extracting a related magnetism thesis. But the really interesting thing about extending the magnetism thesis to cover inductive concepts is that induction is so ubiquitous that magnetism thesis would apply to all sorts of high-level concepts, for normative and social kinds, for example. That hope of a dramatic extension, I think, is frustrated.

I follow Godfrey-Smith (2002) in distinguishing between two kinds of induction: *extrapolative* and *interpolative*. A paradigm of extrapolative induction would be the classic inference from all observed emeralds being green to all emeralds being green. Notice that we do not merely make a claim about the colour of emeralds in the local population we have sampled—in this time period, in this region of space, etc. We take ourselves to be justified in the unrestricted generalization that all emeralds are green. A paradigm of interpolative induction would be inferring the proportion of balls of a certain colour within an urn from sufficiently many random drawing of balls from that urn. If after sufficiently many random samplings, if 100% per cent of observed balls are green, one concludes that all the balls in the urn are that colour. Interpolative induction in this most straightforward form rests on the sampling from the relevant population being fair. Pollsters should not infer the proportion of opinions in a population by straight generalization from a biased sample (like asking only people who live in fancy houses their views on the government).[15] It'd be unreasonable to infer to the *unrestricted* claim that 20 per cent of *all balls whatsoever* are green on the basis of the balls you've seen drawn from the urn (even if this was the first time you'd seen a ball) because you obviously haven't randomly

---

[15] Actual opinion poll methodology doesn't assume random sampling, but instead corrects for known biases in the sample. But that's a matter for another day.

sampled the population of *all balls whatsoever* but only *all balls within the urn*. But that means that something quite different must be going on in the emerald induction, where we reach the truly unrestricted claim on the basis of a set of observations that are clearly not a random sampling of all emeralds whatsoever.[16]

I think it's pretty plausible that extrapolative induction has some connection to IBE, and it's here that I see the scope for some kind of magnetism thesis. The positive case that we saw above involving fundamental properties was inference to an unrestricted conclusion, and so a case of extrapolative induction, so we have a proof-of-principle. Let us therefore consider the paradigm introduced above: the inductive generalization to *all emeralds are green*. What we would require is that the straight generalization *all emeralds are green* be the simplest hypothesis entailing *all observed emeralds are green*. I can't see we have any grounds for thinking this true. Indeed, I would expect that the best explanation of this local regularity would not be the straight generalization, but rather a much more detailed theory about how certain crystalline structures reflect light. It is perfectly consistent with the set-up so far that this detailed theory is more elegant than the hypothesis *all emeralds are green* when the latter is spelled out in fundamental terms, especially since the detailed theory needn't mention the rather unnatural property of *being green* at all.[17]

If the epistemology of extrapolative induction involves IBE, and if as we have been assuming simplicity is elegance-in-ontologese, then the story must be indirect. Here is a candidate. Suppose we are entitled to assume

---

[16] Jackson (1975) argued that good induction comes with side-constraints, and the correct response to Goodman's puzzle of induction is that grue-induction violates these side-constraints. With Godfrey-Smith, I think that Jackson's side-constraints are very plausibly thought of as part of statistical methodology that underlies interpolative induction, like fair sampling of the population. However, that leaves open what we should say about extrapolative induction, since it is not ordinary statistical inference.

[17] Things would be much simpler if simplicity is identified with elegance-in-an-entrenched-language. Then insofar as *emerald* and *green* are among the entrenched properties, *all emeralds are green* has a very good claim to be the best hypothesis—it is after all maximally simple. So a Goodmanian epistemology of induction on explanatorily entrenched properties seemingly falls out of IBE dogmatism on the entrenchment variation. That may be taken as a virtue of the approach; but equally, it could be taken as showing that it delivers implausible verdicts that straight generalizations are better hypotheses than detailed explanations. One option here is to argue that the straight generalization is indeed the best explanation of *all observed emeralds are green* alone, but that as the data-set expands and more vocabulary gets entrenched, the best unified explanation of our data overall will include the detailed theory mentioned above. I will not attempt to settle these issues here.

that the best explanation of why *all observed emeralds are green* involves the operation of a uniform mechanism M in each case (in the actual case: a common crystalline structure leading to distinctive refraction profile), such that in regions where M is operative, all emeralds will be green. What now is the best explanation of the fact that M is locally in operation? I submit that the straight generalization—that M is globally in operation—may well be the simplest hypothesis that entails this. But if M is globally operative, then all emeralds whatsoever are green. Sally may be utterly ignorant of what M might be, yet if she is entitled to presuppose that there is some such M, she is justified in concluding all emeralds are green.

Nothing in this requires the properties inductively generalized upon (being an emerald, being green) are natural. Suppose that the mechanism specifies that light of a certain wavelength L is produced when white light hits an emerald. That property needs to be pretty natural, but that need not be greenness, nor even a property that entails greenness. Greenness could, for example, be a role-property multiply realizable by distinct, fairly natural properties that each play a role in different underlying explanatory mechanisms at different worlds, without being at all natural itself. The upshot for our purposes is that *greenness* need not be an explanatory concept in order to be an (extrapolative) inductive one, and that the magnetism thesis doesn't extend to the concept green just in virtue of its being used in induction. The most we could get is the indirect tie to naturalness just outlined, and that only for extrapolative inductive concepts that work the way I have just outlined.

The case of interpolative inductions seems quite different. Godfrey-Smith (following Jackson) argues that in the case of interpolative induction, the Goodmanian idea of a special *class* of concepts or properties that are 'apt for induction' rests on a mistake. Bad interpolative inductive generalizations of course exist, but are properly explained by bad statistical methodology— biased samples and the like. And a concept of explanatoriness tied to elegance in ontologese seems just the wrong starting point for understanding the statistical inferences involved—distributions of arbitrary properties can arise by pure happenstance, and random sampling is still a good way to detect them.

The magnetism thesis may yet apply to normative and social kinds, and the other high-level kinds that populate the manifest image of the world. But to make the case for this, one has to make the case directly that they are explanatory concepts. There's no short cut through pointing to their undoubted role in (interpolative) induction.

3.6 Conclusion

The predictions of substantive Radical Interpretation are always conditional on normative assumptions and assumptions about cognitive architecture. I have been assuming a cognitive architecture in which many mundane belief-formations we make are cases where the content believed is treated as explaining data. I have explored the impact on the metaphysics of representation of one family of epistemologies of inference to the best explanation. Reference magnetism, or co-magnetism, will be predicted and explained by this epistemology, rather than having to be added and argued over as a separate side-constraint peculiar to the metaphysics of representation. One can evaluate the plausibility of the conditional (and thus the plausibility of Substantive Radical Interpretation) even if one thinks the epistemology wrong-headed. I am not doing epistemology here, and have not defended the antecedent. I invite the reader to plug in their favoured epistemic stories and explore the consequences.

I myself am attracted to IBE dogmatism, though I spread my credence across the various options for theorizing about simplicity that have been introduced in this chapter (including the particularist non-theory). I am no Goodmanian, at least as regards explanations of observed physical events that call on colours, shapes, motions and the rest of the traditional list. So I am pretty confident that one way or another, IBE-dogmatism gives the resources we need to explain why *green* denotes green and not some observationally equivalent disjunctive property.

My position is compatible with an explanatory pluralism across different domains. What constitutes good explanation in mundane macrophysical contexts may differ from what constitutes good explanation in the physical sciences. Explanation in ethics may differ again, as may explanation of social phenomena. This potential variation will matter, especially when we later appeal to the best theory of social phenomena—social *linguistic* phenomena—in later chapters.

Coda: Inductive Dogmatism?

The epistemic principle that led me to think about the significance of IBE dogmatism for Radical Interpretation was in fact a principle about induction:

Inductive dogmatism

An agent is justified in believing *all Fs are G* on the basis that *all observed Fs are G* if (a) F and G are projectable; (b) the subject has no evidence that F and G are not projectable.

I learned about this from Brian Weatherson, and it is model for IBE dogmatism, with a similar externalist flavour. Inductive dogmatism would ground a reference-magnetism thesis—in this case, that *projectable properties* are reference-magnetic, relative to any concepts that an agent is disposed-by-default to use in induction (inductive concepts)—I invite the reader to reconstruct the argument for this, which parallels the one just given. 'Projectability' here is just as schematic as 'potency' was in my discussion. It was the original home of Goodman's appeal to entrenched properties. If inductive dogmatism were the right epistemology of induction, we would indeed derive some kind of magnetism (or co-magnetism, on the entrenchment proposal), and one which would be relevant to fixing the denotation of all inductive concepts.

In the case of IBE dogmatism, I went further: I showed how a particular supplementary thesis would entail that naturalness is reference-magnetic. One could try out a similar move: suppose we add to the above the thesis that the projectable properties are those that are natural enough, in something like Lewis's sense. Green is natural enough, grue isn't, and that's why the former is projectable, and the latter not. Relative to this thesis about the epistemology of induction, the 'natural enough' properties will be reference-magnetic, with respect to inductive concepts.

Whatever the merits of inductive dogmatism in general, I submit that supplementing it with the naturalness thesis is not at all attractive. Green is a paradigm of a projectable property, so will have to be counted as natural enough. The naturalness version of inductive dogmatism requires that there be no *unprojectable* properties that are more natural than green. In particular, unprojectable, 'gruesome' variants of perfectly natural properties such as *being positively charged* will have to be less natural than the high-level property of green. I don't know of a systematic story about relative naturalness which cleanly entails this, and Lewis's own gloss on relative naturalness as definitional distance from the perfectly natural predicts the opposite.[18] Anyone who takes this route needs to put forward an alternative

---

[18] Suppose that P is epistemically entailed by the property of being observed. (One candidate for P may be: is bigger than an electron.) Given a suitable P, 'all observed Fs are positively

account of what relative naturalness consists in which predicts the right kind of results in these cases, and second, as a matter of exegesis it's pretty implausible that Lewis had this proposal in mind.[19] I am much more pessimistic about the prospects for this than I am for the corresponding link between naturalness and reference magnetism via IBE dogmatism.

(This problem reflects a key difference between the way that naturalness can enter into IBE dogmatism, to the way that it enters into inductive dogmatism. In IBE dogmatism, it enters because the relation *more natural than* is a determinate of the relation *betterness*. So the active ingredients are comparative facts like: green is more natural than grue. In the case of inductive dogmatism, what we work with is an absolute distinction between the projectable and unprojectable properties, so this comparative claim is not enough—green needs to be above a certain threshold of naturalness, and grue below it. It is the thresholds that cause the problems.)

---

charged' will epistemically entail 'all observed Fs are either P and positively charged or not P and negatively charged'. This is the gruesome variant of positive charge, and generates a grue puzzle (in the relevant sense). Surely, defining greenness will take longer than defining this gruesome variant of positive charge.

[19] Dunaway and McPherson advocate a rich conception of natural properties, according to which any property that features in serious scientific explanations will be natural. A major question for someone who seeks to develop this view will be: do colour properties count as natural or not? If they do, given the human-specific character of green, we need more information on the sense in which their theory preserves the idea that naturalness is an objective feature of properties. If they don't, then there will be work to be done to justify the claim that a threshold exists which has green on one side, and all the gruesome variants of any natural property on the other.

4

Radical Interpretation and the Referential Stability of Wrongness

In chapter 2, I drew out the way in which Radical Interpretation gives conditional predictions about patterns of reference for logical concepts. In Chapters 3 and 4, the phenomenon of reference magnetism was derived within the theory, as well as its consequences for concepts on which we are default-disposed to generalize inductively. I've mostly used observational concepts (the traditional list of primary and secondary qualities) and natural kind terms as examples of its application.[1] These examples have tended to come from the descriptive rather than normative side of our conceptual scheme. But a theory of the foundations of content that cannot say plausible things about the content of normative concepts is a bad theory, so we should test Radical Interpretation by applying it to concepts like *moral wrongness* just as much as the concept *green*.[2]

In the previous examples given, the first-order normative theory that has been relevant has been epistemology: the provision of good reasons for belief. But there's absolutely no reason why good reasons for belief should always be the thing we look to in predicting and explaining patterns of reference. The provision of good reasons for action, or for affective reactions, are given equal billing in the foundational story about content that we are exploring.

[1] Some (Dunaway and McPherson 2016) have argued that reference magnetism can explain some of the striking features of normative concepts. However, to deploy the resources of the previous chapter for this purpose, we would first have to argue that moral concepts feature in extrapolative induction. This is not something discussed or defended by the authors, since they are assuming a framework for reference magnetism in which it is just a brute fact that reference is fixed by a trade-off between eligibility and fit with usage—the latter being conceived as a matter of maximizing truths. This is a self-declared 'toy model' they inherit from much of the post-Lewisian literature, but the difference between it and the current setting is very important at exactly the point at which they are interested. I set out arguments against their proposed explanation on its own terms in (Williams 2018a).

[2] This chapter is based on the material published as 'Normative reference Magnets' (Williams 2018a).

The Metaphysics of Representation. J. Robert G. Williams, Oxford University Press (2019).
© J. Robert G. Williams.
DOI: 10.1093/oso/9780198850205.001.0001

In this chapter, I will draw out what Radical Interpretation has to say about the concept of moral wrongness. In doing so, non-epistemic reasons come to the fore. Despite this difference, the story to be told has the same form as that given in chapter 2, so the reader will be able to appreciate the common structure in play. And in the process, we can illuminate a striking feature of the concept of moral wrongness: its referential stability.

4.1 The Concept *Wrong* is Referentially Stable

The concept *moral wrongness* has a distinctive referential stability.[3] Environment, society and moral opinion may vary dramatically, and yet agents will succeed in thinking about a common subject matter, wrongness, so long as deliberation and sentiments are internally regulated in the right way. Schematically: there is a property P, applying to actions, which our concept of moral wrongness picks out, and there is also a conceptual role R which our concept of moral wrongness plays. The referential stability thesis is the following:

Referential Stability (Schematic)
Necessarily, if an agent has a concept W that plays role R, then W denotes P.

But what is the concept W? What role R features in the stability thesis? Which property P ends up denoted? I'll take these questions in reverse order.

The property P is the property of being morally wrong. In order to have a concrete thesis to work with, I take a particular candidate specification as a working assumption. Henceforth, I assume, with the Kantians, that P is the property of *violating the categorical imperative*.

The stability thesis talks of concepts and their conceptual roles. As previous chapters, I will make the assumption (not required for Radical Interpretation per se) that the content of mental representation is carried by

---

[3] Or at least, so say I! And so says Hare, Horgan, and many others who are convinced by the moral twin earth examples laid out below. However, whether moral wrongness is really referentially stable in this way is a matter of dispute. This chapter offers something to those on both sides of the issue. To those who endorse stability, I show that Radical Interpretation (together as ever with auxiliary normative and architectural assumptions) explains this puzzling phenomenon. The explanation will be compatible with metaethical positions such as synthetic reductionism and non-naturalism, so demonstrates their compatibility with referential stability. Those who reject stability are free to read the derivation to follow as a *reductio* of the theory of content. Either way, we make progress.

individual states which have language-like structure, the analogues of words being concepts. And just as previously, we will be making a contingent assumption about a pattern in the causes and causal consequences of tokening some concept, to specify role 'R'. Drawing on the tradition which connects moral judgements to (moralized) reactive emotions, I assume that W plays role R iff the judgement that an agent's action is W makes one blame the agent for so acting (absent a judgment that they have an excuse); and the judgement that the agent's action is not W inhibits one from blaming them.[4]

In sum, I'll be working with the following concrete version of the referential stability thesis:

Referential Stability (Concrete)

Necessarily, if an agent has some concept W, such that for any act A:

- When the agent judges x's A-ing to be W, this makes them blame x for A-ing (unless they judge that the agent had an excuse);

and

- When the agent judges x's A-ing not to be W, this prevents them blaming x for A-ing;

then

- W picks out the property of *violating the categorical imperative*.

Different views about the distinctive role played by the moral wrongness concept, or about what it is for an act to be morally wrong, will lead to rival

---

[4] A presupposition must be that *blame*, strictly speaking, is an emotion linked specifically to morally wrongness, and that 'epistemic blame', or 'blaming oneself' for a prudentially unwise but morally okay course of action, is loose speech. If that is denied, then more work would be required in order to narrow down the sentiment to its specifically moral instances. For discussion of this tradition (traced to Mill (1863)), see Darwall (2010) on reactive emotions and moral concepts. Compare Skorupski (2010, p.292): 'It is morally wrong for x to A iff, were x to A from the beliefs that are warranted in x's epistemic state then either x would be blameworthy for A-ing, or extenuating circumstances would apply to x's A-ing' (for Skorupski, blameworthiness is the existence of sufficient reason to feel the sentiment of blame). Skorupski here offers a biconditional analysis, rather than (directly) a description of a conceptual role. There is a connection to (versions of) the conceptual role described, however, for agents who accept the equivalence and feel the way that they judge they have reason to feel. There is a closely related analysis in Gibbard (1990, p.43): 'what a person does is morally wrong if and only if it is rational for him to feel guilty for having done it, and for others to be angry at him for having done it'—except that Gibbard uses 'anger' where Skorupski uses blame (and identifies guilt with self-blame).

versions of the stability thesis.[5] The reader might doubt whether the particular working assumptions I have made are correct. This will not matter. The core argument to be given can be stated schematically, in terms of any role R and property P, and will be valid for any way of filling these in. The reason for making the working assumptions is simply heuristic: a concrete instance will be easier to digest and evaluate. But if, for example, the reader endorses classic hedonistic utilitarianism, and a conceptual role that focuses on first-personal deliberation rather than reactive emotion,[6] they are invited to check that the argument still goes through on their preferred substitutions. I will flag points at which these differences may matter.

4.2 Moral Twin Earth Gives Us Reason to Believe in Referential Stability

I will presuppose in what follows that stability holds, and that the challenge is to predict and explain that datum (though later I'll propose a refinement.) Foes of stability will need to recast what I establish as a conditional connection between Radical Interpretation (with auxiliary premises) and stability, which they will *tollens* where others *ponens*. I will not try to defend stability itself here. But to understand the view, it is useful to know the reasons that friends of stability have (or think they have) for endorsing it. Accordingly, I here recap the 'moral twin earth' case that motivates many.[7]

Suppose the citizens of Utilitas are disposed to blame other agents for taking hedonically suboptimal options. The citizens of Kantopia, on the other hand, blame other agents when they take actions that they cannot will as a general law. We fill in the scenario so each citizen has a concept

---

[5] I say 'rival', but in fact, due to the conditional nature of the thesis, one might endorse multiple stability theses—a variety of conceptual roles, playing any of which is sufficient for denoting moral wrongness.

[6] Wedgwood (2001) offers a first-pass suggestion for a conceptual role for moral wrongness: that the judgement that A-ing is morally wrong leads to the judgement that not A-ing is (all things considered) better than A-ing. Wedgwood also considers variants of this role which do not make judgements of moral wrongness overriding. Though Skorupski, as cited in n. 4, offers a normative-sentimentalist analysis of wrongness, he argues that moral judgements have an overriding role in practical deliberation, by leaning on a connection between reasons to feel blame and reasons to act (Wedgwood 2001, pp. 298–9). Scanlon (2007) emphasizes the first-personal deliberative role in his discussions of the concept of moral wrongness, though he emphasizes a 'higher-order' role in which (possibly implicit) beliefs about what is right and wrong control how other, more specific, considerations figure in deliberation.

[7] Horgan and Timmons 1992; also see Hare 1952. For recent dissent and references to the literature, see Dowell 2016.

W (*wrongness*) that is linked to blame in the way described earlier. The epistemic conditions under which they judge that the concept is instantiated vary by citizenship. Crucially, we are invited to agree that when a citizen of Kantopia tokens a thought with conceptual content *it is W to kill an innocent to save many lives,* and a representative of Utilitas tokens one with content *it is not W to kill an innocent to save many lives,* the two have conflicting views on a common topic. If that is indeed the case, there can be no equivocation in what their respective concepts of wrongness denote: there is some P that they both pick out. This is so even though their views on the extension of W, and so their suggestions as to what property P might be differ. (On our working assumption, P is the property of violating the categorical imperative, so the Kantopians moral theory is largely true, while the citizens of Utilitas go wrong.)

A specific 'twin earth' thought experiment such as this supports an instance of the universally quantified referential stability thesis, and referential stability in full generality will be supported if analogous verdicts are accepted for other communities (including ourselves) who have a concept W that plays the blame-centric role.

4.3 Radical Interpretation Predicts the Referential Stability of Wrongness

Substantive Radical Interpretation predicts and explains referential stability if the following is true: only by interpreting W as wrongness do we make the patterns that are built into the conceptual role it plays reason-responsive.[8]

Let us work this through for one concrete case. Sally has learned that Harry has cheated on his exams, and judges that Harry's cheating is W. She has also learned that Harry engaged in tactical voting, and judges that this is not W. What property does her tokening of W denote? Assuming that

---

[8] Wedgwood (2001) stands to the discussion of logical concepts in Peacocke (1992) as this explanation stands to my discussion of logical concepts in chapter 2. I would particularly highlight the way that the current account entirely bypasses a central element of Wedgwood's account: his attempt to define a notion of validity that covers attitude-formation for mental states that don't have truth-apt content. Wedgwood is led to that project by an attempt to apply Peacocke's general format of a 'determination theory' to the case at hand. In my view his generalization is successfully criticized in Schroeter and Schroeter (2003). Radical interpretation as the underlying explanatory theory allows us a more successful generalization of these ideas. See also van Roojen (2006,2018).

Sally's tokenings of W play the blame-centric conceptual role, I'll argue that Substantive Radical Interpretation entails that W denotes *wrongness*.

First, W plays the wrongness-role in Sally's cognitive economy: Sally's judgement that Harry's cheating is W, for example, makes her blame him for that act (provided she doesn't take him to have an excuse). Moreover, her judgement that Harry's tactical voting is not W makes her not blame him for tactical voting.

Second, according to Substantive Radical Interpretation, the correct interpretation is the one that makes Sally maximally reason-responsive, and so in particular must make the way she handles [A is W] judgements maximally reason-responsive. Additionally (and in parallel to the 'inferential role determinisms' assumed previously), I assume 'conceptual-role determinism for wrongness': the interpretation on which Sally is most reason-responsive overall is one on which her concept W (which plays the blame-centric role R) denotes something that makes the link between her W-judgements and blame most reason-responsive. Absent this assumption, it might be that although a given interpretation does best at making the links between W-judgements and blame most reasonable, this is outweighed by other countervailing factors; essentially it is the assumption that 'all else is equal'. I discuss the assumption later, but for now I ask the reader to just take it on board.[9] Putting Substantive Radical Interpretation and conceptual role determinism together, we derive the following: the correct interpretation of Sally is one that makes the link between her W-judgements and blame most reason-responsive.

The third and final element in the explanation are normative premises that tell us what it takes to make the right kind of sense of the blame-link:

[9] Some theorists think of conceptual roles as psychological natural kinds, and assume that any concept whatsoever comes equipped with its own specific conceptual role. That is not at all the way I am inclined to use the term. For me, conceptual roles are no more than a patterns in the way we deploy a concept with a certain theoretical interest—in the present context, they label the patterns used to articulate the stability thesis. I do not assume there is any topic-neutral way of picking out a conceptual role, and so I am not inclined to see the conceptual role determinism thesis as an instance of a more general thesis connecting 'conceptual roles' to the theory of reasons. If one were more of a realist about conceptual roles than I (contrast Peacocke 1992), then you might regard it this way, and I am not opposed to that reading. Just to put a different view on the table to temper that way of thinking: one might think of conceptual role determinism as resulting from the following stipulation: let us call nothing a conceptual role unless it relates to the theory of reasons so as to make conceptual role determinism true (given that stipulation, the key question is whether the blame link *is* a conceptual role in the first place). For now, I simply rely on the condition, and discuss its status later.

1. A substantively rational, reason-responsive agent would be such that judging that Harry's cheating was wrong and unexcused makes them blame Harry for cheating (directly and indefeasibly).

2. A substantively rational, reason-responsive agent would be such that for any feature F other than those that entail wrongness, the judgement that Harry's cheating was F (and unexcused) would not make them blame Harry for cheating (directly and indefeasibly).

3. A substantively rational, reason-responsive agent would be such that: the judgement that Harry's tactical voting was not wrong, would make them refrain from blaming Harry for tactical voting (directly and indefeasibly).

4. A substantively rational, reason-responsive agent would be such that: for any feature G other than those that wrongness entails, the judgement that Harry's tactical voting was not-G would not make them refrain from blaming Harry for tactical voting (directly and indefeasibly).

By (1), an interpretation of Sally on which W picks out *moral wrongness* (that is, *violating the categorical imperative*) will make her W-involving dispositions reason-responsive. By (2), only interpretations which denote features which entail moral wrongness can do the job. In particular, this rules out interpreting Sally's concept W as denoting *failing to maximize hedons*, since *ex hypothesi* such an interpretation will not make Sally reason-responsive. Notice: this is so even if Sally herself were a convinced utilitarian, and so mistakenly thinks that to be W is to fail to maximize hedons.

This doesn't quite get us to the conclusion that W denotes *moral wrongness*. For all that (1) and (2) tell us, we might interpret Sally's W as denoting something more specific than moral wrongness which nevertheless entails it—perhaps the property of *being deceptive in pursuit of self-interest*. That is why we need (3) and (4), which tell us what kinds of properties would make sense of the link between Sally's negative W-judgements (that she thinks that it is not W to vote tactically in elections) and the fact that this blocks her blaming Harry for his avowed tactical voting. The pattern of links between Sally's negative W-judgements and blame is not reasonable under the over-specific interpretation of W as *deceptiveness in pursuit of self-interest*, since on that interpretation Sally wouldn't have excluded the act as blameworthy in some other way. The interpretation of W as wrongness, however, does make sense of this second aspect of the conceptual role of Sally's W.

In sum: from these four normative premises, together with Substantive Radical Interpretation and conceptual role determinism, we reach the conclusion that Sally's concept W denotes moral wrongness. To derive referential stability in full generality, we simply schematically generalize the description of the case and the content of the normative premises.[10]

I finish this section with two clarificatory comments, with worries deferred to later.

First, the explanation I offer is consistent with the obvious truth that the causal history of a particular episode of blame can involve all sorts of property-ascriptions. Suppose again that Sally is a convinced utilitarian, and thinks (*ex hypothesi* incorrectly) that to be morally wrong is to fail to maximize hedons. Sally judges that Harry's cheating fails to maximize hedons, and this ultimately leads her to blame Harry for cheating. The path from judgement to blame here is indirect: she will infer from her hedonic belief and her background moral views to the conclusion that Harry's cheating is wrong, which is what most immediately makes her blame him for cheating. This is why the premises have the 'direct and indefeasible' rider. This is crucial to the plausibility of the uniqueness claims in premises (2) and (4).

Second, a structural point: the normative premises are not conditionalized to agents with suitable aims, tastes, or preferences—it is assumed that any reason-responsive agent whatsoever will satisfy them. Theorists such as Railton (1986) and Boyd (1979, 1982, 1988) would reject the implicit assumption that (moral) reasons in question are categorical in this way. They argue instead that moral reasons are conditional (albeit conditional on features that are deeply entrenched in human nature). My argument presupposes that Railton and Boyd are mistaken on this point. This is not merely a working assumption (as with my identifications of R and P earlier) but essential to the argument as stated. However, if Boyd and Railton are correct and moral reasons are hypothetical rather than categorical, an adjusted version of the argument will nevertheless go through. One would alter (1) and (2) by making them conditional on the agent having aim T. One would derive a restricted form of stability: for all agents with aim T, and a concept W that plays role R, W denotes P. This is not the full, unconditional stability that is my target, but some might prefer the package deal of hypothetical moral reasons and restricted stability. It still allows

---

[10] See Williams 2018a for the necessary schematic generalization.

agents with utterly divergent views of the extension of W to denote *moral wrongness*, since sharing aim T is *prima facie* independent of whether one subscribes to Kantianism, Utiliarianism, or something else entirely. I will set this aside and persist with my original formulations.

4.4 Conceptual Role Determinism is a Significant Side-premise

Conceptual role determinism is the thesis that the most *overall* reason-responsive interpretation of x's concept of moral wrongness W is one which makes certain local and specific aspects of their mental economy (namely, the link between W-judgements and blame) maximally reason-responsive. This was the assumption that allowed an interpreter to ignore possible trade-offs between different ways that W is deployed in an agent's mental economy, and concentrate on the conceptual role alone. Similar premises were involved in the derivations in chapter 2, there in the guise of 'inferential role determinism'.

Some may worry: 'Conceptual role determinism was a premise in the explanation of stability, but we haven't yet heard anything to explain why it should be true, in general. And if it isn't, then we are not entitled to claim that referential stability has been established in full generality.' Call the following the 'Refined Stability Thesis':

Referential Stability (Refined)
Necessarily if an agent has a concept W that plays role R *and conceptual role determinism holds* for W, then W denotes P.

The objector is pointing out that original stability thesis did not include the italicized restriction, and so what the argument establishes is not what was originally advertised. I am going to concede the point, but argue that the refined (not fully general) version of stability is what we should have been targeting all along.

First, consider a case where conceptual role determinism plausibly fails. Suzy has a concept W that plays the blame-centric conceptual role. However, Suzy in addition has a basic indefeasible disposition to infer *act A is W* from *act A does not maximize hedons*.

No single interpretation of W can make Suzy entirely—practically and epistemically—reasonable. Interpreting her concept W as *moral wrongness* (that is, as *violating the categorical imperative*) will make her W-judgment forming disposition unreasonable. Interpreting her concept W as *failing to maximize hedons* will make unreasonable the way her W-judgments link to blame. Suzy deploys W in multiple ways, and these ways are in tension with one another. We're not entitled to conceptual role determinism for Suzy's W: that would be to assume that it is more important for maximizing overall reasonableness to make sense of the way W relates to blame than the way that W-judgements are formed. I see no principled basis for that assumption. Henceforth, I will take it that (suitably elaborated) Suzy provides a case where conceptual role determinism fails.

Suzy has an extremely strange (almost tonk-like) moral concept, in which she treats a person's failure to maximize hedons as *analytic* grounds for blaming them. Mere ordinary moral error does not afford exceptions to conceptual role determinism. Since ordinary moral error is common, and it will be important that exceptions to conceptual role determinism are rare, I pause to examine these cases.

For an illustrative example, consider our interpretee Sally. To be wrong (we are assuming) is to violate the categorical imperative, but Sally mistakenly thinks to be wrong is to fail to maximize hedons. However, Sally was responsible in reaching this moral belief: she considered a range of actual and possible cases, and consulted and argued the issue through with trusted kith and kin. Ultimately, weighing her evidence, she endorsed utilitarianism. The contrast with the way that Suzy formed her W-beliefs is stark! I say:

i. Sally has the reasonable (though mistaken) theoretical moral belief that to be wrong is to fail to maximize hedons.

ii. Sally has a reasonable direct and indefeasible disposition to blame those whom (she judges) act wrongly without excuse.

iii. Given (i) and (ii), Sally has a reasonable (if mistaken) derived disposition to blame those who (she judges) fail to maximize hedons without excuse.

The first claim is simply an observation about Sally's epistemic practice. The second summarizes the normative assumptions at the heart of the earlier argument. Having a (derived, defeasible) disposition to blame those whom she judges fail to maximize hedons is inevitable given (i) and (ii) and a modicum of rationality. (iii) is surely reasonable, if the underlying (i) and (ii) are.

So I suggest that there's no reason to doubt that conceptual role determinism holds in Sally's case. To be sure, by reinterpreting her moral concept

W so it denoted *failure to maximize hedons*, we would avoid attributing false beliefs. Under that interpretation, she would have reasonable *and accurate* W-beliefs. But the increase in accuracy would come at the cost of making the basic blame-dispositions in (ii) unreasonable. In Suzy's case at this point, we were faced with a nasty trade-off between epistemic and practical reasonability. In cases of ordinary moral errors like Sally's, we have a trade-off between reasonability on the one hand, and accuracy on the other—and that sort of trade-off simply doesn't threaten conceptual role determinism.[11]

(The contrast between Sally and Suzy highlights a way in which the exact details of the agent's mental structures are central to my explanation. Both Sally and Suzy are disposed to blame someone, when they judge that that person has failed to maximize hedons without excuse. In Suzy's case, in effect I say that there's no way of interpreting this so that Suzy is reasonable, since that is (*ex hypothesi*) not a good reason for blaming someone, and it's a *basic* feature of Suzy's mental economy that she treats it as if it is. But exactly the same pattern in Sally is perfectly reasonable, I say, since the disposition is not basic, but derived from two individually reasonable states.)[12]

Let me turn now to the significance of (rare) exceptions to conceptual role determinism. The first thing to note is that cases like Suzy's show more than that I have failed to derive the original, unrestricted, referential stability thesis. If Suzy's case is possible, then it provides a counterexample to the (determinate) truth of that original thesis. After all, Substantive Radical Interpretation applied to Suzy says that the correct interpretation is the one that makes her most reasonable. But we said above that it was not determinately the case that interpreting her W as *moral wrongness* made her most reasonable. So despite the fact that W plays the blame-centric conceptual role in Suzy, it does not determinately denote moral wrongness.

---

[11] The same thing goes for less theoretically opinionated agents who have no overarching theory that structures their moral thinking—the analogues of (i) for an ordinary untheoretical agent will be a range of hard-to-systematize context specific judgements of the form: Harry judges that what x did was wrong on grounds it was F, G, H. The analogue of (iii) will be a derived disposition to blame x for so-acting, on the basis that it was F, G, H. But each instance of (i) is reasonable, then again the induced instances of (iii) will be reasonable, and there will be no interpretative pressure to set against the need to make reasonable the blame-links in (ii).

[12] A reader for *Philosophical Review* noted (correctly!) that this opens up a couple of ways to cause trouble for my account: either to argue that such nuances (between basic and derived dispositions) cannot make a normative difference; or to argue that the moral twin earth intuitions that motivate stability are insensitive to such differences, so they cannot play the crucial role that I'm attributing to them.

I contend, however, that this is an independently plausible thing to say about Suzy's case, a datum that a successful theory of reference should respect. So the failure to derive an unrestricted referential stability thesis is an excellent thing! The cases that motivated referential stability (and were problems for rival accounts) are cases such as Sally (an agent subject to ordinary moral error), or the citizens of Utilitas and Kantopia. In all these motivating cases, say I, conceptual role determinism holds. The motivation that friends of referential stability had for their universally quantified claim was simply that such parade cases are representative of the general case. But the generalization is not obviously warranted, and we have seen that cases like Suzy's show it to be flawed. It is reasonable methodology to use a metaphysics of reference as a tool to predict and explain the scope of the generalization. It is in this spirit that I offer the refined stability thesis.

There is an alternative strategy the interested reader may wish to explore: to add content to the conceptual role R itself, over and above the links to blame, from which conceptual role determinism can be derived. Suzy's W, we would then say, does not play the relevant role R, and so she is outside the scope of the thesis anyway. If one found a way to do this, it would elegantly deal with these problem cases. (Compare inferentialist harmony constraints and Suzy's case to that of the unharmonious 'logical concept' *tonk*.) The strategy is independently interesting, but I see no reason to prefer it to the simple refinement of stability above. After all, if conceptual role determinism followed from R itself, then the original and refined versions of stability would be equivalent.

4.5 The Derivation Doesn't Assume that Wrongness is a Reason

Some may worry: 'The normative premises in the "derivation" of referential stability are highly contentious. They tell us that Sally is being substantively rational, reason-responsive when she reacts to a judgement that Harry's cheating is *wrong* by blaming Harry for cheating. But that is a misdescription! The reason that Sally has for blaming Harry for cheating is not the thin property of *wrongness*. It is the more specific *wrongmaking features* of his act—it's deceitfulness, say.'

The objector may elaborate this in various ways. To think that wrongness is a reason (for feelings of blame, as much as action) is to 'double count' reasons (Dancy 2000, 2004). Or perhaps 'Someone who is moved primarily by overall moral verdicts, such as an action's being wrong, rather than the individual grounds for such verdicts, has been said to have a kind of moral fetish, rather than being truly morally good' (Darwall 2010, p.136, alluding to Smith 1994). Finally, one might worry that the kind of normative premises I rely on encourage a view of moral psychology where there must be 'one thought too many' (Williams 1981)—where the move from the classification of Harry's cheating as deceitful to blaming Harry must await the classificatory thought that deceit is wrong.

My derivation is innocent of such charges. To start with the 'one thought too many' worry: my premises are entirely consistent with thick moral judgments prompting blame. Sandra's judgement that Harry's cheating is deceitful can make Sandra blame Harry for cheating, in exactly the same direct way that a judgement of wrongness would do. (The uniqueness premise I relied on was that only features that entail wrongness can directly make a reason-responsive agent feel blame, which of course allows for Sandra's case.) Nor can I see anything in the account that gives primacy to the thin over the thick in this respect. Some think that the right analysis of thick moral concepts already involves the thin concept of wrongness (Elstein and Hurka 2009), and given that view, one might be tempted to defend the explanatory primacy of a wrongness-blame conception. But that's no commitment of mine.

Turning to the other concerns, I am also neutral over whether an act's *being wrong* is itself a *reason* to blame the agent. The normative premises that I used in my explanation (like Substantive Radical Interpretation itself) are formulated in terms of what a substantively rational, reason-responsive agent would feel or do, and not what normative reasons that agent has for feeling or acting that way. I have not taken a stance here on the relation between reason-responsiveness and the theory of reasons. Dancy (2000, 2004) and anti-Dancians (Heuer 2010, Darwall 2010) will take very different views of this question. It is open to anti-Dancians to identify a reason-responsive agent with an agent who believes, acts or feels for normatively good reasons. Dancians, however, think of normative reasons as always sparse and specific, and a consequence will be that we'll often know that there are reasons to feel a certain way, without being able to identify what those reasons are. Suppose Sally knows that Harry has tattled, and knows that this was either spiteful or deceitful, but lacks the background context that would let her determine which it is. The thing she does know (that it was either-spiteful-or-deceitful) is not itself a normative reason for anything, *ex hypothesi*. Any plausible Dancian theory of reasons will need to accommodate the fact that in Sally's disjunctive-information situation, she should blame Harry for tattling, despite her inability to identify a (sparse and specific) reason to blame him. It will need to theorize what it is for an agent to be 'reason-responsive' in cases of limited information. The case of wrongness is analogous. If Harry has spitefully tattled, but all Sally knows is that Harry's tattling was wrong (which entails that there is reason for her to feel blame), as a reason-responsive agent, she should blame him for tattling.

4.6 The Story Applies Even to the Morally Depraved

A final worry might be put:

Your explanation of stability is all very well in cases like Sally's, or to sensible Kantians or Utilitarians. After all, we take such theories seriously, so it's no accident that we are happy to class adherents as responding to reasons when they blame someone. We expect them to blame people who are worthy of blame a lot of the time, diverging only in recherché cases. But what of agents in the grip of an utterly depraved moral theory—valorizing personal honour and blaming others who indulge in acts of mercy. They too may have a concept W that is linked to blame in the way envisaged. But are they being reason-responsive when they blame someone who is disposed to help those in need for their kindness?

In elaboration of the worry, imagine a depraved moral code (the Klingon ethic) built around the preservation of personal honour and the elimination of impurity. We imagine that Sarpek the Klingon's opinions about which acts are immoral diverge utterly from ours, so that any time where we are both inclined to classify an act as 'morally wrong' the convergence is purely accidental. Unlike my approach in 4.1, I am not inclined to make any further tweaks to the statement of stability to exclude Sarpek. Let us assume that he has false, repugnant views specifically about morality.

The Klingon-ethic worry is initially simply a challenge: does interpreting Sarpek's W as *moral wrongness* make him reason-responsive? The relevant premise in the argument (instantiated in the way relevant to Sarpek's case) is the following:

(*) Any reason-responsive agent would be such that: the judgement that Tim's kindness was wrong (and unexcused), makes them blame Tim for his kindness.

When presenting the argument in section 2, I gave an instance like this for Sally, but then noted that to get the general stability conclusion we needed to generalize it to all agents and acts. The question here is whether that generalization was legitimate. Here are three rival descriptions of Sarpek's case:

A. Sarpek (all things considered) ought not blame Tim for her kindness—such feelings on his part would not be reason-responsive. Kindness is not something blameworthy! His moral judgements are not reason-responsive either. For example, perhaps (as Harman has argued) false moral judgements are *morally* wrong even if epistemically justified.[13]

B. Sarpek (all things considered) ought to make exactly the moral judgements he does. They are the only justified opinion to reach, given his anti-social upbringing and misleading experience, and *pace* Harman, epistemic factors determine what one ought to believe. Further, though Tim is not blame*worthy*—from an objective point of view, she ought not be blamed—Sarpek would not be responding to the reasons he has if he didn't blame her, given his course of experience.

C. Combining elements of the above: Sarpek's moral judgements are reason-responsive (given his misleading course of experience) but is not justified in feeling blame towards Tim.

Which description is correct is contested territory in first-order moral theory, and I won't try to adjudicate it here. (It may vary on different ways of filling out Sarpek's case.) I will trace the consequences of each for the present account. Descriptions (A) and (B) pose no threat to the wide-scope premise (*). If (B) is the correct, then morally depraved agents fit seamlessly into the story given in this paper. (A) is more threatening, since depraved agents will be *unreasonable* in both believing and blaming. Rival interpretations, on which W denotes something other than *wrongness*, could make him *epistemically* more reasonable, albeit at the cost of being unreasonable in linking *those* judgements to blame. On this description, depraved moral agents such as Sarpek might be like Suzy from 4.1. They would thus not pose

---

[13] Harman (2011, sec. 4) holds that we have a moral obligation to believe relevant moral truths. Applied to this case, the Harman position would be that Sarpek's wrongness-judgement was morally blameworthy (and I assume not overall reason-responsive) even if Sarpek were epistemically perfect (contrast p.462). I think Harman's case here is most plausible if restricted to cases of morally depraved beliefs, rather than ordinary moral error such as that of Sally in 4.1.

a new threat to my argument, but they would make the Refinement to Stability introduced in section 4.1 more significant.

Description (C) is the only one on which (*) itself comes under pressure. The following triad is uncomfortable: (all things considered) it is reason-responsive to believe that *p*, reason-responsive to lack sentiment *s*, and yet reason-responsive to have a disposition to have feel *s* when one believes *p*. If we hold fixed the first two normative claims, there is pressure to give up the third claim (*). On reflection, though, I recommend we should not give it up even so. Instead, we should say that it is impossible, in Sarpek's situation, to be perfectly reason-responsive: he is condemned either to believe inappropriately, blame inappropriately, or have an inappropriately run mental economy. If we retain (*) in this spirit, then the explanation of stability applies to Sarpek just as before. We make him more reasonable if we interpret him as having genuinely moral judgements connected to (*). Further, these moral judgments themselves would be reasonable, so unlike description (A), there is no countervailing pressure. He is, admittedly unreasonable in blaming Tim for her kindness, but that doesn't look like a flaw that could be removed by judicious reinterpretation, so there's no *more reasonable* rival interpretation in the offing.

It is a theme of this book that the metasemantic verdicts that Substantive Radical Interpretation delivers turn crucially on first-order normative theses—often interesting and contestable ones. The case of Sarpek highlights some of these connections.

4.7 Conclusion

Radical Interpretation predicts the referential stability of the concept *morally wrong*—conditional on the expected pair of assumptions about cognitive architecture and first-order normative assumptions. This is again conditional: if the concept of wrongness is linked to sentiments of blame in the way described, and if the normative assumptions hold good, then that concept denotes moral wrongness (no matter what false beliefs about who or what is wrong our subject may have). The reader should be able to see how to generate many other conditional predictions of this kind, for alternative hypotheses about the conceptual role of wrongness—again, if it had a distinctive role in practical deliberation, and given the assumption that only things that are wrong should be treated that way in deliberation, then again we would predict and explain stability.

In the previous chapter we saw a way that relatively natural properties counted as reference-magnetic. This was derived from their role in a normative theory: the epistemology of induction. Here we see that moral wrongness is all by itself a reference magnet, being stably referred to over drastic differences in first-order opinion. This is also due to the way that moral wrongness features in a normative theory. In Radical Interpretation, this is characteristic: reference magnetism is always and everywhere normative reference magnetism.

5

Reducing Mental Representation?

My target is a reduction of the representational to the non-representational. Substantive Radical Interpretation is the central element in a three-stage strategy for achieving this. As formulated so far, it targets a reduction of mental reference and truth conditions. That prompts two questions: can Radical Interpretation really work as a reduction? And: would a reductive account of mental *reference* sufficient to give a reduction of mental *representation*? Answering these questions requires we step back from the nitty gritty of the last few chapters where I drew out the consequences of Radical Interpretation to look at the shape of the account as a whole.

What prompts the first question is this: we are attempting to pair truths about belief/desire with more fundamental, non-representational truths. Radical Interpretation's description of the latter involves appeal to 'interpretations which best rationalize' certain facts. But what is it for an interpretation to best rationalize a thing, if not for the beliefs and desires ascribed by that interpretation to make sense of it? If spelling out the key ingredient in the putative 'more fundamental truth' still involves belief- and desire-talk, then this is no reduction.

What prompts the second question is this: there are central, aspects of representational content that go beyond reference. In particular, co-referential concepts (Hesperus, Phosphorus) can differ in Fregean sense. A reduction of reference alone would, apparently, leave the job half-done.

The plan for this chapter is to address the concerns in turn. In each case, I develop the worries, point to options for responding that readers may want to explore, and then discuss at more length what I see as the most interesting theoretical avenue.

5.1 Not Every Good Metaphysical Project is a Foundational Project

This section and the next tackle the first of our two questions, concerning the reductive status of Radical Interpretation. This section sets the context,

The Metaphysics of Representation. J. Robert G. Williams, Oxford University Press (2019).
© J. Robert G. Williams.
DOI: 10.1093/oso/9780198850205.001.0001

contrasting different kinds of projects in the metaphysics of representation. The next section articulates a worry about casting Radical Interpretation in a foundational role, and responds to it.

What is a foundational metaphysics of representation? One that gives a more fundamental description of the representational facts. Prosecuted in a traditional way, it would show us how to pair truths about representation systematically with corresponding truths about the non-representational world. Paired truths will have to be necessarily equivalent to one another, since they are claimed to pick out the same state of affairs under different descriptions.

What would a foundational metaphysics look like when written down on a page? It would be sufficient to specify biconditionals that give explicit definitions of the target representational vocabulary, where the definiens only involve 'more fundamental' vocabulary. I've showed Substantive Radical Interpretation leads to definitions of the representational vocabulary 'believes that' and 'desires that'. I'll remind the reader how these go in the next section. Reductive explicit definitions are a neat way to give a foundational theory, since by substituting definiens for definiendum in an arbitrary truth involving the target vocabulary, one can derive the 'more fundamental' truth with which it is paired. We should not fetishize explicit definitions, however: they are simply a means to the end of communicating the foundational pairing. In the event that explicit definitions won't fly (perhaps because, as alleged in the next section, the target vocabulary is tacitly present in the definiens), we should revisit the issue of whether they were the best way to present the reductive content of the theory.[1] However, for the purposes of this chapter, I'll pretend that the tenability of Radical Interpretation as a foundational project turns on defending the reductive status of these explicit definitions.

We should contrast foundational metaphysics with a more neutral metaphysical project: the search for systematic articulations of patterns involving both representational and non-representational facts, beyond those found in semantic theory proper. A paradigm of this is Kripke's causal-historical

---

[1] My 'Requirements on Reality' (Williams 2012) discusses the methodological issues explicitly. A key thought is that while the base truth paired with a target truth better not involve the target vocabulary, it is not at all clear why we shouldn't help ourselves to whatever we need (including target truths themselves) in giving a humanly comprehensible specification of the pairing of target and base truths. See also my 'Fundamental and Derivative Truths' (Williams 2010) for ways of exploiting this distinction in connection with the metaphysics of sets and mereology.

account of the reference of ordinary proper names. According to one version of this story 'Aristotle' denotes the particular individual it does because (i) that individual was dubbed 'Aristotle' over two millennia ago by those who introduced the name; (ii) there is a historical chain of transmission from that day to this, whereby the name was passed from user to user, such that (iii) each new user of the name intended to use the name to refer to the same individual as their predecessors in the chain of transmission. Kripke himself emphasizes that this is not a story that would reduce referential facts about names (or the mental analogues of names) to the non-representational facts, and disclaims reductive ambitions. And while any advocate of the causal-historical account will think referential truths about names will reliably covary with the causal-historical relation that (i)-(iii) picks out, this needn't commit them to claiming that these pairs of truths are necessarily equivalent. I take the Kripkean account to be a correct and illuminating contingent generalization about the reference of (some) names. I also take it to have theoretical as well as intrinsic interest: Stalnaker, for one, explains a variety of linguistic behaviour by assuming that speakers are aware of these kinds of generalizations.[2] It is a good metaphysical theory, but I see no reason to distort it by attempting to make it part of foundational theory.

What goes for ordinary proper names (and proper-name-like concepts) can go for many other concepts. We might hope, over time, build up a patchwork picture of the most striking or interesting patterns of reference involved in our thought and talk. In the past three chapters I have appealed to links between inferential roles of logical constants and their denotations, the role of naturalness in influencing the denotation of explanatory concepts, and the way that conceptual role can determine the denotation of moral concepts. The best foundational theories should fit with the local patterns identified by these means, either by making them part of its theory or by (in combination with auxiliary premises where necessary) predicting and explaining them. Substantive Radical Interpretation does not make the local patterns part of its foundational account, but it does, I have argued, achieve this 'recapture' in the three cases just mentioned.

Not all fans of Substantive Radical Interpretation will see it as a foundational theory. Instead, one might regard it as having a status just like the illuminating local generalizations just canvassed. What it would provide, on this conception, is a *non-reductive, non-foundational* metaphysics of

---

[2] See the essays collected in Stalnaker (1999).

representation, a single global generalization accompanying, and compatible with, the patchwork of local generalizations. Insofar as it recaptures all the more local generalizations, then it is a unifying theory, and so will be of special interest.

In the 'building block' approach to foundational metaphysics of reference (see chapter 2) we have a precedent for the move I am making, of taking what might otherwise be seen as a non-foundational theory and assigning it a foundational role. The building block approach is this: to take the patch-work of local generalizations about particular concepts and *turn them into* a foundational account of representation facts. To do so while cleaving to the traditional reductive picture of metaphysical foundations, the building blocker needs: (1) to purge each local generalization of target representational vocabulary; (2) to argue that the paired truths are necessarily equivalent; and (3) to extend the patchwork indefinitely, so that *every* lexical item in a public language or simple concept is given a reductive story. Add a few bells and whistles (e.g. give some foundational account of the representational signifi-cance of concatenating words or concepts together into whole sentences or thoughts), and one has in prospect a reductive account of the truth conditions of thoughts that are 'built out of' simple concepts/lexical items. What I'm doing is essentially a dual to the building blocker's approach.

The building blocker, I think, also owes us a recapture project: they should recapture Radical Interpretation, insofar as the latter involves illu-minating global generalizations about reference. I'm sceptical about their prospects for success, just as I'm sceptical about whether they can imple-ment the three steps above that define their programme (the third seems especially challenging). But both the building blocker and I are joined in opposing a less ambitious approach to this whole area, where foundational metaphysics of representation is given up and replaced with a simple trade in non-foundational generalizations. The next section evaluates whether Radical Interpretation can bear the weight of this foundational ambition.

5.2 Radical Interpretation can be a Reductive Account of Reference

Substantive Radical Interpretation says the following about belief:

1) x believes p (to degree d) iff the correct interpretation of x says that x-at-t believes p (to degree d);

2) The correct interpretation of an agent x is that one which best rationalizes x's dispositions to act in the light of the courses of experience x undergoes.

Chaining these together, we have a candidate foundational theory for facts about belief. The challenge was that this didn't even have the right shape to be a foundational (reductive) theory, since it fails to eliminate appeal to the target representational states from the analysans.[3]

The first worry one might have concerns (1), since the term 'believes' appears on the right as well as the left hand side of the biconditional. This worry can be handled by formulating the proposal more sharply. An interpretation is an abstract object, and for illustrative purposes, I take it to be a function that maps time-slices of an agent to pairs of functions from propositions to numbers. You and I know that the first element of the pair is what the interpretation says about the agent's belief at that time, and the second element of the pair is what it says about desire. But the interpretation itself is just a set-theoretic construction. The sharper formulation of (1) is therefore (1+):

(1+) x believes p (to degree d) iff the first element of the pair which is value of the correct interpretation i at x-at-t is a function which maps p to d.

No appeal to belief or other intentional primitive appears in this sharpened formulation.

The more serious worry concerns (2), and the appeal to an interpretation (which is just a set-theoretic construction, remember!) 'rationalizing' or 'best rationalizing' an agent. The first step is to unpack the appeal to 'best rationalization' in terms of the comparative rationality associated with the range of interpretations:

(2a)   Interpretation i best rationalizes x's dispositions to act A given their evidence E iff interpretation i makes x rational to degree k (given E/A) and no interpretation makes x rational to a greater degree than k (given E/A).

---

[3] Of course, the right-hand-side appeals to the representational states of actions/intensions, and perceptions/experience. But that's okay: those first-layer representational states are already in line for a further reductive explanation. The concern here is that the representational content of belief might be being reduced to truths that involve, inter alia, truths concerning the representational contents of beliefs.

This step (which I will not question) sets up the key issue: how to understand 'i makes x rational to degree k'. The 'i' in question, remember, is a complex set-theoretic construct (that's how we sidestepped the circularity challenge over (1)). But sets of sets of sets of functions aren't the sort of things that 'make agents rational' in any familiar sense. I owe further explanation of what this means.

Dangers lurk if we go for the most natural gloss. This relates the phrase to the much more familiar notion of a possible agent (under a belief-desire-evidence-action-physical description) being more or less rational:

(2b)   Interpretation i makes x rational to degree k (given E/A/P) iff if it were the case that:

(i) x believes that p (to degree d) at t iff the first element of $i(x$-at-$t)$ maps p to d, (ii) x desires that q to degree d iff the second element of $i(x$-at-$t)$ maps q to d, (iii) x has evidence E and action-dispositions A, (iv) x's physical setup and context is P, then x would be rational to degree k.

This sharpening of 'making rational' would be perfectly okay if one were not in the business of giving a reductive, foundational theory of belief and desire. It would be okay, for example, if Substantive Radical Interpretation were being presented as a non-reductive piece of theory about belief and desire from which more local and specific theories of reference could be derived—the non-foundational but global and unifying account mentioned in the last section. But given the reductive ambitions of my project, I can't *use* the terms 'belief' and 'desire' in sharpening (2). So while foundationalists like myself can agree that (2b) is a perfectly true biconditional, we cannot offer it as an analysis of 'making rational'. But again: given its relata, it's not something we can plausibly ask anyone to take as primitive.

Here is the strategy for finding the missing analysis. First, I suppose that the rationality of an agent is determined by the possession or absence (or perhaps: possession to various degrees) of rationality-making features of their beliefs and desires. In some cases the rationality-makers will be intrinsic features of a set of beliefs and desires, in other cases, they will be relational features that turn on the agent's evidence, action-dispositions, or context. Such features will include structural factors such as the consistency of beliefs, means-end coherence of beliefs, desires and intentions. They will also include constraints of more substantive rationality such as the justification of perceptual beliefs by facts perceived, or the right kind of influence of morality within practical reasoning. Any purported list of rationality-making features will be extremely controversial. I only assume that some such list exists. Suppose now we have these systematized and written down.

We then generate a new list, by finding for each rational-making feature F a corresponding feature F* of abstract interpretations (note the assumption that we can find such a feature in each case! I come back to this below). Example: *having coherent beliefs at t* may be on our list, and an agent has this feature when their degrees of belief satisfy the constraints of probability theory. The corresponding feature coherence* is the probabilistic coherence of the function from propositions to numbers that is the first element of the value of the abstract interpretation for *a-at-t*. So where coherence figured on the original list, coherence* goes on the new list. Rinse and repeat, all the way down.

The rationality-making features on the original list determine overall degree of rationality. So as well as the list, I suppose we have available a recipe: an aggregation function f such that for any agent a, a's degree of rationality is a function of the truth values of the propositions *a has F, a has G, a has H*... where F, G, and H range over all rationality-making features. The aggregation function will not appeal to any aspect of a's representational mental states: any such factor should be isolated as an argument place of the function.

Given this, we say that the abstract interpretation i makes x rational* to degree k iff $f(|F^*a|, |G^*a|, |H^*a|, \dots) = k$. The starred features were by construction free of appeals to representational mental states; so is the aggregation function f. The above definition therefore sharpens the load-bearing notion of 'rationality-making' in a way that is foundationally and reductively kosher.

There is an exemplar for this strategy: the characterization of perfect structural rationality as a property of credence-utility pairs. According to some formal epistemologists, whether an agent is perfectly structurally rational is determined by the patterns in that agent's degrees of belief and desire (e.g. whether the agent's degrees of belief in an inconsistent pair of propositions sums to 1, whether their degree of desire in a proposition is the weighted average of their degree of desire in a partition of that proposition, with weights fixed by their degrees of belief). The aggregation of the features to determine perfect structural rationality is very simple: the agent is perfectly structural rational (so far as their belief/desire goes) if it has both features, otherwise, is not perfectly structural rational.

My bet is that this strategy can be implemented, not just for the special case of perfect structural rationality, but in general for degrees of substantive rationality. I hold, for example, that that there are features (perhaps relationally specified) of interpretations that correspond to beliefs being *justified* or 'held for good reasons'. I imagine that justification* will appeal to facts about what the relevant evidence supports, and which contents support which other contents, and use that to determine propositional justification of the contents attributed by the interpretation. It will appeal to non-representational facts about dependencies between the vehicles of content, and require that the pattern of propositional justification is matched by corresponding patterns of dependence between the vehicles ('belief-states') in order to determine the extent of doxastic justification attributed by the interpretation. And so on.

The appeal to 'substantive rationality' in substantive rational interpretation is a term of art. I've been careful to pin down exactly what I need to assume about it to derive particular results exactly because I don't expect my readers to know its contours already (although I did offer various regulative glosses on it early on). We know it has to be more than just structural rationality, on pain of the bubble puzzle—that gives us one lower limit to the notion. We now see that not just any attractive feature of agents can be thrown into it, on pain of vitiating reduction—that gives us a corresponding upper limit.

An example for readers to consider: Timothy Williamson (2007) defends a knowledge-maximization constraint on interpretation.[4] He is also a prominent sceptic of the project of analysing knowledge in other terms (as unGetteried justified true belief, for example). I suspect that if he is right

---

[4] He starts from the compelling but elusive idea that perceptual demonstrative concepts pick out an object that is the causal source of an associated stream of perceptual information, on which basis we form perceptual beliefs. Some interpretations of the demonstrative would make these perceptual beliefs false; others would make them true; but Williamson says that we get the right results if we choose the interpretation that makes the beliefs so formed items of knowledge. For example, interpreting the demonstratives as concerning objects in some far away duplicate of the present scene might maximize truth, but in the absence of the usual causal interactions between us and the objects, it would not count as knowledge. By appeal to knowledge-maximization, he hopes to be able to formulate a precise local theory of demonstrative reference—characterizing the 'right kind' of causal channel between object and belief indirectly as channels sufficient for knowledge. See McGlynn (2012) for critical evaluation of Williamson's proposals in this area. Since knowledge-maximization is meant as a general constraint on interpretation, he can also hope to unify the theory of demonstrative reference with the local accounts of other species of reference. Williamson has not developed the knowledge-maximization project systematically. One way to undercut the interest of the recapture explanations he offers would be to demonstrate that 'knowledge-maximization' delivers poor or wrong results when applied to examples beyond the demonstrative.

on the latter point, then the best account available of what property of interpretations corresponds to maximizing knowledge will be in the counterfactual style, involving classifying beliefs as knowledge or not. And that would not be compatible with the foundational ambitions for Substantive Radical Interpretation. This is not a criticism of Williamson himself! He is not pursuing the kind of foundational, reductive metaphysics that I am, but rather the kind of illuminating non-foundational variants of Radical Interpretation I described in the last section. What we see is that some ways of developing an account of substantive rationality to plug into Radical Interpretation are available to him but not to me.

The reductiveness concern that has been occupying me here is best seen not as an objection to a fully formulated foundational metaphysics of representation, but as a constraint on how a partially specified foundational metaphysics should be developed. It could *lead* to objections, if meeting the constraints led to a demonstrably unsatisfactory theory. But carrying out such demonstrations (while policing the constraints) should be the critic's focus; they will not make much progress trying to show that my style of account is in principle impossible.

5.3 Radical Interpretation Gives Foundations for Sense as well as Reference

I cast Radical Interpretation as a reductive metaphysics of representation. The last two sections have concentrated on whether it is really reductive. I now turn to the question of whether it really reduces *representation*. This section presents the challenge of explain sense as well as reference, rebuts an initial worry, and registers a natural revision of the Radical Interpretation project. The next section presents a way of dealing with the foundations of Fregean sense that leaves Radical Interpretation unchanged, and gives star billing to the recapture project of the last three chapters. I finish, then, by considering the prospects of extending that project.

Frege taught us that reference is not all there is representation. Someone can rationally believe *that Hesperus rises in the evening* but simultaneously doubt *that Phosphorus rises in the evening*. The referential representational content of these mental states is identical, since Hesperus is the same object as Phosphorus—it is the planet Venus. Since it seems irrational to both believe and doubt one and the same content, this drives us to think that there is more to content than reference. Putting a label to the unknown quality: the co-referential concepts *Hesperus* and *Phosphorus* differ in *sense*.

Two clarifications before we begin. First, note that I have been using 'concept' for a mental *vehicle* of content. It is not to be assumed that concepts so construed are Fregean senses. Concepts so construed *have* Fregean senses, just as they *have* referents. Second, I have often moved without comment between (i) 'Harry believes that *p*', (ii) 'Harry has a belief with content *p*', and (iii) 'The correct interpretation maps one of Harry's belief-states to *p*'. This is sloppy, but for the most part has the virtue of glossing over distracting distinctions. In this section, however, we need to sharpen things to avoid confusion. In (ii) and (iii), '*p*' ranges over certain entities, 'propositions', and friends of Radical Interpretation can maintain that this pair is equivalent even while disagreeing about whether the contents in question are sets of possible worlds, or structured propositions, or Fregean thoughts, or whatever (a discussion we're about to have). But in (i) '*p*' functions differently, appearing in sentence-position rather than name-position. To connect (i) to (ii) and (iii), we would need to iron out the syntactic mismatch. We might try: Harry believes that *p* iff for some *x*, Harry has a belief with content *x*, and *x* is the proposition that *p*.[5] However, we may not wish to do this. A Fregean about belief might endorse Radical Interpretation as an account of how the possible-worlds content of belief states is fixed (see the discussion to follow). This Fregean should reject the biconditional, since it would entail the paradigmatically un-Fregean result that the subject's beliefs were closed under necessary equivalence. What follows is a discussion of what kinds of content-attributions to belief states our metaphysics of representation can and should underpin. I'll come back to the question of how this relates to truths about belief-attribution at the end of the chapter.

I will assume that Fregean sense is a genuine aspect of representational content. Radical Interpretation in my hands has been to this point a story about the metaphysical foundations of reference and referential truth conditions. I want to show that it can be extended to an account of the metaphysical foundations of sense.

You might think that 'extending' is the wrong word—that Radical Interpretation could only ever work as a metaphysics of sense. Let me play out the

---

[5] A further question is whether the operator 'the proposition that' is a legitimate thing to appeal to in the context of a reductive project. See the close of the chapter for further discussion of this.

line of thought. Consider a paradigmatic case where differences in sense matter. Alf believes that Hesperus rises, and doubts Hesperus rises, and is thereby irrational; Beth believes that Hesperus rises, and doubts Phosphorus rises, and is perfectly rational. Alf and Beth's attitudes have identical referential content, and differ only at the level of sense. This looks like trouble for a referentially focused Radical Interpretation! When one of my abstract interpretations assigns <Venus, is rising> as the referential content of both a belief and a doubt of a single individual, it leaves entirely open whether this counts as a rational flaw (as it is in Alf's case) or not (as in Beth's). So the referential interpretation alone provides not enough information to determine how rational the person is—but determining degree of rationality is essential to Radical Interpretation.

I'll explain why I think this line of argument is flawed later. But it points the way nicely to a sense-friendly generalization of Radical Interpretation. The key would be to adjust our claims about what 'propositions' or 'contents' interpretations ascribe to subjects' mental states. The selection among interpretations will be on the basis of how rational they make the subject. And if, as urged above, interpretations ascribing reference are too coarsegrained to determine this—and if the additional information we need is at the level of Fregean senses—then we should insist that interpretations map vehicles of content onto Fregean senses, not referents.

In order to implement the suggestion, one needs a prior theory of what sorts of things Fregean senses are. Here is one suggestion that plays well with the above picture: senses are *referential intensions*—functions from (centred?) possible worlds to reference. The intensions associated with *Hesperus* and *Phosphorus* respectively would need to differ—for example, in a situation where there are distinct heavenly bodies that are first visible in the morning and evening respectively, the two will pick out distinct things. Contemporary Fregeans such as David Chalmers argue that we have good reasons to believe that there are referential intensions ('primary intensions') that do exactly this. So here is the package-deal: we suppose that 'interpretations' assign senses (primary referential intensions) to concepts. Our metaphysics then flows on as before: we pick the most rationalizing senseascribing interpretation as correct, and the correct interpretation fixes the content of our mental states at the level of sense. Referential intension (together with which world is actual) fixes reference. Reference is therefore fixed *en passant* by a sense-focused Radical Interpretation.

This is a possible way of extending Radical Interpretation, and I am not opposed to it. But it does require a very particular theory of Fregean senses to implement, and the package-deal could be undermined by attacking that particular theory of sense. The next section shows, however, that Radical Interpretation is more robust than this, by showing how a second, very different theory of sense can be combined with the story so far.

5.4 Non-foundational Theories of Reference can be Foundational Theories of Sense

This section presents a very different model of how the foundational theory of reference and sense relate, drawing on work by Gareth Evans. It will be important for these purposes that Radical Interpretation focused on interpretation ascribing reference alone is in good order, so I start by re-evaluating the argument of the previous section that suggested the opposite.

The alleged problem was this. Alf believed that Hesperus rises, and doubted that Hesperus rises, and was thereby irrational; Beth believed that Hesperus rises, and doubted that Phosphorus rises, and is perfectly rational. Alf and Beth's attitudes have identical referential content. If all the information we are given by an interpretation is the referential content of their attitudes, apparently we don't have enough to determine whether or not they are rational. But we were supposed to be selecting the correct interpretation based on how rational it made the subject.

What's right about this is that the referential content of a pattern of attitudes alone does not determine whether or not the subject is rational. But neither is this determined by adding in facts about the level of sense, for non-representational relations between attitudes also matter for rationality. If Derek forms the belief that someone is writing about him, causally based on his justified belief that Cathy is writing about him, then he's rational (so far as that goes). If Elsie forms the belief that someone is writing about her as a result of paranoia, with no causal basis in any particular individual instance, then that is irrational, even if she also happens to hold the justified belief that Cathy is writing about her. Generalizing: rationality turns on facts about the way the gears grind in an agent's head, not just on the patterns of representational states that such grindings gives rise to.

Once we recognize this, the Alf/Beth case doesn't at all undermine a Radical Interpretation that works with reference-assigning interpretations. Alf believes the referential content <Venus, is rising> and doubts the same content, and this is internally coded using the very same resources. That makes him irrational—a verdict that depends on both content and background coding. Beth believes the referential content <Venus, is rising>, and doubts the very same referential content, but her internal coding in the two cases is different. That makes her not irrational. We need more than a pattern of attitudes and their referential content to determine rationality, it is true. But the radical interpreter has got a lot more to play with than that. In particular, they are allowed to appeal to relevant facts about the way the subject's internal gears grind, so long as they are themselves non-intentionally specified. So to get a convincing argument against reference-focused Radical Interpretation, one would need to show that referential interpretation together with the full non-intentional specification of the agent's cognitive workings underdetermine rationality. But I submit that this thesis is false. Senses are often very useful in allowing us to express generalizations about rationality, particularly in ways that abstract from differences in cognitive machinery between individuals. But even an indispensable expressive role for senses in formulating neat generalizations about rationality would not show they are needed as part of the supervenience base for determining rationality.

With Radical Interpretation as a foundational theory of reference back on the table, we can look afresh at how to extend it to a foundational theory of sense. Here I draw upon work by Gareth Evans (1982). Evans takes himself to have inherited it from Dummett and ultimately Frege.[6]

Here's the idea in brief. First, identify a relation between Sally and what she's thinking of, in virtue of which she counts as thinking about *that*. Then abstract on this: anybody who thinks about *that* in virtue of standing in the same relation to it as Sally does will share something important in common with Sally: they'll both be thinking about it in the same way. We then make and defend a theoretical identification: we identify these 'ways of thinking about' with Fregean senses.

Some examples: suppose that the planet Venus is the brightest heavenly body visible to Alf in the evening. We can then suppose that Venus is the referent of *Hesperus* (as used by Alf) in virtue of the description *brightest heavenly body visible to me in the evening* being associated with that concept in Alf's cognitive economy. If the same goes for Beth, then she and Alf are using the concept *Hesperus* with the same sense. If Cathy associated a different description with a *Hesperus* concept, then even if it is also satisfied by Venus, the sense of the concept is different, because the 'account' of how

---

[6] I'm very grateful for discussions with Richard Kimberly Heck, Rachel Goodman, Gail Leckie, and Imogen Dickie on these points.

it refers to what it does is different from the previous two cases. Likewise, if Derek has a non-descriptive concept, which refers to Venus in virtue of the historical chain of acquisition and transmission, and not in virtue of description-satisfaction, then that will be concept with a distinct sense.

Generalizing: take a relation R that holds between the subject *s* and Hesperus, such that R(*s*, Hesperus) is what makes it the case that s's *Hesperus*-thought is about Hesperus.[7] For Evans, the sense of *Hesperus* is the property of *standing in relation R to Hesperus*. At a further step of abstraction: given a relation R that holds between a subject-at-*t* and O, such that R(*s*, O) is what makes it the case that s's C-thought is about O, then for Evans the sense of C is the property of standing in relation R to O.

Key to this Evansian construction, clearly, is the identification of relations R between subject and object *in virtue of which the subject is thinking about an object* (with minor variations, this could be taken to be a relation between concept in the subject's head, and the object that concept denotes). And the natural candidates for filling in R are the non-foundational local generalizations about reference discussed earlier. It is at this level that the Radical Interpretation recaptures accounts such as the causal theory of ordinary proper names, or descriptive theories, or inferential role accounts of logical constants, and so forth.

To sum up: on this account, Radical Interpretation remains our foundational metaphysics for reference. Once reference is fixed by this mechanism, we can step back and look at the patterns that emerge. We can and should 'recapture' these patterns by deriving them from Radical Interpretation and auxiliary hypotheses, in the manner of the last three chapters. By articulating these patterns in reference as a local generalization, we give ourselves the tools to describe agent's attitudes not just in terms of what they think about (reference) but the way in which they think about it (sense). Evans' conjecture is that these abstractions from reference will play the theoretical role that Frege associated with senses—particularly in allowing the formulation of powerful generalizations about rationality.

A theme throughout this chapter has been the status of local theories of reference—these served as non-foundational foils to Radical Interpretation in the first section, and take centre stage in the Evansian account of sense. I said early on that such local theories may emerge sporadically. If they are

---

[7] Rather than taking the first relatum of R to be the subject, we could take it to be an inner state of the subject. That's how I would like to go.

just patterns in reference that bubble up on occasion, there is no particular reason to think that there is such a story to be given for each and every concept. I do not know what a local theory of reference for the intensifier *very* would be like, for example. I find the building blocker's approach to the foundations of representation implausible, exactly because they commit, without any particular justification, to the universal availability of local theories for every concept whatsoever. It's worth noting that if local theories of reference are sporadic in this way, and senses are Evansian abstractions from local theories of reference, then this would mean that some but not all concepts will have Fregean senses.

This story reverses the direction of explanation of the first account. On that account, Radical Interpretation focused first and foremost on giving foundations for sense, and in doing so fixed reference *en passant*. Here, Radical Interpretation focuses primarily on giving foundations for reference, and in doing so, fixes sense *en passant*. Which implementation of Radical Interpretation you should go for is not my business here, for I am not evaluating first-order issues about the best way to theorize about propositional attitudes. I can cut my cloth to suit the customer's requirements.

5.5 Conclusion

For the purposes of my project, I develop Radical Interpretation in a foundational way. That opens it up to challenges to my theory of representation, based not on problems to do with the truth of the biconditionals I endorse, my warrant for endorsing them, or the consequences I draw out, but with its foundational status. I have presented the strongest such challenge I know, and shown how it can be resisted. I have not needed to depart from a traditional formulation of the reductive project to do so. If I'm wrong here, in ways that can't be patched by articulating more sophisticated notions of 'foundation', not all is lost. Radical Interpretation would still be interesting on a non-foundational construal, as a unifying and global metaphysics of reference predicting and subsuming many others.

If I want to reduce representation, I must provide a foundational theory of all aspects of representation. Fregean sense, I've been supposing, is an aspect of representation. So I had better have something to say about it. I've presented two approaches. One is to tweak the target of Radical Interpretation, by letting interpretations ascribe Fregean senses, not simply reference. A second is to leave Radical Interpretation as a theory of reference, and to build an account of Fregean sense on top of it. Very different theories of Fregean sense are built into these two approaches, but by giving both options, I demonstrate the relative autonomy of my account from either.

What has been achieved? I have made a case that Radical Interpretation gives us a foundational metaphysics of truths such as the following: Harry deploys a concept whose denotation is greenness; Harry has a belief whose truth conditions are the set of possible worlds in which grass is green; Harry has a concept that has the Fregean sense [green]. I have not given you a neat biconditional that allows you to reduce truths systematically like this: Harry believes that grass is green and 2+2=4. It's not enough for this that Harry has a belief B with the coarse-grained truth conditions that grass is green and 2+2=4, since Harry satisfies that condition if he believes that grass is green and is entirely ignorant of basic arithmetic. It might be sufficient that Harry has a belief with those truth conditions under the right modes of presentation, but pinning down 'the right modes of presentation' for an arbitrary belief-attribution is notoriously tricky. Even if I were able in a given case to find necessary and sufficient conditions for the belief-attribution being true in a single case like 'Harry believes that green is green', that is not yet to give a systematic account that tells us for arbitrary p what it is for Harry to believe that p. Cases where the p in question is not be expressible in my language are going to be particularly demanding (the task can seem easier than it is, if we only proceed on a case-by-case basis disquoting the complement of a belief-attribution expressible in my language).

Here is a way of completing this story. First, use Radical Interpretation to characterize the contents of belief in a way that's as fine-grained as belief-attributions (or perhaps some cleaned up version of belief attributions with some of the idiosyncrasies of natural language stripped out). Second, appeal to the following biconditional: Sally believes that p iff (Ex)(Sally has a belief with content x, and x is the proposition that p). This is legitimate only if the term-forming operator 'the proposition that' is something we're entitled to appeal to in the context of a foundational metaphysics. I finish by flagging the issues that arise.

It would be bad for my foundational project if I had to make an unanalysed appeal to representational truths about propositions. Prima facie, 'x is the proposition that p' is in the target zone here—it seems pretty much the same claim as 'the proposition x represents that p'. It could be something that has a proper place in foundational theory, but one would need to show how to define it up from more obviously legitimate resources.

In some theoretical contexts, that's done fairly easily. For example, if propositions are sets of possible worlds, then P is the proposition that p iff for all w (w is a member of P iff were w the case, then p). The resources on the right hand side are legitimate parts of the reductive base.[8] But in general, the situation is murky. For example, the Fregean holds that 'the proposition/thought that Hesperus is shiny' and 'the proposition/thought that Phosphorus is shiny' denote distinct things. 'The proposition/thought that' so construed is a hyperintensional term-forming operator, in the sense that it changes its denotation under substitution of necessarily equivalent expressions within it. I want to see a definition of this term-forming operator worked out fully before I start leaning on it.

My target is therefore not ordinary belief-attributions directly (at least pending resolution of the issue just flagged), but rather a more theoretical description of subjects' beliefs and desires characterized by their sense, reference and truth conditions. Radical Interpretation, I submit, is a reductive, foundational metaphysics of these representational truths.

---

[8] Of course, one can press on. What is it for 'w to be the case'? Isn't this to say that w represents things as being as they are? But here we find representation again. This takes us into issues about the metaphysics of modality, which is not my topic, but if one wishes to have a working model to combine with what I say, consider Stalnaker's own gloss on worlds as maximal properties of the whole of reality. For a world, so construed, to be the case is for it to be instantiated. But instantiation is not a representational notion.

Conclusion to Part I

Radical Interpretation says that for Sally to have some belief, that belief needs to be attributed by the correct interpretation of her. What makes an interpretation correct is that it best rationalizes her dispositions to act, in the light of her courses of experience (we haven't said yet anything about how we're to understand and ground 'dispositions to act' and 'courses of experience'—this is the task of Part III). Because of the bubble puzzle, we see that if this story is to fly, rationalization must be read as the requirement that we depict Sally as substantively rational, that is, reason-responsive: that as far as possible she is doing as she ought, doxastically and practically. We have seen that this has afforded a basis for responding to underdetermination arguments such as the bubble puzzle, as well as to more local and focused arguments, such as the skolemite challenge to grounding our ability to generalize over absolutely everything, and the permutation challenge to grounding our ability to think about the solid objects in front of us, rather than their permuted images (small furry creatures on the other side of the galaxy). More generally and positively, it affords a basis for predicting and explaining local patterns of reference and constraints on reference: for understanding why inferential cognitive architectures lock us onto logical properties, why the cognitive architectures that link judgements of wrongness to sentiments lock us onto moral properties, and how inductive practice can induce a metasemantic pressure towards attributing natural content, which in turn can explain how our concepts of observational properties really do manage to pick out those properties.

My forays into predicting patterns of local reference have been selective. I don't see any reason to expect that there will be an interesting story to be told, just on this basis, about any concept you can throw at me: for many of our concepts, the most we can give may be the 'holistic non-theory': we use the concept in many and various ways, with no particular theme emerging as dominant, and what fixes reference is just whatever makes best sense of the whole mess. I am relaxed about that prospect: the foundational story is

The Metaphysics of Representation. J. Robert G. Williams, Oxford University Press (2019).
© J. Robert G. Williams.
DOI: 10.1093/oso/9780198850205.001.0001

Radical Interpretation, and these are simply patterns emerging from the underlying dynamics—there's no reason to expect that every concept will feature in some such emergent pattern. (We've just seen that this may have implications for how extensive a theory of Fregean sense we can extract from the overall project.)

Since the chapters above are selective, one might wonder about what other areas are plausible candidates for the 'recapture' treatment given logical, explanatory, and moral concepts above. Here I survey some likely candidates and resources for continuing the story.

First: concepts that are introduced by explicit definition. For example, the concept *grue* was introduced by associating it with a particular condition: *something is grue iff$_{def}$ either it is green and first observed before year X, or is blue and not first observed before year X*. And it's pretty obvious that in virtue of this, the concept *grue* denotes the property *being green and first observed before year X, or being blue and not first observed before year X*. Generalizing, if C is introduced by the definition *Cx iff$_{def}$ Dx*, then the concept C will denote the property of *being D* (or, being more careful about use and mention: the concept C will denote whatever property the complex concept 'D' denotes). This is our claim about the local pattern of reference for terms introduced by explicit definition. It is something that an adequate foundational theory should recapture. In order to do so, a first step is to characterize the cognitive architecture associated with the explicitly defined concept that the notation 'iff$_{def}$' signifies. Perhaps this requires that the concept-possessor treat the substitution of C for D and vice versa as *primitively compelling* in the sense of the previous chapters. The second step, in the style of the previous chapters, is to argue that *given* this cognitive architecture, and plausible premises about rationality, Radical Interpretation can predict that 'C' denotes the property of *being D*.

Second: concepts introduced by *implicit* definitions. Suppose that a concept is introduced by laying out a whole theory in whose axioms it figures. Perhaps ZFC-set-membership is introduced via the axioms of ZFC, or a theoretical concept *charge* is introduced via a role in electromagnetic theory. There is a local generalization about reference here too, though we might fight about how exactly it should be formulated. Here's a candidate: a concept C implicitly defined by theory T denotes whatever property is denoted by the complex concept *T(C/X)*, i.e. it denotes the concept of playing the C-role in T. If we think that 'Something is C iff$_{def}$ it plays the C-role in T' is treated as a definition by the relevant thinkers, than this could be reduced to the previous case.[9]

The first and second generalizations are only appropriate for 'pure' cases, where nothing else metasemantically interesting is going on—grue is a decent approximation to this, I think. More generally, though, the definition is just one of a number of metasemantically relevant aspects of the concept's deployment. Concepts introduced via successful scientific theories may be implicitly defined via the surrounding theory and also deployed in explanations, and I argued in chapter 3 that potent (perhaps: natural) properties are reference magnets for explanatory concepts. Where we have a defined concept that is deployed in explanations, we will get interaction effects. If the property P picked out by 'plays the C-role in T' is impotent/unnatural, but there's another P* that *nearly* plays the C-role, and is *more* potent in that it explains what T is deployed to explain, then Radical Interpretation may well predict that P* rather than P is the referent of C. This is an example where the foundational theory may issue predictions in cases where we don't have a neat local generalization to hand.

A third case related to the above are concepts that come equipped with conceptual analyses. These could be analyses involved in a descriptive theory of names, for example, or the analyses of 'pain' offered by analytic functionalists in the philosophy of mind. In such cases, there is a concept already in use, and the conceptual analysis is something that looks very much like a definition. If we have a broad enough understanding of what it is to 'treat a biconditional as a definition', then such cases might already fall under the generalizations we have just been pointing to, but these are cases where we can expect interaction effects to abound. When a concept is introduced for the first time via a definition or via a theory, we have a very good handle on how it is deployed—initially only in ways that flow from its definition or from the relevant theory. But in the general case, the role of the concepts for which we put forward an analysis could be almost anything. They could, for

---

[9] The gloss just given is appropriate when there is just one 'new' concept, and all the rest are presupposed. Lewis endorses a generalization in which clusters of new concepts are introduced together, and explicit definitions of each are extracted by existentially generalizing over variables corresponding to all but one of the cluster. I am suppressing various niceties in Lewis's treatment (Lewis 1970)—for example, his treatment is about implicit definitions in language, not thought, and involves some subtle manoeuvres such as paraphrasing a theory into a form where there are singular terms for each 'introduced' property. That matters, since the way he goes beyond Carnap and Ramsey's work turns crucially on a particular treatment of reference-failure for singular terms.

example, have a significant *practical* role, of the kind we discussed in connection with the concept of *wrongness*—or not. They could be already deployed in explanations—or not. They could feature in further primitively compelling inferential patterns—or not. One should expect a complex interdependency between the success-conditions of analysis, the under-standing of 'treating as a definition' and the right way to formulate a local generalization about reference. Definition and analyses thus provide rich pickings for future recapture projects.

A fourth target for recapture is the Kripke-style causal-historical pattern of names (better: the mental analogue of names). A fifth is the pattern that characterizes the reference of perceptual demonstratives. For detailed treat-ment of the local patterns characteristic of these cases (and of descriptive names), I point the reader towards Imogen Dickie's monograph *Fixing Reference*. Dickie does more than just formulate the local patterns—she herself is engaged in a recapture project. She does not endorse Radical Interpretation, so she is not doing exactly what I would want to, but it is a close cousin. Its overarching principle is the principle 'Reference and Justi-fication'. This, roughly, tells us that holding the denotation of other terms fixed, the correct interpretation of any ordinary singular concept for ordin-ary objects is whatever would justify the canonical belief-forming practices involving that concept. Dickie uses this principle together with assumptions about epistemology and assumptions about the cognitive and social archi-tecture of demonstrative, descriptive, and name-like thought, to recapture local theories of reference. From the perspective of Substantive Radical Interpretation, Dickie's Reference and Justification principle picks up on one aspect of a broader reason-maximization principle. If Dickie's deriv-ations are successful, I think I can borrow them for my own project. If they're not quite successful, I have some additional constraining resources to offer.[10]

Sixth, the concept of *same person as*, I think, is apt for a treatment similar to the one given in chapter 4 for moral wrongness. To be sure, on the epistemic side, there are various criteria that we use to reidentify a person across time, but I doubt that our actual practice discriminates between the

---

[10] For example, I do not think that she does enough to show that Reference and Justification alone would rule out observational duplicates of ordinary objects as the referents of perceptual demonstratives. I think that the wider set of resources that Radical Interpretation provides can help. Perceptual demonstratives are intimately linked to action, as well as belief-formation, and making demonstrative intentions rational can, I think, help explain aspects of reference-determination that epistemology alone cannot.

philosophically most interesting candidates, or that our judgements about counterfactual cases are sufficiently determinate to be probative. But personal identity is absolutely central to moral and prudential practical reasoning, being linked to responsibility, self-sacrifice for later-greater-good, and the like. I conjecture that the same-person-as relation is involved in moral and prudential practical reasons, and that the primary pressure that fixes the reference of this concept will be the pressure to rationalize the way we deploy the concept in practical deliberation.

One could go on. One fascinating topic, for example, is how political and social kinds are handled in this framework. Here, paying attention to the difference between sampling and extrapolative generalization will be particularly important: social class, racial categories or gender, for example, undoubtedly feature in sampling generalizations, but it is much less clear that there are true extrapolative generalizations to be had here. Connectedly, a bias towards *more natural* referents looks like a highly committal place to start, when thinking about the denotations of concepts of the social world. And of course, many concepts of social kinds are politically loaded, and this normative aspect will matter to what Radical Interpretation predicts.[11] But these must be topics for another day: it's now time to move on, and start looking at the next layer of representation: that of public language.

---

[11] In the case of social kinds, the kind of magnetic clustering produced by having a direct linguistic expression, as described in Part II, may be especially significant, and suggests a broader way by way in which properties of the way the language is used might be necessary to understand why the associated concept means what it does.

PART II

LINGUISTIC REPRESENTATION

Radical Interpretation took the primordial intentionality of experience and action and transformed it, via rationalization, into the intentionality of belief and desires. In these two chapters, a further transformation is proposed, whereby certain human artefacts—words and sentences—acquire representational properties. In the three chapters to follow, I give an account of this transformation, and so a metaphysics of the topmost layer of the three-layer metaphysics of representation.

The essential prerequisite for everything to follow in this triad is the first section of chapter 6, which gives an overview of the way that the convention-based metaphysics of linguistic representation will work. The metaphysics has two elements: a specification of 'base facts'—conventional associations between sentences and propositions, and story about selection—what makes a linguistic interpretation correct, in light of those base facts. After that, the reader can choose their own adventure. Those taking the main line by reading in order will find, in the remainder of chapter 6 ways of refining the initial account of base facts to drop various apparent presuppositions: a presupposed ontology of sentence/word-types, a presupposed division of subjects into language-using populations, and the presupposition that declarative sentence-types always express belief.

Next in the main line is chapter 7. This lays out Lewis's characterization of linguistic convention, the central resource used to the base facts. Here I focus on a prerequisite for there to be any conventional associations, so characterized: that for each sentence there is some shared mental content that language users throughout the population associate with that sentence. Finally, Chapter 8 turns to the other half of the metaphysics of linguistic representation by giving an account of how interpretations are selected by the base facts—a combination of fit and simplicity.

The Metaphysics of Representation. J. Robert G. Williams, Oxford University Press (2019).
© J. Robert G. Williams.
DOI: 10.1093/oso/9780198850205.001.0001

Those whose main interest is in the way that language inflects the metaphysics of mental content should consider an alternative reading order which starts with the first section of chapter 6 and skips straight to chapter 7. Those who want to get the proposed theory of linguistic representation under their belt as quickly as possible should start with the first section of chapter 6 and skip straight to chapter 8.

6

From Mental Representation
to Linguistic Representation

This chapter introduces the convention-based metaphysics of linguistic representation that I favour. The story makes free use of the resources of second-layer intentionality that we covered in Part I of this work. Section 6.1 outlines the complete account, with two working primitives: conventions and 'best theory' that will be examined in detail in the next two chapters. The account appears to presuppose that we have some independent grip on the typing of utterances into sentences, and the grouping of agents into language-using populations, and in section 6.2 I refine the formulation so that these are characterized 'endogenously'. The account also appears to presuppose that declarative sentence-types always express beliefs with standard factual content, which appears to rule out of court various classic and contemporary 'expressivist' theories of morals, modals, and the like. Section 6.3 discusses how to generalize the theory. These sections pre-empt some big picture concerns about the metaphysics of representation, but only the first section is essential to the comprehension of the material in Chapters 7 and 8.

6.1 Correct Linguistic Interpretation is Determined by the Best Theory of Linguistic Conventions

In the case of mental representation, the metaphysics I advocate takes this form: there is a space of abstract interpretations, which map states or stages of agents to contents. The job of the metaphysician of mental representation is to give an illuminating story about which of these abstract interpretation is correct, from which we 'read off' facts about what a person believes or desires. In the case of linguistic representation, the situation is similar. There is a space of abstract interpretations which map linguistic expressions to contents. The job of the metaphysician of linguistic representation is to give

The Metaphysics of Representation. J. Robert G. Williams, Oxford University Press (2019).
© J. Robert G. Williams.
DOI: 10.1093/oso/9780198850205.001.0001

an illuminating story about which of these linguistic interpretations is correct.

As well as an illuminating account of correctness, however, we must start from the right space of interpretations. Will the vehicles of linguistic content be individual utterances, utterance-types, sentence-types, or individual words? What kinds of contents are assigned to linguistic entities? My space of linguistic interpretations will contain functions that assign contents (semantic values) to individual words. Via compositional rules, each will thereby assign contents to well-formed expressions including sentences. I will be targeting the contents of words and sentences of a shared public language.[1]

A key role is played by biconditionals such as:

- The correct interpretation maps N to O iff N refers to O.

Just as at the analogous point in the metaphysics of mental representation, I propose that we read the biconditionals with the direction of explanation flowing from left to right: what it is for a name to refer to something is for the correct interpretation to say that this is so. This makes obvious the need for an illuminating account of what it takes for an interpretation to be correct.[2]

Just as my starting point for the metaphysics of belief and desire was David Lewis's brief remarks on (mental) Radical Interpretation, my starting point here is Lewis's theory of linguistic representation.[3] His account of correctness for compositional interpretations[4] I take to be the following:

---

[1] One issue that I won't get into here is whether these linguistic intensions should be functions *in extension* or *in intension*—where the former would be the familiar set-theoretic constructions that map words to contents, while the latter are individuated as finely as the axiomatic specification of one of the former mappings.

[2] I use reference to illustrate, but I think the fundamental kind of semantic values assigned to names are more likely to be functions from context-world pairs to referents—in which case the above kind of biconditional will tell us what it is for the name to have an entity of that kind as semantic value, and the reference relation will be characterized indirectly, as the value of function so-associated at the actual world and context.

[3] The most important text here is Lewis (1975), but see also Lewis (1969, 1974, 1992).

[4] A 'compositional interpretation' because the interpretations *may* contain compositional rules, but it is an open issue, in this framework, whether the semantics determined by an interpretation is fully compositional. It is consistent with the view to be developed below that the best theory of the conventional associations of truthfulness and trust for a public language is non-compositional. It's perfectly possible that we lay down compositional rules for disjunction, say, but also write in an ad hoc exception, say for disjunctions occurring in the antecedents of conditionals. We might well have good empirical grounds for thinking that this will not ultimately be the simplest way to write down the semantics for English—because, for example,

- The correct compositional interpretation of the public linguistic expressions E of population P (and the semantic rules for the expressions they form) is that interpretation which is the best theory of the propositions conventionally associated by P with E-sentences.

This is a story with two elements. First, there is an appeal to a range of base facts: conventional associations in a population, between sentences and propositions. Second, there is a relation of 'best theory' which selects the correct interpretation, by appeal to the actually-obtaining base facts. Both elements will receive attention.[5]

In the case of linguistic representation Lewis paid most attention to one central aspect of the base facts—conventional associations between whole sentences and propositions (this is a striking contrast to the case of mental representation, where the relevant base facts were little discussed by Lewis). Here is how I propose to understand the key notion:[6]

we think that a more thorough-going compositional theory is a well-supported hypothesis about the structure of individual linguistic competence. But fully compositionality for public languages is not an issue prejudged from the get-go.

[5] In Williams (2007), I characterized interpretationism in general as marked by this kind of two-step approach, where a range of data fixed by usage at the sentence-level is identified, and then semantic facts are fixed by best theory of that data. I intended this to cover at least Davidson (1984) and the 'global descriptivism' which, supplemented with naturalness, is discussed and seemingly endorsed by Lewis (1984). The latter has been widely influential, but a crucial disanalogy to this setting is that its data consists of pairings of sentences with truth values, not propositional contents. This makes it a harder theory to get to work, though a simpler one to work with.

[6] Lewis talks of 'languages' which are abstract objects that map sentences to propositions (for him, these are sets of possible worlds). He then gives an account of what it is for a language L to be in use by a population P. The account he gives is essentially the one given here, though he states truthfulness and trust thus: 'to avoid uttering any sentence of L unless one believes it to be true in L ... to tend to respond to another's utterance of any sentence of L by coming to believe that the uttered sentence is true in L'. There are two things to note here. First, Lewis's characterization of the beliefs is metalinguistic: members of the population are to believe that sentences are true in L. Second, rather than characterize a set of (conventional) regularities, one for each sentence, as I do, he characterizes a general regularity governing all sentences of L. The first point I don't think is significant. L, recall, is an abstract function from sentences to propositions. Assuming sentences are necessary existents, if L maps S to proposition p, then S *being true in L* is necessarily equivalent to p. Lewis in this paper took the content of beliefs to be individuated only intensionally. So for him, for Sally to believe that S is true in L just is for Sally to believe that p. So there is no deep difference between his metalinguistic and my proposition-orientated formulations. There may be more at stake over whether each individual regularity of truthfulness and trust is a convention, or whether the totality of such regularities are collectively a convention. It would only be a minor tweak to my characterization to follow Lewis in this. A third difference is that Lewis's languages, since they are functions, will map each sentence to a unique proposition, whereas as I will emphasize below, the set of conventional associations can associate a given sentence with multiple propositions. In general, a 'language' (function from

- Sentence S is conventionally associated with proposition p by population P iff there is the following pair of regularities within P: all members of P will utter a token of type S only if they believe p, and all members of P will come to believe p if they hear another utter a token of type S; and further, these two regularities are entrenched in the beliefs and preferences of members of P so that they count as conventions.

These two regularities are known as 'truthfulness' and 'trust' respectively. Lewis has a lot to say about the final clause—what it takes for a regularity to count as a convention. In the next chapter, I will be cracking this open to look at the details, but for now 'convention' like 'best theory' is a working primitive.

To state the obvious: people are not always honest, nor always trusting. Some sentences ('I did not do it') may be more often used dishonestly than honestly. Audiences may rightly fail to trust certain speakers (the accused in court, the politician on the radio) and may be disposed on some subject matters will ask for further evidence rather than take interlocutors at their word immediately. Following Lewis, we may refine the regularities we are looking for, requiring conformity only in 'serious communicative situations' where the speaker has no interest in deception, and where the audience takes the speaker to be a relevant authority. I take such restrictions as read.

That there is a conventional association between a sentence and a proposition does not mean that the proposition is the representational content of that sentence, if we understand 'representational content of a sentence' as a matter of what the sentence literally means, i.e. what the world has to be like if the sentence is to be literally true. Here are four issues that illustrate the difference:

1) As stated, you have a conventional association between sentence and proposition only when that sentence actually figures in conventional regularities. But most well-formed sentences of English will never be uttered (after all, they are infinitely many of them), and many are uttered only on a few scattered occasions.[7] Most English sentences,

---

sentences to propositions) is in use in Lewis's sense iff it maps sentences to propositions with which they are conventionally associated in my sense.

[7] Strictly, sentences that are never uttered feature in arbitrary regularities of truthfulness and trust (as will sentences that are uttered, but never in a 'serious communicative situation'). Vacuously, an unused sentence S, S is only uttered when the uttered believes p, and so on, for

including some we deploy and are well understood and certainly do have representational content, are not conventionally associated with a proposition.

2) I see no reason to assume from the get-go that there will be only one proposition conventionally associated with a sentence. For example, I will utter 'Harry is a bachelor' only if I believe Harry is unmarried. And someone hearing me utter this will likewise form that belief. This is regularity of truthfulness and trust, and I don't see why it shouldn't count as a conventional regularity (checking this against Lewis's definition of convention, which we'll introduce later, also makes me think it should count as a convention for him). But of course, this particular conventional association is not a good candidates to be the sentence's 'literal meaning'

3) I see no reason to assume from the get-go that the literal meaning is going to be some simple construction out of the plurality of propositions conventionally associated with the sentence. One reason for this is the influence of pragmatic factors. 'Some students performed well at the exam' implies but does not state not all did.[8] Speakers in a serious communicative situation will utter this only if they believe that not all students performed well, and audiences will come to believe that not all performed well on hearing it. This regularity too will likely count as conventional by Lewis's lights. So any account of literal meaning would somehow have to disentangle pragmatic from semantic effects.

4) Indexical sentences are not conventionally associated with the truth-conditions they express. A utters 'I am sitting' while believing that A is sitting. B will utter the same while believing B is sitting. C, hearing one or the other utter that sentence, will form one or the other belief on different occasions. So even though 'I am sitting' as uttered by A says that A is sitting, that proposition is not conventionally associated with the sentence (there's not even a regularity of truthfulness and trust here). If there's a conventional association to a proposition here, it will be to something else, for example, what Chalmers (2002) would call the 'primary intension' of the sentence: A, B each believe that speaker

every p. However, none of these vacuous regularities is a plausible candidate for a convention. Lewis (1992) endorses this conclusion, pointing in particular to sentences so long and complicated that we would expect, if they were used, that their use would be rife with performance errors.

[8] Grice (1975).

of the context is sitting, and C forms that belief upon hearing each utterance.[9]

To summarize: conventional associations encapsulate some interesting properties—interesting representational properties, even—of a core range of sentences which are in reasonably regular use and which ordinary speakers can handle with ease. But the job was to ground the representational properties of linguistic artefacts more generally, and I want to ground the kind of representational properties that are cited in semantic theory. My target therefore includes truth-conditions for each of infinitely many well-formed sentences of English, including the many that are never used. And I want a story that grounds reference of individual words and phrases. For all of this, conventions are no good unsupplemented: we need the second stage of the project. That will be the focus of the next chapter. Here, I continue laying the groundwork.

6.2 There's No Need for a Separate Metaphysics of Words and Populations

The basis for linguistic convention makes essential appeal to the *sentence-types* uttered by language-using *populations*. Without the first, we haven't even said which occurrences are relevant to the regularity (it would be like claiming that *blahs* drive on the left, without saying what a *blah* is). Without the second, we won't know whether a string of occurrences counts as a

---

[9] A standard model for primary content is a set of centred worlds, and one candidate for a content both A and B believe is the set of centred worlds at which the person at the centre is sitting. This won't be a content that C believes in response to the utterance, however. One option here is to characterize truthfulness and trust slightly differently: truthfulness for sentence S in set of centred worlds p requires all members of the population utter a token of S only if they believe p, but trust requires that all members of the population form the belief $p+$ only if they believe p, where $p+$ shifts the p's centre from whoever is speaking to a member of their audience. Another idea (which is in effect what Lewis 1975 proposed) is to appeal to Kaplanian character, thus: S is conventionally associated with character C by population P just in case all members of P utter S in context c only if they believe p, and all members of P come to believe p when they hear someone utter S in context c, where p is, in each case, the proposition obtained by applying character C to context c. In order to make this work, we would need to add to the characterization of the 'serious communicative context' to which we restrict attention the further condition that speaker and hearer are fully informed about relevant aspects of the context. There is a danger here of fooling ourselves into thinking we have achieved too much: there will be regularities of truthfulness and trust in this sense not just with the sorts of characters that are plausibly semantically associated with the sentence, but also with characters that map contexts at which the sentence is not uttered to arbitrary propositions.

regularity (cars driving on the left is a regularity in the UK, but not worldwide). The ontology of word-types has generated a small literature, in which it's become clear that it will be an uphill task to identify sentence-types as types of shapes or sounds.[10] This should prick the conscience of a reductively minded metaphysician of representation. Perhaps there is no way to pick out sentence-types independently of semantic facts. Perhaps only semantic facts make the ambiguous homophones/homographs 'bank' and 'bank' distinct words. The second task again affords ammunition for the anti-reductionists. What way could there be to pick out a population that uses a single language, if we ban appeal to the fact that they are all users of that very language?[11]

Leckie and Williams (2019) suggest that we should give up on the attempt to specify populations and sentence-types exogeneously, i.e. prior to and independent of semantic facts. Instead, we submit that populations and sentence-types arise as part of parcel of the metaphysical theory that delivers the semantic facts—they are endogenous to our metasemantics. I will follow the story we defend in that paper by refining the proposed characterization of base facts as follows:

- (Endogenous) Given an utterance u, <P, T, L> are the conventional associations relevant to utterance u iff P is a population, T a typing relation and L a set of sentence$_T$-proposition pairs such that:
- for all <S_T, p> in L, conventions of truthfulness and trust relating S_T to p prevail in population P.
- The speaker/hearer of u is a member of the population P
- u is a member of some equivalence class of the typing relation T.

Instead of fixing the conventional associations *presupposing* a particular population and typing relation, (Endogenous) treats the population and typing relation as variables whose values are fixed in whatever way is necessary to produce conventions of (Truthfulness) and (Trust). The correct word-typing for English is as described by the T-role in this structure for a population that includes the utterance I am presently making. The membership of the language-using population of which I am a part is as described

---

[10] For an excellent review of problem cases and the relevant literature, see Nick Tasker (2017).

[11] I'm here very grateful to discussions with my co-author Gail Leckie as well as to conversations with my colleague Roger White, which first got me thinking about these issues.

by the P-role in that same structure. And finally, the content-sentence pairings that are the basis for facts about linguistic representation in English can be read off that same triple.

Endorsing this account does not foreclose saying other, more immediately illuminating things about words and populations. If a reader thinks that they have an exogenous way of specifying a language-using population and a typing relation that feature in linguistic conventions, then all the better for (Endogenous)—that typing relation and population will be an illuminating independent specification of a typing relation that features in a set of conventional-associations, according to our formulation. I'm very pessimistic that an illuminating characterization could be done in a reductive fashion, without appeal to linguistic representation, but it's much more plausible that one could, in part by appeal to semantic facts, give a theory which characterizes of the language-using population and a typing relation. These sort of features would be part of a non-foundational metaphysics of word types and language-using populations (compare the discussion in chapter 5 on non-foundational metaphysics of mental reference and their relations to foundational theories).[12]

In sum: since the reductive characterization of words and populations is given by (Endogenous) and not by an exogenous characterization, the project of saying interesting things about types and populations that figure in languages in use doesn't have to be burdened by any reductive constraint. Metaphysically speaking, the bounds of the population, the relevant types, and the contents conventionally associated with sentences, are all jointly and simultaneously grounded in facts about patterns of linguistic usage and attitudes of speakers and hearers.

I'm not too worried about this account undergenerating populations or sentences—after all, if you feed in an intuitive characterization of sentence-types and language-using populations, it'll do exactly as good a job of counting those as conventional as it would if we were to treat that typing

---

[12] For example, in Tasker (2017) an intriguing account of the nature of words is offered, building on work in the metaphysics of artefacts by Amie Thomasson. An account of word-individuation (or at least, various necessary and sufficient conditions) is offered as part of the package, built on the more general model of individuation of artefact-kinds. But Tasker is clear from the start that among the determinants of word-individuation for him are facts about the semantic properties of the individual word tokens, their recognizability to a certain audience, and so forth. Tasker's account might be exactly what we need to understand how words work, but also entirely unsuitable to be slotted in as an 'exogenous' account of words. However, so long as word-types as he characterizes them figure in linguistic conventions, his account is consistent with (Endogenous).

and population as exogenous. Undergeneration objections are best seen as objections to the account of convention, not as worries about the way we are handling words and populations. The thing we need to guard against is overgeneration. By choosing crazy typing relations and gerrymandered populations, in principle we might be able to find all sorts of dubious regularities connecting uses of sentences (so typed) to attitudes, that intuitively would be *not* be genuine conventions and would be a bad basis for a theory of linguistic representation.

I will not adjudicate the issue here, but instead point the interested reader to Leckie and Williams (2019) where the overgeneration issue is the primary focus. That paper gives a typology of potential sources of overgeneration may happen, for example, by subdividing genuine populations and types (typing utterances by brown-eyed people separately from blue-eyed people); merging separate types together, or tailoring the population or typing so as to bias the resulting regularity (e.g. by restricting it to population who apply 'red' to more orangey things than is the norm). The response involves working through such cases in turn, and arguing that none of them produces a genuine example of overgeneration. There are plenty of gerrymandered regularities of truthfulness and trust, to be sure—but we argue, none of them are regularities count as conventions, at least by the lights of the definition of that notion that Lewis gave.

6.3 The Mental States Expressed by Declarative Sentences Need Not be Beliefs

Conventions of truthfulness and trust give us an excellent handle on what it might mean to say that a sentence-type conventionally 'expresses the belief that p'. If the kind of attitude expressed by declarative sentences is always and everywhere belief, then we lose nothing by leaving that implicit, and concentrating just on the relation between the sentence and the content, p. That is in effect what is presupposed in the convention-based account as formulated above.[13]

---

[13] I concentrate on the issue as it arises for declarative sentences, where it raises special challenges. Another issue is whether we should extend the convention-based story to non-declarative sentences used in non-assertoric speech acts. Associating such non-declarative sentences with conventions of sincerity and submission as detailed below is one idea; the idea that all such sentences might be regarded as circumlocutions for reflexive declaratives is another. Thanks to Thomas Brouwer for pressing me on this issue.

If I made that assumption, however, I'd lose some of my audience. Some philosophers that that moral sentences express planning states of mind, that epistemic modal sentences express a state of uncertainty, and that conditional sentences express states of conditional belief.[14] So this final section will sketch how to tailor the story to their concerns (having outlined how it can be done, I'll go back to the belief-universalism assumption in future sections).

The first thing to note is that there is a very natural way to understand what these expressivist claims about particular sentences come to, using the resources we already have on the table:

- There is a conventional regularity of: (i) uttering 'x ought φ' only if one's contingency plan for x's situation is to φ, and (ii) coming to so plan when one hears the utterance 'x ought φ'.
- There is a conventional regularity of: (i) uttering 'It might be that p' only if p is compatible with what one believes, and (ii) adjusting one's beliefs to make them compatible with p when one hears the utterance 'It might be that p'.
- There is a conventional regularity of: (i) uttering 'if p, q' only if one believes q on the supposition that p, and (ii) adjusting one's beliefs to come to believe q on the supposition that p, when one hears the utterance 'if p, q'.

In place of (Truthfulness) and (Trust), we find here a sincerity condition—one utters the sentence only if one has the expressed attitude—and a submission condition—one forms the expressed attitude when one hears another utter the sentence. Truthfulness and Trust are just what sincerity and submission come to for the special case of belief.[15]

Are there such regularities? One might wonder whether someone uttering the words 'Harry ought to φ' regularly leads their audience to plan to φ in

---

[14] John Macfarlane has recently advocated that any *vague* language should be treated in the Gibbardian expressivist fashion. If he is right, then pretty much all natural language expresses plans as well as beliefs. See Macfarlane (2016) and Williams (2016c) for my response and development of the view.

[15] These are not the only ways of formulating the connections in the conventional framework—for example, perhaps closer to the dialogical role of epistemic modals would be to present them as a test: the 'sincerity' condition remains the same, but on the 'submission' end, the regularity is that the speaker checks that p is already compatible with their beliefs, or else challenges the utterer. But the simple generalization above will give us enough to work on right now.

Harry's circumstances. And after all, sometimes such normative claims are contested—where someone is saying that Harry ought to change career, or do more exercise, or avoid white lies. In those cases, we don't respond to bare assertions simply by incorporating the plans expressed into our own—we would tend to ask for a bit more explanation and justification. But of course, the same could be said of contested factual claims. If someone claims that the government will fall next week, we want to know how they know before we'll take them at their word. These are violations of the 'trust' regularity for belief, unless we add the caveats I am taking as read: to restrict it to situations where the speakers have no interest in deception and hearers regard speakers as relevantly authoritative. The same restrictions to suitable communicative scenarios are, unsurprisingly, required in this case. (It's worth remembering one can come to plan to φ in x's situation, without changing your contingency plans for any situation. For example, if you hear someone say 'Harry ought to change career', one might hold fixed one's opinion about the circumstances in which changing-career is the thing to do, and simply come to believe that Harry is now in one of those circumstances. Lots of communication using normative sentences can take this form.[16]) Such regularities, I contend, are also good candidates for being conventional.

All of the above could hold, and it could still be the case that:

- There is a conventional regularity of uttering 'x ought φ' only if one believes x ought to φ, and of coming to believe x ought to φ upon hearing 'x ought φ'.
- There is a conventional regularity of uttering 'It might be that p' only if one believes it might be that p, and of coming to believe this upon hearing 'it might be that p'.
- There is a conventional regularity of uttering 'if p, q' only if one believes that if p, q, and of coming to believe this upon hearing 'if p, q'.

As I mentioned early on, typically sentences will conventionally express many different beliefs. There's no reason to think that they shouldn't express both beliefs *and* other attitudes. There are some interesting questions about explanatory priority, however, which take us to the heart of expressivist treatments of normativity, epistemic modality, and conditionals. For

---

[16] For an excellent extended discussion of communication for expressivists, see Perez Carballo and Santorio (2016).

remember, the beliefs we can legitimately appeal to in grounding linguistic content are only those that we can in turn ground via the second-layer story of Radical Interpretation. And someone might doubt that the best rationalization of the subject's behaviour by itself requires we attribute normative, modal or conditional *beliefs*, in addition to planning states, states of uncertainty, and states of conditional belief. That would leave us in the following position: as we approach linguistic content in phase three of our grand plan for theorizing representation, there are sentences for which we are not in a position to appeal to belief-centric conventions of truthfulness and trust, since the belief-states that they might express have not yet been assigned content in the phase two. The semantic facts that we can ground by means of the story just given will then be restricted to a fragment of language that leaves out these problematic bits of vocabulary. If we can make use, however, of conventional associations to non-belief attitudes already grounded in phase two, then an unrestricted, though expressivist, grounding of semantic facts is available.

There are some blind alleys to be avoided. In the belief-centric setting, the key 'datapoints' that a semantic theory had to fit were the range of propositions 'conventionally associated' with each sentence, where those were the contents of the beliefs the sentence conventionally expresses (i.e. that figure in conventions of truthfulness and trust). We can't just mechanically transfer this to other attitudes: for example, the content of the plan expressed by 'Harry ought to change career' might be: that one changes career in Harry's circumstances. But we wouldn't want a semantic theory to assign that factual content as the semantic value of the normative sentence. The semantics needs to fit with a planning state, not a factual belief that the plan has been executed.

More constructively, I see two options here. One is simply to mark the differences in the data, so that instead of consisting of sentence-proposition pairs, the data will be sentence-attitude-content triples. That defers the central task of spelling out what it is for a linguistic interpretation to 'match' such enriched data to the second stage of the metaphysics of linguistic interpretation. That would be attractive for a classic form of expressivism where linguistic theory itself was supposed to take the form of an 'attitude semantics' that associated attitude-content pairs with sentences. (Disclaimer: I do not defend the possibility of such an attitude-semantics: if it is not tenable, then that's a problem for these expressivists independent of my kind of metasemantics.)

The other approach is to do some pre-processing of the data, in order to transform it into a uniform format. To illustrate this, I take my lead from

(Gibbard 2003). Let a world-hyperplan pair be the combination of a complete description of how the world is factually, together with function from all possible choice situations to one of the options available in that situation. To accept a world-hyperplan pair is to believe that the world fits the description given by the world component, and to plan to φ in circumstance c iff the hyperplan maps c to φ. To accept a set of world-hyperplan pairs is to rule out any combination of world and hyperplan that is outside that set—this amounts, in the general case, to a set of conditional commitments to plan a certain way if the world is thus-and-such.

I will assume that our metaphysics of second-layer representations gets us to a point where we can read off what a subject's conditional plans are, in this sense. We can then redescribe the combined belief/planning states of this agent in terms of which sets of world-hyperplan pairs they accept. And that means we will have earned the right to redescribe the first statement below as the second, for a suitable q (set of world-hyperplan pairs):

- There is a conventional regularity of (i) uttering 'x ought φ' only if one plans to φ if in x's place, and (ii) if one hears 'x ought φ' uttered, then one comes to plan to φ if in x's place.
- There is a conventional regularity of uttering 'x ought φ' only if one accepts q, and of coming to accept q upon hearing 'x ought φ'.

Once things are presented in this format, we can extract the data the semantic theory is to fit, since we now have a new, more general kind of conventionally associated content: the combined belief/planning states q. The combined semantic theory will then have to assign generalized contents that can be assessed for fit or lack of fit with the contents assigned in the data. This is a good description of what many contemporary expressivist semantic theories do. (Disclaimer: I do not take a stand on the tenability of their project: if it is not legitimate, then that's a problem for Gibbardian expressivists independent of my kind of metasemantics.)

The crucial technique here is the Gibbardian transformation of a description of a subject's psychology as the acceptance of enriched content—that's what allows us to articulate the convention in a way that provides a target for compositional interpretations. So if we want to replicate this metasemantics for other kinds of expressive content, we need to perform the analogous redescription. It might be, for example, that to underpin epistemic modals, we need to describe an agent as accepting a set of world-information state pairs, representing combinations of factual states of the world and states of their own factual information to which they are open. To underpin epistemic modals, we need to credit the agent as accepting a set of world/update-function pairs. And if this is to be a single story across the board, we will need to combine these and others into a highly complex summary of a possible opinionated psychology: a world/hyperplan/information/update/etc. tuple. Then, on the basis of the facts about mental content already established at the second layer of representation in more familiar terms, we say which of these possible opinionated psychologies belong to the subject.

Whatever way we go, the claims we'll need to make are contentious. But the contentiousness is part and parcel of the expressivist treatment, not due to the kind of metaphysics of mental and linguistic content I am offering. The existence of the conventions that tie the target sentences to non-doxastic attitudes, the Gibbardian redescriptions, and the availability of compositional interpretations of language are all points at which one might reasonably raise an eyebrow—but you should take up your questions with the expressivists who advocate the approach, not with me. What I have been arguing for in this section is simply that I do not stack the decks either way—expressivists as well as more traditional cognitivist projects can happily buy into the metaphysics of representation I offer.

6.4 Conclusion

This chapter has developed the outline of a metaphysics of linguistic representation, and then freed it of apparent commitments in two respects. I have said that, properly formulated, there will be no appeal to exogenous theories of word-types or language-using-populations—and that's a good thing, since they would represent serious vulnerabilities in the overall reductive project. I have shown that the 'cognitivist' setup whereby every sentence expresses a belief is just a simplification (one that I'll continue to indulge in for pragmatic reasons) not an essential feature of the account. With these two preliminaries handled, we are ready to move on to investigating in the next two chapters the two most load-bearing components of the metaphysics: the appeal to convention and to the relation of 'best theory'.

7

Linguistic Convention and Shared Mental Content

I say: the basis upon which linguistic representation is built is convention. Facts about conventional associations between sentences and content are understood as follows:

- Sentence S is conventionally associated with proposition p by population P iff there is the following pair of regularities within P: all members of P will utter a token of type S only if they believe p, and all members of P will come to believe that p if they hear another utter a token of type S; and further, these two regularities are entrenched in the beliefs and preferences of members of P so that they count as conventions.

In the previous chapter, I looked at some of the explicit commitments of conventional association: the way in which it appeals to words and populations, and the assumption that the attitude conventionally associated with a sentence is always a belief (I continue with this simplifying assumption for convenience here). In this chapter, I focus on a final presupposition of the account. In order for S to be conventionally associated with p, according to the above, all member of the relevant population must believe that p, in the right circumstances. Apparently the mental contents available to members of the population must be shareable, and shared, else the account will fall apart. We'll see that this generates a problem that takes some detailed work to overcome.

This chapter starts by giving more details about Lewis's account of conventions, moves on to articulating the shared content presupposition and makes a prima facie case that my second-layer metaphysics of mental content won't vindicate it. I put forward two responses and draw out some consequences of the one I favour.

The Metaphysics of Representation. J. Robert G. Williams, Oxford University Press (2019).
© J. Robert G. Williams.
DOI: 10.1093/oso/9780198850205.001.0001

7.1 Lewis's Account of Linguistic Conventions Set Out

Lewis's (1969, 1975) account of convention was as follows. A regularity R is a convention in a population P iff within P, the following hold, with at most a few exceptions:

- (Conformity) Everyone in P conforms to R.
- (Belief) Everyone in P believes that everyone in P conforms to R.
- (Reason) This belief gives everyone in P a good reason to conform to R himself.
- (Preference) There is a general preference in P for general conformity to R rather than slightly-less-than-general conformity to R.
- (Alternative) There is an alternative possible regularity R' such that if it met (1) and (2), it would also meet (3) and (4).
- (Common Knowledge) All of (1–5) are common knowledge.

And of course the regularities that are conventions according to Lewis's treatment of linguistic content are the following:

- (Truthfulness) Members of P utter *s* only if they believe *p*.
- (Trust) If a member of P hears another member of P utter *s*, she tends to come to believe *p*.

We find here appeal to second-layer representation both in the characterization of the regularities, and also throughout the characterization of what it takes for a regularity to be a convention.

The details of Lewis's account have generated extensive discussion, but I will not be considering here whether, for example, the various clauses are overdemanding or need refinement.[1] I will be focusing instead on presuppositions that I expect it to share with successor accounts.

7.2 Individualistic Descriptivism Seems Incompatible with Linguistic Conventions

In order for 'I am in Paris' to be conventionally associated with a specific content *p*, members of the population need to be having a belief with

---

[1] For an overview of such discussions, see Marmor (2009).

content p whenever they utter that sentence. This follows just from the characterization of (Truth) and (Conformity).

We have already met one worry about this consequence of the characterization. In the last chapter, I noted that there is variation across Harry and Sally in the truth conditions of the beliefs they entertain when uttering an indexical sentence such as 'I am in Paris'. I noted that by switching the focus to the primary contents of such sentences, we can identify the needed conventional regularity:

- Harry utters 'I am in Paris' only if he believes the speaker of the context is in Paris.[2]
- Sally utters 'I am in Paris' only if she believes the speaker of the context is in Paris.

But this is a common content associated 'I am in Paris' only if Harry and Sally's *Paris*-concepts carry the same content. Suppose contemporary descriptivists were correct, and each person's *Paris* concept is associated with an idiosyncratic set of descriptions, albeit ones that in each case are uniquely satisfied (or best satisfied) by one and the same city. Then a more accurate way to write the above would be:

- Harry utters 'I am in Paris' only if he believes the speaker of the context is in the city with Notre Dame cathedral, the museums, located on the Seine...
- Sally utters 'I am in Paris' only if she believes the speaker of the context is in the city that was invaded by the Prussians in 1870, that is the capital of France, that was subject to major terrorist attacks in the 2010s...

It's possible that Harry and Sally's idiosyncratic descriptive fixes have considerable overlap. But post-Kripke, it's standard to point out that this doesn't appear to be an essential feature of the practice at all—two competent language-users might not overlap on almost any information about

---

[2] Or more precisely: Harry utters 'I am Paris' if he believes something true at a set of centred worlds where the centre is in Paris. I'll stick to the more succinct formulations in the main text, but it's important not to be suckered into thinking that something like the non-verbalized words 'the speaker of the context' have to be running through Harry's head in order for this to be true.

Paris. (Indeed, when first introduced to the name of a city in a pub, one might have virtually no identifying non-linguistic information at all.)

I have my own account to offer here, but before this, let me survey a few initial defensive moves. I do not want to rest on these, but if readers are keener on them than I am, then they would be alternative ways to stabilize the overall account I am developing.

The first defensive move is to point out that there is a commonality of content across Harry and Sally's Paris-beliefs—both of them associate the concept with descriptions that correspond to a single object. And contemporary descriptivists (of the 'two-dimensional' variety) tend to say that there is a legitimate sense in which Harry and Sally have beliefs whose *content* doesn't involve the complex descriptions, but simply the object those descriptions pick out. This is Chalmers' (2002) 'secondary' content of belief. So if we worked with secondary content, rather than primary content, then we could characterize a regularity.

But of course, there are other pressures within the convention-based metasemantics to favour primary content—if we rewrote the two Harry/Sally regularities above using secondary content, we would have:

- Harry utters 'I am in Paris' iff he believes Harry is in Paris.
- Sally utters 'I am in Paris' iff she believes Sally is in Paris.

We regain shared material at one end of the content but lose it at the other. The dialectic might be further developed: e.g. we might find some kind of nuanced hybrid content which at some components (indexical ones) is primary, and at others (name-like ones) is secondary. So one might, for example, represent each belief with a structure whose elements are n-tuples of the various kinds of content that can be associated with the belief-state, and we pick out a regularity of truthfulness and trust by holding some fixed and allowing others to vary. I don't know how that would go in detail, but a reader is free to explore such possibilities if they think it promising.

A more general problem in the vicinity, however, is that there may be no convergence even at the level of secondary content. The two idiosyncratic fixes might not, after all, home in on the same object. The best satisfier for Sally's description might be Paris-broadly-construed, which includes outlying suburbs. The best satisfier for Harry's description might be central Paris. The challenge again is to explain in a principled way how the shared content that is presupposed is secured by the individualist metaphysics of mental content that we have on the table.

A second defensive move to be explored is to look to common-core beliefs *entailed by* everyone's Paris-beliefs. Perhaps everyone competent with the term knows that Paris is a city (even that is controversial, I think). Every relevant English language-user presumably knows that Paris is called 'Paris'. So perhaps we can at least find the following regularity:

- Harry utters 'I am in Paris' iff he believes the speaker of the context is in a city called 'Paris'.
- Sally utters 'I am in Paris' iff she believes the speaker of the context is in a city called 'Paris'.

The common-core proposal faces a nasty dilemma. First, if 'calling' is indeed an essential part of this common core, one owes an account of this proto-semantic notion, which if the hierarchical 'headfirst' structure of the metaphysics is to be sustained, will have to be spelled out prior to and independent of semantic facts. Second, if 'calling' is left out of the common core (for fear of circularity) then it is very unlikely that what's left shared among the whole community will be sufficient to discriminate Paris from Rome, Madrid, etc.

One option for analysing the calling relation is to appeal to the kind of descriptions that recapitulate metasemantic theories developed in philosophy. Perhaps O is called N when O is at the far end of reference-preserving chain of transmission which terminates in the relevant token of N, or when O is the dominant causal source of N-utterances.[3] This doesn't eliminate presuppositions of shared content, for the concept *calling* (and concepts of words) will need to be shared, and we would have to explain how that is compatible with the individualistic metaphysics of mental representation. But why would this be easier for *calling* than for *Paris*? Positing a calling relation for names is, moreover, just the tip of the iceberg. Idiosyncratic descriptive fixes arise for words for natural and social ontology in many categories—Burge's examples of 'sofa' and 'arthritis' being two paradigms (Burge 1979). By the back door, we'd end up committed to an analysis of 'calling' for each prima facie variable term. Commitment to the piecemeal calling-analysis would undercut much the appeal of the convention-based

---

[3] Compare Lewis (1984) on causal descriptivism.

approach (compare the 'building block' approach discussed in chapter 5. I'd really rather not go there!).

The incompatibility between individualistic descriptivism and convention-based metaphysics of linguistic representation, if genuine, would be an interesting result. It is an awkward ad hominem against the source of this convention-based approach to linguistic representation, David Lewis. He often seems to express sympathies with these kind of individualistic descriptivist theses about proper names, and so while his convention-based metasemantics presupposes subjects have attitudes with shared content, his descriptivist take on ordinary proper names is prima facie inconsistent with it. (I'll later offer some ways of responding to the argument on behalf of the individualistic descriptivist.) To this point, however, the friend of convention-based treatments of linguistic representation could take away the message that they had better avoid individualistic descriptivism about proper names, and so I want to set up the puzzle briefly in more general terms.

7.3 Radical Interpretation Seems Incompatible with Linguistic Conventions

The metaphysics of mental representation of Part I is individualistic in structure. Individual subjects are up for interpretation, and the constraints on success are to make *that subject* as rational as possible. Since the content of each subject's *Paris* concept is determined separately, on the basis of the idiosyncratic role it plays within her own cognitive economy, the null hypothesis should be that the contents assigned to counterpart concepts possessed by different thinkers will be distinct, albeit similar. If one wants a specific example: I earlier (Ch. 5) sketched how one might recapture a kind of descriptivism within Radical Interpretation, using hypotheses about classes of truths that are 'treated as definitions'. But notice that what one subject 'treats as a definition' will likely vary from what others do. So the descriptivism that is recaptured will be one that incorporates individualistic variation in content.

The null hypothesis is therefore that, according to Radical Interpretation, content varies between subjects even when those subjects have concepts that play analogous roles in their cognitive economies. If I want to argue that nevertheless there *is* shared content, the burden is on me. In some cases, the explanation of shared content is already at hand. If two thinkers are endorsing the same tautology, I can appeal to an earlier story to say why their logical constants pick out particular logical contents (*and, not, every*), and I can appeal to another story to say why they both think about *wrongness*, even if they are rather different in their deployments of that concepts. Reference-magnetism of potent or natural properties can help in special circumstances, for example, in explaining how two different theorists lock onto the same content *charge* despite introducing via different idiosyncratic takes on the subject. That can work when there's only one relevant potent content, and when the explanatory role of the concept in question is central enough that charity allows us to override individual differences in order to save explanatoriness. (This is one way in which the selective reference magnetism of chapter 3 differs importantly from the unselective, universally applicable reference magnetism often associated with Lewis's metaphysics of content.)

Unfortunately, these special cases only scratch the surface. They do very little to show how thinkers can think the same thoughts about sofas, Paris, their friends, shoes and string and sealing wax, and so on and so forth. After all, it'd be perfect consistent to endorse each of the stories above, and also think that individualistic descriptivism is the right account of the *Paris* concepts. But a convention-based metaphysics of linguistic representation requires that the majority of sentences in use feature in conventions, and so for these purposes we can't afford for shared content to be an exceptional phenomenon restricted to some interesting special cases. Shared content must be common enough to cover the whole vocabulary of public language.

To tie things up, I present a master argument for the incompatibility of a convention-based foundation for linguistic representation (CONV), and Radical Interpretation as a foundation for mental content (RI):

1. If RI is correct, then shared mental content is exceptional.
2. If shared mental content is exceptional, then propositions being conventionally associated with sentences is exceptional.
3. If propositions being conventionally associated with sentences is exceptional, then CONV is incorrect.

Therefore: RI and CONV are not both correct.

The argument is strong because it can be read schematically; *any* reading of 'being exceptional' which makes all the premises true will support the conclusion. As a friend of both RI and CONV, I need to give you reasons to think that some premise will fail on every reading.

The view I favour is that (1) is false—RI predicts and explains why shared mental content is the rule, not the exception. But I can only argue for that if I am granted a particular assumption. After developing the view on which RI generates shared content, therefore, I'll consider how the story goes if one denies my assumption, and make the case that premise (2) will then fail (I recommend that friends of individualistic descriptivism take this line). The crucial thing is that whichever way you go, the two stages of my foundations for representation are reconciled. The final section of this chapter steps back to draw out how the presence of public language inflects mental content.

7.4 Given One Assumption, Radical Interpretation Predicts Shared Mental Content

I claim that Radical Interpretation predicts shared content as the rule, not the exception. To set this out, I'll continue to use the two individuals' concepts of *Paris* as the example. The mechanisms in play will not turn on the details of the case, and so the bias to shared content is an effect that generalizes.

To get my story going, I need one central assumption which concerns the way belief attributions work. Let P_h be the content assigned to the belief state that Harry reports by uttering 'the Louvre is in Paris'. Let P_s be the content assigned to the analogous belief state of Sally's. I assume:

When Harry has a belief with the content *Sally believes that the Louvre is in Paris*, then his belief is correct iff she has a belief state with the content P_h.

This is how you would naively expect things to be. Harry is deploying his own concepts when entertaining *that the Louvre is in Paris* and P_h is the content of that thought. Seemingly, he is attributing that very content to some belief of Sally's.

Harry's belief that *Sally believes that the Louvre is in Paris* is correct only if Sally has a belief with the content P_h, and since (absent wild coincidence) the only relevant belief state in Sally's head has content P_s, then Harry's belief about Sally's belief will be true only if P_h and P_s are the same. Absent shared content, Harry's belief-attribution misfires. This misfiring is not one-off but systematic, happening no matter how good (by everyday standards) the evidence he has about Sally, whenever analogous concepts in their heads differ in content. The case for misfire doesn't turn on the details of the *Paris*-concept. If we generalize the assumption in the natural way, then when x has a belief with the content that y believes that p, x's belief is correct iff y has a belief with the content that p. The argument above will show x's beliefs about y's beliefs misfire whenever their contents diverge. The conclusion is that ordinary belief-attributing methods are only generally reliable where there is generally shared content.

This matters to Radical Interpretation. That theory tells us that the correct interpretation of a subject is the one that makes that subject most (substantively) rational. We need to make Harry, as far as possible, responsive to reasons. If we make a whole class of a subject's belief-forming methods systematically unreliable, then absent special pleading, we have failed. The conclusion to draw is that the correct interpretation of Harry will make his belief-about-belief forming methods reliable, unless somehow this comes at too high a price.

How could we make Harry's belief-about-belief forming methods reliable, given what we have seen? One way would be to reinterpret his concept *believes that*. But the assumption that I made at the start has taken option off the table, for the time being. The only other way is for interpretations to attribute shared content. In our case study: the content attributed to Harry's the-Louvre-is-in-Paris belief state would have to be the same as the one attributed to the analogous belief state in Sally's head. Doing this may well come at some cost. Perhaps Harry but not Sally treats as primitively compelling the inference from *Paris is F* to *the city of Notre Dame city is F*. An interpretation that attributes shared content may well have to find rational fault with either the presence of this inferential disposition in Harry or its absence in Sally. I put it to the reader, however, that irrationality around the edges is a price worth paying for the global reliability of belief-attributing methods.

So this is the moral that I suggest we take from this setting: that Radical Interpretation favours interpretations on which Harry and Sally's *Paris* concepts are assigned the same content. These considerations are silent about what this content is. It could be shared referential content, or it could be some aggregated descriptive content, but whatever we say, it will be shared.

I started this discussion by saying that the convention-based foundations for linguistic representation presupposed shared content. This seemed a problem for Radical Interpretation, as the individualistic structure of interpretation-selection threatened to make shared content the exception, rather than the rule. But I submit that the opposite is the case: there will be a very general bias towards shared content (at least if we assume that content of *believes that* is held fixed). The bias towards shared content is circumscribed, since it will be operative only for contents that we attribute to others. If someone thought something analogous to *Paris*-thoughts but lacked the ability to metacognize altogether, the explanation just given would lapse. If someone had 'private' concepts that they reserved for their own use and assumed others lacked, then again the explanation would lapse. But the convention-based story about linguistic representation assumes from the get-go that we are dealing with creatures with who have attitudes about others attitudes, and the contents that need to be shared in order for the story to fly are exactly those that language-users are disposed to attribute as the contents of other's beliefs when they utter the relevant sentences. So the bias to shared content is exactly what we need to escape the master argument given earlier by denying the first premise: shared content is not in the relevant sense exceptional.

7.5 If the Assumption Fails, Linguistic Conventions Don't Require Shared Content

I started from an apparent incompatibility between two theories: the claim that there are conventional regularities of truthfulness and trust linking public sentences to propositions, and the apparently individualistic slant of Radical Interpretation. I've concentrated so far on dissolving the tension by arguing that, against initial appearances, Radical Interpretation predicts shared content. To get this prediction, I needed to make an assumption about the content of agents' concept of belief—that when x has a belief with the content that y believes that p, x's belief is correct iff y has a belief with the content that p. You could undermine my story by denying that. In this section I'll show that in doing so, you'll end up dissolving the tension in a different way.

Here is what I what I take it that those who deny my assumption will want to say. When Harry has the complex thought *Sally believes that the Louvre is in Paris* I was assuming it had the content BEL(Sally, p), where p is the proposition expressed by Harry's thought *that the Louvre is in Paris,* and BEL is the belief-relation that was the target of the first part of this book. The rival proposal is that the content of that belief-state is rather: BEL*(Sally, p), where p is the proposition expressed by Harry's thought *that the Louvre is in*

Paris, and BEL*(Sally, p) iff ($\exists q$)(BEL(Sally, q) & R(p, q)). Harry would not be characterizing Sally's beliefs directly via the propositions he has the wherewithal to entertain. He would be characterizing them indirectly, as having contents suitably related (the 'R' relation above) to the propositions that he himself is in a position to entertain. So long as the content of our heroes' first-order Paris-beliefs are R-related, on this account Harry will have a true belief that Sally believes that the Louvre is in Paris, despite the lack of shared mental content.

This revised understanding of the content of *believes that* in belief-attributions is what I expect someone independently committed to indi-vidualistic descriptivism, for example, to say in response to the threat of unreliability. So now let's take this proposal, and see how it impacts the alleged need for shared content in linguistic conventions. To rehearse the line of thought: if there is to be a conventional regularity linking the use of 'the Louvre is in Paris' to some content p, minimally it needs to be that everyone in the population utters 'the Louvre is in Paris' only if they believe that p (that's required in order for there to be conformity to the regularity of Truthfulness). We were then worried that there simply was no p such that everyone in the population utters 'the Louvre is in Paris' only if they believe p, at least if p is going to be specific enough for the account to be at all plausible as a base for linguistic representation.

The key principle, however, is itself a (quantified) belief attribution, one stated in the theorist's language. If we apply the analysis above to what the theorist is saying, we get:

- Everyone in the population utters 'the Louvre is in Paris' if they BEL some proposition R-related to the proposition that the Louvre is in Paris.

Mutatis mutandis for the more complex belief-attributions that occur else-where in the characterization of convention. The addition of the R-relation within the account of convention itself, however, changes everything. There is a proposition (namely, the proposition that the Louvre is in Paris) such that each member of the population utters the sentence only if they believe that proposition. Indeed, there are many such propositions. Harry's take on the cluster of R-interrelated propositions associated with 'the Louvre is in Paris' is *the Louvre is located in the city with Notre Dame...* Sally's take is *the Louvre is located in the city invaded by Prussians...* There is a conven-tional regularity linking one to the sentence if and only if there is a conventional regularity linking the other to the sentence. So there will be conventional associations between the sentence and both of these.[4]

The prima facie case for incompatibility between individualistic variation in mental content and the existence of conventions dissolves if belief-attributions work this way. And, always supposing there is a suitable way to fill in 'R' so the sketch just mentioned works, then an interpretation of each agent can interpret their *belief* concept as denoting the appropriate BEL* relation, and guard against the threat of systematically misfiring belief-attributions without having to attribute shared content. Those who are independently committed to individualistically varying descriptivism about names, for example, should explore this route. More sceptical readers may wonder whether there's really a way to make good on the promise, and find the magic R-relation that will set the whole structure going. I count myself among the sceptics, which is why I favour the story that has no need of it.[5]

7.6 The Interpretative Pressure to Shared Content Generates a Social Externalism

I recommend that we bind the metaphysics of mental and linguistic content together by endorsing the simple account of beliefs about beliefs, and embracing the bias towards shared content that falls out of it. This means that in what follows, we can take appeals to conventional associations between sentences and propositions at face value, and this is good news for the primary focus of these chapters: the metaphysics of linguistic representation.

These foundations for shared content also show us something new about the structure of the metaphysics of mental representation. Prior to this discussion, I had only talked about content-determining factors which

---

[4] If the whole cluster of idiosyncratic *Paris*-propositions are conventionally associated with a public-language sentence, what will the upshot be when we come to select a semantic theory that has to be as good a match as possible to them? One idea is that if the semantic interpretation assigns a content to the sentence which matches any member of the cluster, it will thereby match with all the rest. After all, if the relation expressed by *believes* doesn't discriminate among R-related contents, then it would be no surprise if we were to count assigning a proposition R-related to a conventionally associated content as 'matching' well enough. And it would be no surprise if in the end, public language did not have determinate content.

[5] If someone gives me a *candidate* to be an R-relation, then that generates the following challenge: explain why interpretations that attribute shared content and assign simple content to *believes* beat interpretations that attribute individualistic varying content and assign the more complex content to *believes*. Though it's hard to respond to this in the abstract, one thing to be said in favour of the former is that if *believes* is an explanatory concept, then all else equal it will denote the most potent/natural content, which may break the tie in favour of the shared content package.

were independent of what any other person thinks. These happen to be special cases where we can theorize about interpretation-selection individualistically. But what I am now putting forward is an case where the rationality of x turns on facts about what y's mentality is like, and vice versa. We should formulate Radical Interpretation in a way that acknowledges this possibility, and which makes clear why it induces no circularity in the foundational account of mental content. Here's how.

What we need are 'global' interpretation functions that map each thinker to a 'local' interpretation of that thinker. Local interpretations are, as before, mappings of states of that thinker to content-attitude pairs. One evaluates the correctness of a global interpretation function pointwise, with the constraint being to maximize the substantive rationality of each individual. If it happened to be the case that the substantive rationality of each individual was determinable independent of the interpretation of others, then this procedure gives you exactly the same results as finding the most rationality-maximizing interpretation of each individual in isolation, and gluing the results together. When that atomizing assumption fails, selecting the best global interpretation function will still deliver results. A demand for shared content is exactly a case where atomization fails.

The constraint to select a global interpretation function that maximizes individual rationality leads to some interesting interaction effects, which connect to Burgean social externalism (Burge 1979). Let's suppose I will take testimony from my doctor on matters concerning the presence or absence of arthritis; she won't take testimony from me on the same issues. Since we treat each other as thinking arthritis-thoughts, by the story given in this chapter there will be a bias towards attributing common content to us. Beyond this, the case is interestingly different from one where there is no hierarchy in testimony. In the current case, let us take it that the conceptual role of my concept of *arthritis* involves some easily defeasible links to observations, and a central and overriding role for testimony. In making me rational, you don't have to worry too much about making my defeasible observation-links justified, since I myself am not very deeply committed to them, and they are certainly of secondary importance compared to the role that experts' testimony plays in shaping my beliefs. By contrast, an arthritis expert won't revise their beliefs on who has arthritis in what circumstances on the basis of just anyone's say-so. The recognitional aspects of the conceptual role for their concept of *arthritis* are prominent and stable. If an interpretation makes a nonsense of those capacities, there is a significant cost in rationality; if an interpretation makes a nonsense of my arthritis-recognition capacities, that's at most a slight cost. Messing up my doctor's recognitional capacities even brings costs for me, since I won't be properly responding to reasons if the experts on whom I rely are badly messing up.

What all this leads to is the following: the primary concern in evaluating the global interpretation function, so far as *arthritis* concepts, go will be to vindicate the belief-forming methods of experts—those with non-defeasible belief forming methods, to whom we *hoi polloi* defer. Via the shared content constraint, we *hoi polloi* inherit the contents of the elite.

The story about shared content can also illuminate what goes on in cases of concept-acquisition triggered by language. These are a kind of limiting case, where the global bias to shared content is all we have to go on in assigning individual content to a concept. Suppose that when Zed encounter a public-language word W for the first time, he coins a new concept C, and deploys the latter in patterns of attitudes exactly as if there were convention to utter W-sentences only if one has the C-belief. Because he assumes others will conform to the regularity of Truthfulness, Zed will form the belief that Ada believes that dogs are C when he hears her utter 'dogs are W', and will form the belief that Beth believes that all Cs are mammals when he hears her utter 'all Ws are mammals'. Because Zed conforms to the regularity of Trust, he forms corresponding belief-states: *dogs are C, all Cs are mammals*, and his reasons for these beliefs are the beliefs he attributes to the smart people around.

How do we maximize Zed's rationality here? The first-order C-beliefs that Zed possesses are rooted in Zed's beliefs about others C-beliefs. We have seen that in order to make belief-attributing methods rational we need to attribute shared content. So the primary prediction here is (all else equal) Zed's concept C will pick out whatever content *others* associate with the word W. But by construction in this case, all else is equal! Zed's C denotes whatever others' denote with the concepts they associate with W. In this pure case, the role of C in belief-attribution is so central that language becomes a means through which Zed inherits mental content from others in his linguistic community.

According to the three-layer model of representational content, mental content is metaphysically prior to linguistic content. Nothing that I've said here is inconsistent with that. The role of language is, in each case, to trigger patterns of belief attribution. What I have appealed to here as a constraining factor for mental interpretations is the demand to rationalize mental content: patterns of beliefs about beliefs. There is no appeal to specific facts about what words mean that might cause one to revisit the relative priority of thought and language. But it's right to say that on the account I've sketched, public language inflects mental content. We are by now familiar with idea that, compatibly with an underlying foundational story, there is room for non-foundational theories that articulate illuminating patterns holding between concepts and their denotation. Often in spelling these out, it is useful to appeal to the idea of a 'conceptual role' of a given concept, which picks out some of the central ways in which the concept is deployed. What we've been seeing here is that 'expressibility by word W in a public language' can be an important part of the conceptual role of a concept. Some concepts lack this, but where the concept-word link is present, we find the bias to shared mental content.

7.7 Conclusion

This chapter started by laying out Lewis's characterization of linguistic conventions, and pulling out a seeming commitment of them: the commitment to shared mental content as the rule, rather than the exception. The following argument worried me, since I am committed to both Radical Interpretation (RI) and the Convention-based treatment of linguistic representation (CONV):

1. If RI is correct, then shared mental content is exceptional.
2. If shared mental content is exceptional, then propositions being conventionally associated with sentences is exceptional.
3. If propositions being conventionally associated with sentences is exceptional, then CONV is incorrect.

Therefore: RI and CONV are not both correct.

I haven't questioned the third premise, but I have argued that either premise 1 or premise 2 fails. If subjects' *believes that* content works in sophisticated ways, then I have argued that we can deny the second premise. But I favour an alternative, where those concepts work in relatively unsophisticated ways. I've argued that under that constraint, the requirement to make belief-about-belief forming methods reliable creates pressure in Radical Interpretation towards shared content. This would mean that premise 1 is false, since the pressure to shared content will be present in all the cases in which we would want linguistic conventions, and also teaches us new things about how the metaphysics of language and thought interact.

8

Elegant Interpretations

In chapter 6, I described convention-based foundations for linguistic representation. The base facts are conventional associations between sentence-types and propositions, and all the discussion since then has focused on fixing the base. But with those foundations in place, we need also to provide a story about how the base fixes the facts about linguistic representation. In my terms: what is the relation to base facts that makes some abstract function from linguistic expressions to content the correct semantic interpretation?

The issue is made pressing because we cannot read off facts about the literal meaning (semantic content) of a sentence directly from the conventions in which it figures. The four focal obstacles introduced in section 6.1 were:

1) Most well-formed sentences of English will never be uttered, and many are uttered only on a few scattered occasions, so won't feature in interesting regularities.
2) There will typically be many propositions conventionally associated with a sentence, and many of them are not good candidates to be its 'literal meaning'.
3) Propositions can be conventionally associated with a sentence because of a mix of semantic and pragmatic factors, and an analysis of literal meaning would have to disentangle these.
4) Indexical sentences will not be conventionally associated with the truth conditions they express, as they express different truth conditions depending on the context in which they are uttered.

These obstacles mean we have substantial work to do in saying what it takes for a linguistic interpretation to be correct. My proposal was as follows: the correct interpretation of a public language is the one that gives you the best theory of the conventional associations in which the sentences of that language figure. The job of this chapter is to spell out what that comes to.

Section 8.1 presents an analogy between the challenge we face and curve-fitting. Section 8.2 gives reasons against developing this analogy in one

The Metaphysics of Representation. J. Robert G. Williams, Oxford University Press (2019).
© J. Robert G. Williams.
DOI: 10.1093/oso/9780198850205.001.0001

particular (neo-Lewisian) way. Section 8.3 presents a way that I recommend developing the analogy. Section 8.4 shows how this allows us to rebut underdetermination challenges and uses this to support my way over its rival. Section 8.5 compares the stance I take here to the stance I took in chapter 3 on explanatoriness and simplicity, and argues that I am entitled to the differences in implementation.

8.1 Finding the Best Theory of Linguistic Conventions is like Fitting a Curve to Data

The best analogy for way that a semantic theory is selected by conventional associations, I think, is that of fitting a curve to data points.[1] Perhaps we run a series of measurements of pressure against temperature in a vessel of fixed volume (a set of pairs of real numbers). We might generate, say, fifty points that can be plotted on a graph one of whose axes marks off different pressures, and one of whose axes marks off different temperatures. By taking several measurements of pressure at a given temperature, we might generate a little cluster of data-points for a fixed temperature. Through these data points, we draw a line of 'best fit'. If we've done the experiment reasonably well, then we'll be able to draw a straight line which passes very close to the data points that we have marked.

The best curve through this data optimizes a trade-off between simplicity and fit with the data. We could have drawn a much more complex curve that would have passed exactly through every point—a listiform enumeration of the data points is in a sense a 'curve' that perfectly fits the data, or a sufficiently high-frequency sine curve could pass through the centre of each cluster of data points. But the linear curve is far simpler, and fits well enough. The lack of fit that remains we explain away by a variety of auxiliary assumptions, such as margins of error in our measuring instruments, or experimental error—or in more interesting cases, systematic departures may be explained by the effect of another mechanism, if e.g. the vessel used expands slightly at high temperatures, leading to the data-points falling away from the curve.

---

[1] This discussion is based on the very illuminating presentations in Sober (2008, 2015). Just to connect back to our discussions of the previous chapter: curve-fitting in the sense that I'll be discussing it here is an exercise in interpolation not extrapolation. It is generalization in the 'random sampling' sense, not the sense that was in play when we were discussing the greenness of emeralds.

The simplicity/fit trade-off in curve-fitting has been extensively explored in the literature on statistical model-choice. Various approaches have been pursued, but many share a feature of identifying simplicity with 'elegance'. For example, suppose we have a practical choice over which polynomial curve to fit with some data. Greater or lesser elegance of a class of curves is fixed by the number of parameters one has to 'fill in' to specify a particular curve. Thus a linear curve defined by $y = ax$ has just one parameter: a. A quadratic curve, $y = ax^2+b$, has two parameters. And in general, as we increase the powers of x, we have more parameters that need filling in. The following is known: by choosing a more inelegant model (set of curves with a greater number of parameters), you can in general find a curve within the model that fits the existing data better, but this comes at a cost: such 'overfitted' curves have a low expectation of *future* fit (think of a complex sine curve that happens to intersect each data point—nobody would trust that curve as a guide to what the next measurement of temperature will be at a given pressure). There are various ways to make this precise. Here is one of the remarkable results in this area. Among a class of curves with the same number of parameters, one finds the 'best fit' to the data. This representative is assigned an 'Akaike information score' based on a particular function of how well that curve fits existing data *minus* the number of parameters used to characterize the family of curves from which it is drawn. If you choose your 'level of complexity' by maximizing this Akaike score with respect to the existing data, and then continuing to fit the curve as data comes in, you will maximize the unbiased expectation of fit with *future* data. The number of parameters is a measure of elegance, so in substracting it from a measure of fit with data, the Akaike information score exemplifies an elegance/fit trade-off. As is characteristic, the way that elegance is measured in Akaike-terms presupposes a fixed way of describing curves. Try to apply this idea to curves specified in a language with a constant symbol for some highly complex sine curve that happens to pass through all our data points, and it will misfire.

This relativity to background language is found in other formal approaches in the same area. Here is one that is very suggestive for our purposes. Solomonoff's 'ideal' minimum-description-length account of model-selection identifies the simplicity of a curve with the minimum length of a program that computes it (the curve's Kolmogorov complexity). This, again, is a measure of elegance. Formal results then decompose the probability of truth of a given theory into a combination of this measure of elegance and a measure of fit. Again, we have the idea that the goodness of a theory is measured by a combination of elegance and fit. Again we find a sensitivity to a background language—in this case, the programming language in which theories are formalized and their minimum length measured.[2] The Solomonoff minimum-description-length measure of elegance is both much more general than Akaike's results on curves, and also extremely close to Lewis's idea of elegance as compactness in a canonical language.[3] The lesson I take from this work on statistical model choice is that elegance is epistemically important, but can't be deployed without fixing the language in which it is measured.

In our case, the data points established by conventional associations are a set of pairs of sentences and propositions, rather than pairs of real numbers. But other than that the task is similar: we are after something which assigns to each item in the first dimension (here a sentence) an item on the second dimension (a proposition). The proposal under consideration is that the selected theory should be the 'best theory' of this data, and guided by the analogy to curve-fitting, the best theory will be one that optimizes a trade-off between a measure of elegance and a measure of fit.

In section 6.1, and again at the start of this chapter, I set out four problems that arose if we tried to simply read off semantic content of sentences from conventional associations. The curve-fitting model of semantic theory selection resolves these difficulties. The first issue was that only finitely many sentences are involved in conventions, though infinitely many sentence-types have semantic content in English. But it's to be expected that when we fit a curve to data, we select something that generates predictions for all sorts of possible data points beyond our dataset.

---

[2] See Grünwald (2004), section 1.2.1. The sensitivity to the background language is constrained in one sense. Any two general-purpose programming languages can simulate each other, by adding a finite-length emulator. This means that for languages A and B there is a constant c such that minimum description lengths of arbitrary data D in A vs. B differ by at most c—where c is independent of the length of D. This is not good enough for our purposes. Indeed, the Lewis trick can be adapted to illustrate this. Suppose the minimum description length of fixed data D in A is k. Then consider a language B which adds to A an additional primitive instruction for printing D. You can emulate any B-program in A just by defining up a new 'print D' command using the k-length programme within A that prints D, and so it is true that the minimum description lengths of data in A and B differ by at most a constant, k. But the theory chosen by the minimum description length criterion in language in B is not the complex k-length set of instructions that is selected in A, but rather, the ultra-compact command "print D". This trivializes the trade-off between description length and considerations of fit. Grünwald identifies exactly this issue as making *practical* appeals to this kind of minimum description length approach language-sensitive, and it is no easier in our highly theoretical context.

[3] Solomonoff was a student of Carnap's, and it wouldn't surprise me if Lewis was aware of his work and had it in mind

The second issue was that many propositions would be conventionally associated with a single sentence, including some that are patently not good candidates to be that sentence's semantic content. One example was the existence of a conventional association between the sentence 'Harry is a bachelor' and the proposition that Harry is unmarried, as well as to the proposition that Harry is male and unmarried. We find precedent in curve-fitting: a single curve can generate (and so be fitted to) many different datapoints pertaining to a single x-axis value. A curve that predicts the pressure is p at temperature k will fit with the data that the pressure it at least p-3, that it is at least p-2, etc. It's perfectly reasonable to require a semantic theory to fit with not just some but all the data about conventional associations between sentences and propositions.

The third issue was that conventional associations result from a mix of semantic and systematic pragmatic factors that need to be disentangled if the semantic content is to be isolated. Compare this to cases where a lack of fit with data is produced because of a systematic distortion (the vessel expanding). In some such cases, the appropriate thing to do would be to adjust our measurement of fit exogenously by taking account of the distorting factor. In other cases, we might let the theory run, and hope that the curve that best fits the data is fruitfully represented as the product of two curves. Both approaches could be implemented in the case of selecting a semantic theory. Our measurement of fit should account for exogenous factors where they are isolable, but also, we should be open to the possibility that the best theory of a range of conventional associations is a combined semantic-pragmatic theory, with semantic content fixed by one component, and conventional-ized pragmatic effects (e.g. conventional implicature, presupposition triggers, etc.) fixed by the other.

The fourth issue was that the kind of content reflected in conventional associations might systematically differ from the sort we think of as seman-tic content proper. Indexical sentences are only conventionally associated with primary content, which does not specify their truth conditions. But just as in the first case, once we've used data to fix a curve, we can use that curve to make all sorts of predictions that go beyond the particular formats that the data comes in. In the current case, the hypothesis would be that semantic theory will need to assign to sentences rich semantic values that tell us whether a sentence is true at a world and context of utterance. That generates predictions for primary content, so can be fitted to the data, but also generates predictions for more properly truth conditional content, and so allows us to read off whatever semantic facts we like.

Without the constraining power of elegance, none of this would make much sense. If all that we had to worry about when picking a semantic theory was fit with the data, then a listiform enumeration of it would be fine. Elegance drives us away from mere lists of the dataset, and toward more compact formulations—a paradigm effect of which is to favour compositional assignments of semantic content wherever possible. Evans (1981) and Wright (1981, 1987) discuss a simple case: a language with ten names and ten predicates and no recursive operations, leading to twenty words but a hundred possible sentences. Listing a theory sentence-by-sentence we have at least a hundred separate 'parameters' to fill in, and we could fit any data we like. Listing it word-by-word, we can get this down, in principle, to twenty 'parameters'. Just as before, the abundance of parameters allows overfitting. Suppose it just so happened that our actual, limited data featured a string of performance errors with a particular sentence S. In the sentence-by-sentence setting, we could 'fit' this misleading data by tweaking one parameter. This, of course, would be a bad guide to the future, as the performance errors shouldn't be expected to continue, and the overfitted model will predict the wrong things about use of that sentence. Sticking with the twenty-parameter, word-by-word model prevents this, since there'll be no easy way to 'fit' to the outliers in the data without failing to fit results for all the other sentences that feature the same words.

'Best theory' in this curve-fitting sense has its original home in an epistemological project—when looking at temperature and pressure, for example, we are interested in finding an underlying curve, in part, in order to form expectations about where the pressure *would* be were we to take a new reading at a new temperature. But a property that is used and refined in epistemological theory can also be used in other theories. My proposed use takes it away from its original home, and deploys it in an account of what makes a semantic theory correct.

8.2 Elegance in Ontologese Would Generate Language-Thought Mismatches

I am proposing that the correct semantic theory is one that optimizes a trade-off between elegance and fit with conventional associations. I have pointed to formal models of this relationship in the literature on statistical model choice, and drawn out analogies. The existence and success of these formal models should raise our confidence that elegance is a real phenomenon. Developing a detailed theory of elegance (or indeed, fit) for the case of semantic theories is well beyond what I can at present offer. Like practical and epistemic normativity earlier, these theoretical norms must remain working primitives. However, we're not entirely ignorant. Elegance, if it is to deserve the name and sustain the analogy, must be a matter of compactness of expressibility in some 'canonical' language. The identity of this canonical language makes a huge difference to what the metaphysics of linguistic representation predicts. The denotations of the basic expressions of this background elegance-measuring language will end up as 'reference magnets' for public language. If F is a basic predicate of the background language, then we can characterize a predicate 'Pr' that denotes F-ness extremely compactly, e.g. by including the clause in the semantic theory: Necessarily, (Pr is true of x iff Fx). In general, the more compactly characterizable a semantic value is in the background language, the more elegant a theory will be that assigns that semantic value. It makes a huge difference, then, whether the background language, for example, only contains predicates for natural properties (a Lewisian proposal, making natural properties reference magnets) or contains predicates for ordinary parts of the manifest image of the world: being green, being a person, being morally wrong.

Readers of chapter 3 should find this discussion familiar. There I discussed the issue of how to think about the components of explanatoriness, and proposed simplicity as one contributory factor. Taking my lead from Lewis's discussion of laws of nature, I explored identifying this with elegance, and more than this: with elegance in a particular background language of 'ontologese', the language whose every term picks out a fundamental aspect of reality.

This proposal would fit nicely with a common understanding of how Lewis's own theory works. Most discussion of his metaphysics of representation focuses on his remarks on language. The received view takes him to be endorsing the view that the relative naturalness of properties is what we have to add to fit-with-use in determining the correct semantic theory. Identifying the canonical background language that fixes elegance would seem at first to mesh well both with that tradition and with the metaphysics of mental content I've already set out.

On closer examination, ontologese as the background language would be a very strange combination with the metaphysics of mental content that I set out earlier. Recall that the impact of natural properties there was selective— relevant only to concepts that have a particular role in inference to the best explanation. But if we now made ontologese the canonical language in which elegance of semantic theory is to be measured, then natural properties would end up as reference magnets for any term whatsoever—in particular, for terms that do not have anything to do with explanatory concepts. So there's a real danger of a mismatch here, where the words we use to express concepts end up with a different denotation, simply because the relative naturalness of semantic values is predicted to matter for word-reference but not for concept-reference.

This points the way to a different way of thinking about a principled choice of elegance-fixing language. A driving idea behind the convention-based metaphysics of linguistic representation is that people use language to express and communicate their thoughts. We should respect the idea of language *inheriting* content from thought, and build into our theory a guarantee that we will avoid the kind of language/thought mismatches that overenthusiastic appeals to Lewisian naturalness would produce.

In what follows, therefore, I first sketch a 'subject-sensitive' account of elegance that will have this effect, and then illustrate the way that it forms a conduit through which the results from the theory of mental content can be transferred to the case of language. Finally, I'll return to the question of whether it's ad hoc to be appealing to elegance in this subject-sensitive way here, when in earlier discussions where simplicity mattered for semantic theory, I took the Lewisian ontologese proposal much more seriously.

8.3 Elegance is Elegance in a Subject's Conceptual Scheme

I suggest the canonical language relative to which elegance of semantic theories are measured is fixed by an interpretee's conceptual repertoire.[4]

---

[4] I'm grateful here to discussions with Callie Phillips on subjective characterizations of simplicity within Lewis's interpretationism. In other work (Williams 2016), I floated the idea of 'parochial' simplicity. This involves the theorist specifying—in a quite ad hoc and parochial manner—some language C that they favour for formulating theories, the compactness of which then provides a measure of elegance. Relative to that choice of C, elegance facts can be handled as before, and shortness of definability from C becomes a determinant of content ('reference magnetism'). If different theorists select different C, they may pick different interpretations as correct, and so in principle come up with different candidate accounts of semantic content. So this approach makes facts about linguistic content (insofar as they go beyond what we can extract from the constraint to 'fit with the conventional base'), if not wildly subjective, at least parochial. In the spirit of conceptual engineering, we might tailor our starting language to iron out surprising or unexpected predictions. I continue to think this approach is interesting— indeed, I think it's the best version of a deflationary approach to linguistic representation (essentially, we deflate a determinant of reference, the eligibility constraint, rather than deflate

For this to make sense, we need have available facts about their conceptual repertoire and its interpretation, and it needs to be spelled out in some medium in which it makes sense to construct theories or deploy definitions. I need, in short, the assumption that there is a sufficiently language-like medium for thought, whose components have fairly determinate content. In Chapters 2–4, I appealed to this idea *conditionally* several times over, but the fundamental theory of mental content remained officially neutral on the matter. I am now going to presuppose it in the very formulation of the account of linguistic content.

The elegance of a theory (for subject x) can now be characterized as the compactness of its expression in x's conceptual repertoire. If x's medium of thought is mentalese, with a certain range of basic concepts, then we can let the elegance of a property be, for example, its minimal description length in that version of mentalese.

I already noted that the denotations of the basic vocabulary of the elegance-fixing canonical language would turn out to be reference magnets for public language. From the proposal just made, therefore, the things that each agent can think about via an atomic concept will be reference-magnetic, for that subject.[5] By contrast to the Lewisian idea that elegance is elegance in ontologese, this metaphysics of linguistic content is silent on whether *natural* properties are reference-magnetic for words. What is magnetic for language depends on what is basic in thought. Sometimes naturalness may be involved in determining the content of thought (if some of the basic concepts are explanatory concepts), and in those cases, it indirectly helps determine the reference-magnets for language. But perfect natural properties for which we lack basic concepts will not be very magnetic at all, and the properties denoted by basic logical and normative concepts, where denotation is fixed by the stories in chapters 2 and 4, will maximally magnetic. The basic phenomenon is magnetism-by-inheritance, not magnetism-by-the-natural.

reference directly). But I do not think it counts as a realist theory of linguistic content, and I am here exploring the prospects for an account of that kind.

[5] You might worry that the interpretation will be inexpressible for theorists who lack semantic and mathematical vocabulary involved in setting out the semantic theory. If that's the case, then I will simply build into this account of simplicity for semantic theories that it should be judged by the subject's conceptual repertoire supplemented with standard semantic and mathematical resources. This is analogous to Lewis's supplementation of predicates with natural properties with other general-purpose resources, in fixing his 'ontologese'.

This proposal gives up on the idea that 'elegance' is a subject-independent theoretical virtue, and so takes seriously the always seductive idea that what is simple/elegant for me may not be simple/elegant for you, and vice versa. That leads to a wrinkle. We are targeting a metaphysics of public language, and a public language involves a diverse population, each with a potentially idiosyncratic conceptual repertoire. The bias towards shared mental content (chapter 7) helps cut down some potential divergences, but it only says that when two subjects have analogous concepts, they are ceteris paribus assigned the same content. It does not guarantee that subjects have concepts that are analogues of each other in the first place. Who within this population gets to set the standards of simplicity? One view is: no one person does, but elegance is indeterminate, with each person's conceptual repertoire providing one sharpening of the notion. Another view is: everyone does, and it is the *pooled* basic repertoire of all our languages of thought that fixes elegance. Other ways of aggregating are no doubt available, and I will not here take a stand on which is best.

8.4 Conceptual-scheme Magnetism is the Best Account of Linguistic Determinacy

The appeal to natural properties as a determiner of correct linguistic interpretation is often motivated as a way of resolving otherwise problematic challenges to explain how our words have determinate meaning. We've already met several such arguments, in the context of *mental* content. But of course, there's nothing to stop someone raising them again now in their more familiar setting of linguistic interpretation. Two in particular that received discussion were *permutation* challenges and *skolemite* challenges. I reintroduce them here:

- **Permuted interpretations.** Where the standard interpretation has 'Tibbles' referring to Tibbles, and 'is sleeping' picking out the property of sleeping, the permuted interpretation says that 'Tibbles' refers to the image under the permutation p of Tibbles, and 'is sleeping' picks out the property of being the image under p of something which is sleeping. Systematically implemented, the permuted interpretation can be shown to produce exactly the same truth conditions at the level of whole sentences as does the standard interpretation. But, apparently, that means that they fit with and predicts the same sentence-level facts about conventions. So we can't explain on this basis the obvious fact that the permuted interpretation is obviously and determinately incorrect.

- **Skolemite interpretations.** Where the standard interpretation has the quantifier 'everything' (in suitable contexts) ranging over absolutely everything, the skolemite interpretation takes it to be quantify restrictedly only over a countable domain (this domain may vary counterfactually, but relative to every counterfactual situation its domain is countable). And (with a few caveats) we can show that the skolemite interpretation and the original are truth conditionally equivalent. But, apparently, that means that they fit with and predict the same sentence-level facts about conventions. So we can't explain on this basis the fact that the skolemite interpretation is obviously and determinately incorrect.

To these, I add a final challenge:

- **Compositionally twisted interpretations.** John Hawthorne (1990) once asked Lewis to spell out what fixed the compositional rules that must be part of any compositional interpretation. One version of Hawthorne's 'Kripkensteinian' challenge is as follows: the standard compositional rules say, for example, that if the semantic value of 'a' is x, and the semantic value of 'F' is the function f (at each world, mapping an object to a truth value), then the semantic value of the sentence 'Fa' is the function that maps a world w to the True iff at w, and f maps o to the True (or, if one wants a fine-grained content, then it is the structured proposition $<f, a>$). But a twisted rule might take the following disjunctive form: if 'Fa' is a sentence that is tokened in the community (by itself or as part of a longer sentence), the semantic value of the whole is determined just as previously. But if 'Fa' is never tokened, then its semantic value is a function that maps a world w to the False iff at w, f maps o to the True (respectively for fine-grained content: it is the structured proposition $<neg(f), a>$, where $neg(f)$ maps o to the True iff f maps o to the False and vice versa). The key thought is this: the linguistic conventions that fix linguistic interpretation are just special kinds of regularities in the way we use sentences. There are no regularities in the use of sentences that are never tokened, and so a fortiori no conventions governing then. Original and twisted interpretation coincide whenever there do exist linguistic conventions, and diverge only where there are none. But, apparently, that means that they fit with and predict the same sentence-level facts about conventions. So we can't explain on this basis the fact that the twisted interpretation is obviously and determinately incorrect.

We have already solved the first two before, at the level of thought.[6] My view is that a desideratum on a theory of linguistic representation is that it efficiently makes use of these earlier explanations in rebutting the challenges they pose for linguistic content. It would be a bad sign if we had to solve the problems all over again for public language. And it would certainly strain credibility if the solution in the case of language was very different from the solution in the case of thought. These considerations, I think, favour the subject-sensitive elegance (inheritance-magnetism) I outlined in the last section.

Here is how the inheritance-magnetism would deal with the challenges. The compositional interpretation of language that gives rise to permuted content will involve axioms assigning *permuted green* as the denotation of 'green', where the standard one assigns *green*. But we may assume *green* is a basic concept for the kind of language user we are thinking of, and *permuted green* is not. The permuted interpretation is going to be less compact than the standard, so by these standards less elegant. Since it has no compensating virtues, it will not count as correct.

The same story goes for the skolemite challenge, under the assumption that the agent has basic concepts for unrestricted generality, but no basic concepts for deviant skolemite alternatives. Expressing the skolemite clauses for 'every' will be overly complex, compared to the short way of assigning it truly universal concept. The skolemite interpretations will again count as less elegant, and hence, incorrect.

The Kripkenstein problem of deviant compositional rules is also resolved. We have every reason to believe that the deviant rule takes longer to write out than the original in an ordinary language-users' conceptual repertoire—

---

[6] Lewis at this point stuck resolutely to modelling belief-content in a coarse-grained way (as a set of worlds, and later a set of centred worlds/individuals) and characterizing the overall beliefs of a time-slice of a person, setting aside any finer-grained division into individual representational states and any compositional structure they might have. That meant that it was only when he reached public language and its compositional structure that he faced these challenges head-on. Nothing that Lewis achieved earlier in securing determinate mental content helped him. Remember, the raw materials for selecting interpretations are conventions of the form: utter S only if one believes *p*; and come to believe *p* if one hears someone utter S. For Lewis the '*p*' here picks up a coarse-grained truth condition. But the permuted and skolemite interpretations fit that sort of data perfectly, exactly as well as their unpermuted and unskolemized originals. So underdetermination loomed for Lewis at the level of linguistic content. Since Lewis had not already had to tackle the challenges at the level of mental content, he did not face the issue I highlight below of ensuring a uniform solution to the same challenge.

after all, the way we have of writing it out is to write down the original, add a conjunct restricting its application, and then add a further disjunction. So an interpretation that builds it in will be less simple than the standard. Again, in the absence of compensating virtues, it is incorrect.[7]

Of course, all these explanations turn essentially on the assumption that thought-content is already determinate in the relevant respects. That is a virtue—it means that we do not have two separate explanations for how the permutation argument (for example) fails, once in thought and once in language. The explanation for why it fails in the case of thought becomes a proper part of the explanation for how it fails in the case of language. That is the ideal situation.

Now, it's certainly true that going for a more 'Lewisian' solution according to which the correct semantic theory is one that trades off fit-with-use against elegance-in-ontologese also gives responses to the three challenges. The responses are exactly the same as just sketched, except that instead of being able to appeal directly to the fact that language users possess concepts of green (rather than permuted green) or universal quantification (rather than skolemite quantification) and so on, we need to add a claim that these are either part of ontologese, or at least more-compactly-definable-in-ontologese than the alternatives. Believers in ontologese will no doubt insist that this is so, and if you trust them, then you'll think that they can rebut the challenges. But this violates the desideratum mentioned above—that we reuse the explanation of determinacy in mental content in explaining the determinacy of linguistic content, rather than solving the problem twice over. This is manifest particularly in the response to the skolemite. The explanation of determinately unrestricted quantification for thought will turn, I argued, on the particular open-ended inferential role of unrestricted quantification. But the explanation of determinately unrestricted quantifiers in language would, on this proposal, turn on the alleged metaphysical specialness of *Everything*—the quality that gets it included in ontologese. Quite aside from the extra metaphysical commitments of the latter story, this seems to me one explanation too many.

A possible response is as follows: these underdetermination challenges can be resisted by appealing to the way that a linguistic interpretation must

---

[7] In the 2007 paper, I presented an underdetermination challenge that doesn't 'piggyback' on the standard interpretation as both these do, and hence one where we lack an immediate prima facie case for it being less natural. This construction targets a kind of interpretationism on which the 'dataset' consists of pairs of sentences and truth values, rather than pairs of sentences and truth conditions. So it doesn't have immediate application in the current context.

fit with determinate (and structured) mental content. That is a way of inheriting solutions to these challenges, but one that is independent of how we handle elegance. If the mental states that sentences conventionally express have green but not permuted-green as a component of their content, then to match this, the structured content of the sentences must do the same. If those mental states involve unrestricted generality rather than skolemite restricted generality as a component of their content, so must the sentences. Considerations of elegance are not redundant, since they would be needed to solve the third, Kripkensteinian, problem—but that's not a case where we already have an existing solution for thought that we want to import.

I think this can't be the right story. It is too optimistic to suppose that for each sentence-in-use in public language, there is a belief whose content exactly matches the structured content of the sentence. Take agents with basic concepts 'unmarried' and 'adult male', but no basic concept for 'bachelor', and whose cognitive architecture has no analogue of predicate conjunction, but only of sentential conjunction. They speak a language with the single word 'bachelor'. The fine-grained belief they conventionally express by 'Harry is a bachelor' is a conjunctive structured proposition: <<Harry, being unmarried>, CONJUNCTION, <Harry, being an adult male>>. But I can't see how a compositional semantic theory associating structured propositions with sentences could end up assigning that conjunctive proposition to the subject-predicate sentence—surely the correct semantic theory will assign to that sentence the singular non-conjunctive proposition <Harry, being a bachelor>, where the property of *being a bachelor* might contain conjunctive structure. The lesson to draw is that a more lax understanding of fit is called for: assigning content, for example, that is a priori equivalent to the conventionally assigned content should be good enough for top marks on the fit dimension. Laxity on fit, however, would reintroduce the determinacy problems, since the permuted and skolemite interpretations assign propositions to sentences that are a priori equivalent to the originals from which they are built. To implement the inheritance idea, we need inheritance via elegance.

8.5 There is Nothing Ad Hoc about What I Am Suggesting

I have used a single set of resources twice over: appealing to elegance in content-fixing for explanatory concepts as part of the metaphysics of mental content, and now also at the heart of the metaphysis of linguistic content. In the former case, a central option was to identify elegance with elegance-in-ontologese. That led to connections between explanatory concepts and naturalness. However, here, I've advocated something different: elegance is elegance-in-mentalese. In the current context, against a background where we are presuming that each agent has fairly determinate mental content, the appeal to elegance-in-mentalese has constraining power. But in that earlier context, it would have none. Whatever I say at that earlier point, it will differ from the proposal I have made here. I want to defend this difference in approach.

The first thing to note is the different underlying contexts of the two discussions. In the earlier discussion, our focus was explanation. Here, our focus is curve-fitting, and I am not committed to viewing fitting a curve to data as an explanatory project. To be sure, curve-fitting is broadly a kind of inductive generalization from observed values to unobserved values. But while I do think that some kinds of induction ('extrapolative' ones) are plausibly viewed as backed by a presumed background explanation, I am sceptical that this is the case for curve-fitting, any more than it is for interpolative inductions such as figuring out the proportions of blue balls in an urn by random sampling, or the distribution of opinions in a population.

We have good reason to think that elegance (in some language) plays a role in good curve-fitting, independently of any connection to explanation. But there's little motivation to think that it is elegance-in-ontologese that plays this role. I've said very little about how, given some arbitrary kind of data and the challenge to fit a curve to it, we should fix the L such that elegance-in-L is epistemologically relevant. My claim is only that in one specific case, that of fitting a semantic theory for public language to conventional associations, that it is elegance-in-mentalese that we should go for. My reason for believing that is because it fits nicely into the overall theory at this point—in particularly, allowing a mesh between thought and language and the inheritance of content from the former to the latter. That's analogous to a claim that in fitting curves to temperature-pressure data we should be concerned with elegance-in-standard-polynomial-vocabulary. I'm as interested as anyone in what the principled fix here is, but we can have good reason to believe these various instances without having a general characterization to hand. And it's only the local instance for semantics I need to formulate the metaphysics of linguistic representation I favour.

Why, then, do we find elegance-in-ontologese turning up in our theory of mental content? I'm open to the view that we do not find it there. My central contention in chapter 3 was that explanatory potent properties were reference-magnetic. One could even think that natural properties were the potent properties without committing to elegance-in-ontologese being involved in the story (see the discussion of Sider in the earlier chapter). Elegance-in-ontologese entered as a reconstruction of Lewis's account of the reason why natural properties got to be reference-magnetic. Although of course other views of explanation are available, the idea that natural properties are particularly relevant to explanation and extrapolative induction is a very attractive one, so if a notion of elegance is constitutive of explanation, that it is elegance-in-ontologese that is involved is an attractive hypothesis.

If we go all the way down this path, with what overall picture are we left? We have the idea that for the purposes of interpolative induction and curve-fitting, elegance-in-L for an appropriate choice of L is important. And we have the claim that elegance-in-ontologese is relevant for explanation and extrapolative induction. There's no incompatibility here! Indeed, it wouldn't be all that odd if simplicity/elegance came in subjective (subject-relative) and objective flavours, and that subjective simplicity is relevant for some kinds of epistemic projects and objective simplicity for other projects. To be sure, it would be nice to have a comprehensive epistemology where we knew exactly how and why and in what form simplicity was relevant to every project. But we shouldn't put all other projects on hold until we have that figured out.

8.6 Conclusion

'Beth' refers to a particular flesh-and-blood human in virtue of the correct linguistic interpretation mapping that word to Beth. I have been defending the view that correctness is determined by a combination of fit with the base facts (conventional associations between sentences and propositions) and the elegance of the theory. I motivated the general fit/elegance account of best theory by an analogy to fitting curves to data, where a lot of sophisticated work gives us confidence that elegance is a real, epistemically important property. In holding that the same property plays a role in the metaphysics of linguistic representation, I have left open many questions about the exact contours of fit and elegance for this particular case, but emphasized that the elegance-fixing language would play a major role. In later sections, I have defended one particular take on what the elegance-fixing language is: it is the subject's language of thought. The upshot is that solutions to determinacy problems directed at language can be inherited from solutions already offered to their analogues in thought.

PART III

SOURCE INTENTIONALITY

Linguistic intentionality is built from the intentionality of beliefs and desires. In Part II, I explained how that can work. The intentionality of belief and desires is built from the intentionality of perception and action, and the story of Radical Interpretation in Part I presented an account of how this goes. But where does the intentionality of perception and action come from in the first place? In these final two chapters, I give an account of this source intentionality, and so a metaphysics of the bottommost layer of the three-layer metaphysics of representation.

The Metaphysics of Representation. J. Robert G. Williams, Oxford University Press (2019).
© J. Robert G. Williams.
DOI: 10.1093/oso/9780198850205.001.0001

9

The Basis of Radical Interpretation

9.1 We Need to Determine Whether the Basis of Radical Interpretation Consists in Representational States

This chapter and the next develop an account of source intentionality: the first layer of representation which Radical Interpretation presupposes. Let me recap where we are up to.

Back in the introduction, I set out an account of the nature of representation (or at least, core kinds of representation) that broke the task into three layers, each building on the next. I then started in the middle, by setting out a story about how representational properties of beliefs and desires are grounded (second-layer representations). That story was Radical Interpretation, and the key thesis was this:

- The correct interpretation of an agent x is that one which **best rationalizes** x's **dispositions to act** in the light of the **courses of experience** x undergoes.

To unpack that story further, I distinguished between the *basis* of interpretation and the *selectional story*. The basis consisted of what our interpretee (Sally) is disposed to do, given various courses of experiences that she might undergo. The selectional story is whatever else is needed to pin down a correct interpretation from these base facts. The key notion there was that of 'best rationalization'.

At that point, I set the question of the grounding of base facts aside, since the immediate problem that we encountered (the bubble puzzle) would arise on any plausible story about these facts and the content they deliver. What we needed to address the problem, I argued, was clarity on the other element of the story—rationalization. The key to resolving the bubble puzzle was to set aside a familiar construal of 'rationalization' as picking out structural rationality or formal coherence. Instead, the selectional story we need is substantive rationality or reasons-responsiveness, which makes a broader appeal to how Sally ought believe and act, given her evidence and

The Metaphysics of Representation. J. Robert G. Williams, Oxford University Press (2019).
© J. Robert G. Williams.
DOI: 10.1093/oso/9780198850205.001.0001

preferences. The story rolled on from there, encompassing predictions about patterns of reference for concepts, and lately, an extension to the representational properties of public language—something that I argued also retroactively inflects the reference of concepts that have direct linguistic expression.

While rationalization has up to this point played the starring role, it is only half of the resources needed to get radical interpretation up and running. Radical Interpretation should be viewed as a story about how one set of representational facts is 'transformed' into another, and we need those 'source' perceptual/action facts to be in place so we have something to work with.

There are two key theoretical choices here.

One has to decide whether or not the basis of Radical Interpretation—the 'courses of experience' and 'dispositions to act'—are defined out of representational states. Prima facie, perceptual states are representational, so if we understand x's course of experience as the sequence of perceptual states that x undergoes, that would be to include representational states in the base. Likewise, describing the actions x performs in various counterfactual scenarios prima facie carries information about the intentions that shape x's behaviour.[1] Some theorists, however, might attempt to get away with explicating these notions in terms of raw behaviour (dispositions of the agent's body to move in particular ways) and sensation (facts about their history of sensory stimulations).

If one does assume that the basis for Radical Interpretation consists in representational states, one has to offer an account of the nature of this kind of 'source intentionality'. At this point, I see a second choice point:

A. Following Pautz (2013), we could pair Radical Interpretation with a non-reductive account of the intentionality of experience and action. To this end, Pautz recommends we take the intentional features of phenomenology of conscious experience as a metaphysical primitive. This would be to abandon the original ambition to ground representational facts in the non-representational.

---

[1] One might think consistently with this that they are most *fundamentally* relational states— relations between subjects and sense-data (Jackson 1977), or ordinary macroscopic objects or property instances (Campbell 2002). But as Logue (2014) emphasizes, this is perfectly consistent with such states having representational content as well—whether that is directly explicated in terms of the relation (e.g. any property of the sense-data one is related to, or the object instantiating the property involved in a property-instance one is related to).

B. Alternatively, we could preserve that original ambition, and so, having reduced belief/desire intentionality inter alia to representational facts about experience, we would need some other reductive story about this 'source intentionality'. This story will have to be prior to and independent of facts about belief and desire representation, so that we don't go round in circles.

At the first choice point, I argue that the basis of Radical Interpretation—what slots in for 'courses of experience' and 'dispositions to act'—will be defined in terms of representational states. On the second choice point, I preserve the reductive ambition and offer a metaphysics of source intentionality prior to and independent of Radical Interpretation. This chapter focuses on the first of these points, and I take my job to be to explore what Radical Interpretation needs, by way of source intentionality. That sets us up, in the next chapter, for my account of how we can get what we need.

9.2 We Need to Appeal to Representational Facts to Individuate an Agent's Options

Radical Interpretation was the thesis that the correct interpretation of an agent was that one which best rationalizes 'dispositions to act', in the light of 'courses of experience'. Those particular descriptions of the relata of rationalization are just placeholders, however, and it is not my task here to analyse experience or action while presupposing that whatever results is what turns up in the basis for Radical Interpretation. Rather, the task is an engineering one: to determine what best fills those slots in the theory. For neutrality, I will label the slots respectively (A) and (E). There are two holistic theory-driven constraints on the engineering task. First, what we appeal to should make Radical Interpretation work. And second, it should be something that we can ground independently of belief/desire.

Radical Interpretation says that (A) and (E) stand in rational relations to belief and desire. On the Bayesian model to which I default, rationalizing an A-fact about Sally is a matter of showing that this is an option that maximizes expected value for her. E-facts, on the other hand, need to constrain the rational evolution of Sally's beliefs.

There's an immediate prima facie problem for one who would try to explicate (E) using non-representational resources, say, as facts about sensory stimulations. It's entirely unclear how a raw sensory stimulation (described by the impingements of wavelengths of light on my retina, for example) could stand in rational relations to a belief change; it is just the wrong level of description to be reaching for. It is the fact that those sensory stimulations are part of me *having an experience as of a red cube to the front of me* that explains why I raise my confidence in the existence of a red cube in front of me. But that description of the sensory stimulations is not available to someone who wants to keep the story non-representational. A response to this might be to recharacterize both the sensation and the belief change allegedly rationally required. For example, perhaps an agent who has an experience with a reddish-cubish quality is rationally required to believe that they have just had an experience with a reddish-cubish quality. Now: it is not at all obvious that we have beliefs about the qualia we undergo, but this is not as self-evidently absurd as attributing beliefs about retinal impingements. And so long as facts about qualia are not themselves representational, this strategy might allow us to avoid appeal to source intentionality, at least for a while.[2]

Another problem with analysing (E) in non-representational terms is what to say of the perverse 'switcheroo' interpretation described by Stalnaker:

> Mary is angry at Fred, her neighbour. She wants him to suffer, and believes that he will suffer is she plays her cello badly at three o'clock in the morning. So she does play her cello badly at three o'clock in the morning. That, at least, is one hypothesis for explaining why Mary did what she did. Here is another: Mary wants Albert to suffer, and believes that Albert will suffer if she plays her cello at three is morning. That is why she did what she did. [...] [T]he defender of the perverse hypothesis, when pressed about the implausibilies in his explanation, elaborates his hypothesis by saying that Mary believes Albert, rather than Fred, to be her neighbour, believes that Albert, rather than Fred, insulted her, believes that Albert's name is 'Fred'. In fact, all the attitudes that sensible observer would say Mary takes towards Fred, the defender of the perverse hypothesis says that Mary takes towards Albert.... The shift from Fred to Albert looks, from the point of view of [this] analysis, like an innocent shift in the conventional units used to describe Mary's attitudes and relate them to each other, and not as a shift in the claims made about the attitudes themselves.
>
> (Stalnaker 1984, p.17)

---

[2] Thanks to Dave Chalmers for suggesting this line to me.

If the basis of Radical Interpretation is representational, then the story can go as follows: Mary perceives Fred making insulting noises, and so rationally forms the belief: *that guy just insulted me*. Here the object of her demonstrative thought is Fred, the same guy that figures in the content of her experiences.[3] The content of the experiences constrains the content of beliefs that are rational to form in reaction to those experiences. Someone who deprives themselves of content-laden descriptions of the experiences in the basis for Radical Interpretation owes some other account of how we manage to rule out Stalnaker's switched interpretations. For example, the qualia strategy sketched above would require beliefs formed in reaction to experience to capture the qualitative character of the scene viewed, but one might worry that the qualitative beliefs so formed are consistent with both de re belief that *Fred* is the neighbour, or that *Albert* is. Someone pursuing that strategy will have to hope that something else in the story about Radical Interpretation can ground *de re* content.[4]

Explicating (A) in terms of raw behaviour seems initially quite promising. The idea that I desire certain goals, and believe that certain behaviour is likely to bring about those goals, has some prima facie appeal at least for a layer of basic actions. I'll set out below why I think here, too, we should appeal to intentional states.[5]

---

[3] Compare my brief discussion of demonstrative thought in the conclusion to part I, and Dickie (2015) for extensive discussion of perceptual links, justification of demonstrative belief, and reference-fixing. Stalnaker uses this story to motivate the indication-theoretic analysis of the notion of belief which I mentioned in the preface, and I am not going to follow him in this, but the general idea that broadly causal factors need to be introduced to explain why the switcheroo interpretation is wrong is something that I support, and implement in my own way in this chapter and the next.

[4] Here's one option. Suppose one is a descriptivist about the concept "Fred". One says it has a primary content like "the actual person who behaves Freddishly near to me", and that "behaving Freddishly" can be ultimately analyzed in qualitative/indexical terms. Beliefs about Fred will then be analytically connected to qualitative beliefs, and we will be in a position to explain why certain qualitative beliefs prompted by experience rationalize Fred thoughts rather than Albert thoughts.

[5] I favour versions of Bayesian theory on which the objects of choice are propositions (as in Jeffrey 1965, Joyce 1999) rather than the Savage-style formulations on which utilities, probabilities, and preferences are defined over disjoint sets (see Elliott (2017) for difficulties with the latter in this kind of context). There are two possible readings of such a decision theory. On the rationalization-by-striving approach, in order to be rational, the subject must be in some state whose intentional content is the proposition that maximizes utility amongst their options (e.g. they must try to q, intend to q, etc.). On the rationalization-by-satisfaction approach, in order to be rational, the subject must be in some state which makes-true the proposition that maximizes utility amongst their options (they must be such that q). The former approach builds in intentionality in the relata of rationalization from the start, but on the latter approach, the proposition might simply be a description of raw behaviour.

Rationalization of Sally's actions/behaviour/choices is a fundamentally contrastive matter. At a moment of choice, she has a number of options. Staring blearily into the cupboard, she can go for muesli or for porridge. Muesli is a rational choice if it's the *better* of the available options, or at least that there's no option that is better than it. That contrastive characterization of rationality immediately entails the following. In situations where Sally has only one option, and enacts it, then this is automatically a rational choice. After all, it is vacuously true that there's no option better than the one and only option she has available. It of course sounds a little weird to evaluate such 'fatalistic' choice situations for rationality—limit cases often sound weird—but there's no reason to think the theory doesn't apply.

It's crucial to Radical Interpretation that we rule out option-fatalistic interpretations of Sally's choice-situations, i.e. those on which she only ever has a single option. If every choice situation Sally faced or might face were an option-fatalistic one, then however we interpret her, she'll count as vacuously rational. What she does would not constrain interpretation at all.[6]

I submit, therefore, that the basis of Radical Interpretation needs more than just facts of the form:

- Sally, in decision situation C, is disposed to A

But instead it needs to contain facts of the following form:

- Sally, in decision situation C, is disposed to A_i out of available options A_1, $A_2, \ldots, A_n$,

Facts about the options-not-taken, as much as the options-taken, are part of the required basis.

I can't see how we can ground these facts about options without appeal to representational facts—facts about actions under intentional descriptions or action-guiding mental states. Let me take a couple of paragraphs to explain my pessimism.

---

[6] Some ways of getting into problems with option-fatalism include: to list options as an extra parameter fixed by interpretation alongside beliefs and desires, or to analyse options via the agent's beliefs, e.g. about what their options are, since then by attributing the agent a belief in fatalism, one can generate option-fatalism and so make their actions vacuously rational. Factors like what an agent believes their options are may matter for some normative evaluations—I'm tempted by the thought that structural and substantively rational action might be associated with different option sets. But we need something more exogenous for Radical Interpretation.

Behaviourism about the basis for Radical Interpretation is attractive for the reductionist about representation because behaviour has a physical signature: the motions of limbs and body parts through space and time. But most obvious fact about options Sally had but failed to take is that they lack this kind of physical signature. The behaviourist about options might respond by pointing to modal facts: there are ways Sally's limbs could have moved but didn't (in close enough counterfactual scenarios). This will not help. The trouble is that we can't plausibly identify Sally's options with all possible behaviours that she can (in close enough possibilities) enact.

Consider, for example, throwing a dart at the bullseye. Hitting the bullseye is not something I have the skill to bring about reliably, but there's a chance that by blind luck my throwing action will happen to be just what it needs to be to hit the bullseye. Maybe this happens one time in every hundred. Now, clearly, standing ready to throw, it's physically possible for my limbs to move in just the right way to hit the bullseye. But that behaviour is not in the relevant sense an option for me.[7] If it was, then I'd be constantly irrational, since performing those limb movements would ensure an outcome (hitting the bullseye) with far greater value than the limb movements I actually perform. That would be a false prediction though—I'm not irrational, I'm absolutely doing my best to maximize my score, but I just lack the fine-grained control over my limb movements to ensure they trace the path mentioned.

The behaviourist about options faces a difficult challenge. She needs to cluster together all these counterfactual trajectories-of-limbs in a way that reflects the limitations of my 'control' over them. It needs to be, for example, that the bullseye-bringing-about trajectory is part of a bundle that also includes another trajectory that makes the dart hit two inches to the right. And here's what seems to be the crucial fact: if I *tried* to hit the bullseye, either one of these trajectories would occur with equal likelihood. But to appeal to what I try to do in performing a behaviour is to appeal to intentional mental states or behaviours under intentional descriptions that, say I, requires explication in representational terms.

What I think is going on here is that the necessary bundling is grounded in the fact that these behaviours are all (actual and counterfactual) implementations of a single action-guiding state. Perhaps in the case at hand that is an intention to *hit the bullseye* which is at chance in whether it leads to behaviour B (which brings about hitting the bullseye) or behaviour B*

---

[7] It's not in the relevant (agentive) sense something I can do. For recent state of the art on agentive modals, see Mandelkern, Schultheis, and Boylan (2017).

(which leaves it two inches to the right). I don't think any account of options will be viable that doesn't appeal, in some way or another, to the mental states that control the behaviour and that fix the level of grain.[8]

So the prospects for explicating the (A) 'disposition to act' element of the basis of Radical Interpretation without at least tacit appeal to representational states are bad. And explicating the (E) 'course of experience' element without representational states looks both implausible and like it stores up trouble. So we have a lot of work to do to demonstrate, in detail, how to do without source intentionality, or else we need to accept that source intentionality is required, and show that we can earn the right to it. I take the second option. I assume that we need a first layer of representational states, prior to and independent of belief and desire, to run the story. In the next few sections, I flesh out what kinds of representational facts will be required.

9.3 An Agent's Options are Action-guiding States

Any account of Radical Interpretation will have to provide an account of what to substitute for 'evidence' and 'actions'—the relata of rationalization. I've argued that any such account will involve descriptions of states under intentional descriptions, and so every account needs an account of this first-layer source intentionality. But that doesn't yet pin down what intentional states feature in the first layer. The rest of this chapter will concentrate on getting clear on a target. That involves taking a stand on how to individuate the options in rational choice, and the most evidentially basic contents of

---

[8] Once it's agreed that intentions are going to be appealed to in the story, I think the appeal of behaviourism-about-options sinks away. One might press a more nuanced but still non-representational treatment here, by insisting that the content of the intentions doesn't matter—behaviours that are possible results of the same single intentional state (individuated by functional role without appeal to content) are bundled together. Here's one observation about this proposal. Mental duplicates (with the same beliefs about their abilities) might have different options in virtue of differences in their possible bodily behaviours. If my hands are tied, but I don't know it, then an upward hand trajectory (that I believe would save the child) would be in the relevant sense impossible for me. Contrast the expected utility of these two propositions: (i) that I form an intention which causes me to flex muscles in a way that would lead to my hands raising, but fail to raise them; (ii) that I form an intention to raise my hands. The expected utility of (ii) may be far higher than the expected utility of (i), since (i) incorporates information not otherwise present to the agent about the worldly outcome of a certain attempt. Accordingly, options glossed in the (ii)-type way will rationalize the attempts of an unfortunate individual to surrender by raising their (unknown to them) tied arms, whereas the gloss (i) would not. This shows the delicate interplay between a metaphysical account of options, and the first-order results about rationalization we're about to discuss.

experience. I set out a pair of answers, and though I motivate them by outlining some puzzles they solve, I won't argue that that they are the only and best way to solve them (personally, I'm neutral on that question). The motivations in each case derive from constraints implicit in familiar Bayesian models of rational decision making and updating on evidence, and so I proceed under the assumption that being substantively rational in part involves being structurally rational in the Bayesian sense. Options and Evidence must therefore be such as to make at least *possible* Bayesian ideal rationality. The reader who doesn't like where this ends up should therefore consider switching out the Bayesian constraints below for some alternative.

The account of options I will run with I take from Brian Hedden (2012). He proposes that first and foremost, what is rationalized by beliefs and desires is the formation of mental states—what he calls decisions. Decisions are action-guiding states. If Sally decides to ford a creek, then in the right circumstances she will set about fording the creek. Decisions are contingently connected to successful creek-fording. Sally may be more or less confident that if she took the decision to ford the creek, then she'd succeed. As anticipated, decisions are representational mental states, albeit the representation of a state of the world that is to-be-brought-about, not a representation of a state that currently obtains.

Here is Hedden's motivation for the claim that what are rationalized are decisions, rather than behaviours or actions or anything more 'external'.[9] Sally is facing a raging creek, and can either attempt the crossing or go back. Going back would be a disappointment, but at least she'd be safe. If she crosses successfully, she'll have a great hike—much better than going home. If she crosses unsuccessfully, she'll be swept downstream and injured. Let's suppose that in fact, she has the ability to cross reliably, though she's not herself at all confident in this (and rationally so, based on her evidence). Hedden evaluates the verdicts a decision theory would give (and so here enters the distinctive Bayesian assumption) under various theories of what your options are.

First of all, suppose Sally's options include *cross the creek*, and *go home*. The expected value of *cross the creek* will be an average of the value of the possible outcomes that result from Sally crossing the creek, weighted by how

---

[9] These kind of cases are considered at length in Pollock (2006), who proposes adjustments to the formalism of decision theory (to incorporate 'null' outcomes) in order to account for them. I am grateful to Gary Mullen for discussion of the points later in this section about option-individuation.

likely each given outcome is to be produced. Crucially, any outcome that results from *cross the creek* will be one where Sally successfully crossed and had a great time. So the value of that putative option is very high—the scenario where she makes the attempt and get swept downstream and injured doesn't factor in at all. The value of this option, so calculated, clearly beats the expected value of going home.

Second, suppose Sally's options are to *decide to cross the creek* and *decide to go home*. The expected value of *decide to cross the creek* is again the average of the possible outcomes of making that decision, weighted by likelihood. And crucially, there's a possible scenario where Sally decides to cross the creek, makes the attempt, and fails. That is a scenario to which Sally gives considerable credence—after all, she's not confident in her ability to cross. So the possibility of trying-and-failing is factored into the expected value calculation if options are construed in this way, and given the considerable disvalue of getting injured, the option that maximizes value is deciding to go home.

The raging creek case illustrates a couple of points. One is that whether or not a given course of behaviour (Sally turning around and walking back to where she came from) is part of a rational course of action is sensitive to the individuation of the options. In the two calculations above, we're holding fixed Sally's abilities, beliefs and desires, and any objective values of the outcomes that might matter. All that differs is the framing of the choice situation in terms of options, yet in one case, what is rationally required is *crossing* and in the other case it is *deciding to go home*. So the case dramatizes again the moral of the previous section: the individuation of options is a crucial part of the theory of rationality.

However, the other thing to extract from the case is an evaluation of the plausibility of various theories of options. Sally really should be factoring in the chances of trying-and-failing to cross the creek, when evaluating whatever proposition ends up corresponding to the 'cross the creek' option. It would be reckless for her to make the attempt, given her well-supported doubts about her ability. The case is evidence for options-as-decisions over the more externalistically specified alternative.

The dialectic can of course continue. The problem with *cross the creek* as an option, it might seem, is that it is excessively external. Perhaps some more basic bodily movements—walking towards and into the creek, progressing to the best of one's ability against the flow—would do better. After all, such descriptions are compatible with not making it to the other side. The problem is that it always seems possible, for any description of an option that entails bodily behaviour, for me to have rational doubts about my ability to perform it (perhaps I give some credence to a demon popping up and freezing me mid-flow). If I'm not certain that I'd succeed in φ-ing, if I tried to φ, then, intuitively, that possibility of trying-and-failing should be factored into rational evaluation of the 'φ' option. Hedden argues that only a mental event, like a decision, is immune from such concerns.

9.4 Which Action-guiding States are Options?

Hedden's label 'decisions' suggests an action-guiding representational mental state that has been *decided upon* by some kind of process of deliberation. Nothing in the motivations he has for identifying options with action-guiding mental states requires we restrict attention to cases involving explicit deliberation. It's best not to confuse a theory of *deliberation* with a theory of *rationalization*—the latter consists in saying which is the *rationally best* option for the agent, given their beliefs and desires, the former consists in an account of how an agent should practically go about determining what's best.[10] All of which is to say: I want to distance myself from Hedden's terminology. What he motivates, I think, is the identification of options with representational action-guiding mental states, of which decisions are just one special case.

To say that options are action-guiding mental states is doesn't yet tell us *which* such states are options. Take two extremes. Planning to catch the train tomorrow is future directed, at a conceptually high level (it represents a state of the world involving *trains*) and is determinable, in the sense that there are many different ways of 'filling in' the plan—choice of train, moment to leave, mode of transport to the station, etc.[11] On the other hand, the intention-in-action[12] that I form when putting one foot in front of the another on the way to the station is present-directed (it guides the movements I'm currently

---

[10] In moral philosophy, it is a familiar point that it is perfectly compatible with a broadly consequentialist account of what makes an option best, that it is best for cognitively bounded agents like us to deliberate in non-consequentialist ways.

[11] Bratman (1987).

[12] I am thinking of intentions-in-action in the way described by Searle (1979), on which they are caused by prior future-directed intentions, and themselves cause bodily movements which are their intentional contents. Searle also describes them as 'experiences of action', albeit experiences that unlike the usual perceptual states involves world-to-mind direction of fit. I'm not sure that is useful terminology, but the analogy he draws seems compelling to me. McDowell (2011) lays out a different model, on which intentions-in-action are identical to prior future-directed intentions, with temporally dynamic content (the intentions-in-action are the present-tensed versions). That model would raise more difficulties when we come to fixing content in the next section.

engaged in) and as such is determinate (I delegate all further details of its implementation to subpersonal systems that control my fine-grained movements). It is also conceptually low-level, involving just basic concepts of the movements of my limbs.

There's a final contrast between high-level and low-level action-guiding states that will be important in the next chapter: the planning state might well not be fulfilled—I can abandon it if a better prospect comes into view, or it might prove impossible to fulfil if a broken train closes the line. An intention-in-action to put one foot in front of the other can also be frustrated, but only in much more extreme cases, of abnormal environments or some internal malfunction on my part. It'll turn out that the metaphysics of source intentionality I'll offer will directly ground the intentionality of the low-level states but not the high-level ones.

Here is the picture I have: in carving a path through the world, we engage in a constant hum of low-level action. We also, more occasionally, form long-lasting high-level plans that are filled in over time in a high-level way. At the sharp end, such high-level planning and intentional formation is implemented in the moment by actions guided by low-level action-guiding states. There is a uniform (Bayesian) story about rational choice that governs both high-level planning (which plans to form) and low-level action-guidance. To be rational, the intentions you form at whatever level should maximize the expectation of good outcomes, by your lights. Metaphysically speaking, we can take the trajectory of this agent through the world and identify what low-level action-guiding states the agent has formed and fix their content via the metaphysics of source-intentionality. We consider, counterfactually, what alternative low-level action-guiding states the agent could have formed, and correct belief/desire-interpretation will have to (all else equal) maximize the rationality of the state formed, compared to the alternatives. This is not to deny that high-level and future-directed planning will be part of the final story, nor to deny that it must be also be rational. But I envisage content being assigned to planning states alongside the assignment of content to beliefs and desires by the correct interpretation. High-level planning states are part of second-layer representation, and not themselves part of source intentionality.[13]

---

[13] An interesting possibility: planning is a mental state which is non-trivial to get oneself into. One can try and fail to plan not to smoke. You fail to plan, if you never acquire the disposition to not-smoke, given the opportunity (which is distinct from forming that disposition, and then failing to carry it through due to a revision of the plan, or abnormal stress levels weakening your will, etc.—dispositions can be finkish or masked). If planning is thought of like this, then the

I've spent two sections identifying what I propose to substitute for (A) 'dispositions to act' in my initial glosses of Radical Interpretation. *Actions* themselves have disappeared from view, replaced by representational *action-guiding states*, as a consequence of accepting the Heddenic identification of what sorts of things are rationalized. The target I propose for a metaphysics of source-intentionality at the action-end will the action-guiding states that feature in a Heddenic account of rationalization.

9.5 We Update on the Fact We Have Perceived Something, Not Just on What We Perceive

The other half of source intentionality was (E), originally glossed as 'courses of experience'. Again, I will outline and provide some (Bayesian) motivations for one substitute for base facts, which will be the target in the next chapter.

The overriding constraint is that what goes in place of (E) must be relata of the relevant kind of rationalization. In the case of (E), what we're looking for is a specification of the way that (intuitively) information about the environment rationalizes a shift from one belief state to another. Something goes on in my visual system, as a result of light hitting my retina. This leads me to form the belief that the lights are green. Given my background belief that *if the lights are green then I am allowed to drive on*, I form the new belief that *I am allowed to drive on*. But under what description do these visual goings-on rationalize the belief change?

On the simplest Bayesian account of rational update of beliefs, one updates one's prior beliefs by conditionalizing on a certain proposition— the proposition which is the 'total information' that one has learned. On that simple model, what we're looking for is a specification of the proposition on which we conditionalize, in any given physical circumstances. This proposition is something I will be certain of, post-conditionalization, and that is

---

relevant options that are most directly implemented when one is planning may be states of *having decided to plan on ϕ-ing*—a plan being more like an action than an action-guiding state, from this point of view. The decisions to plan on ϕ-ing would be action-guiding states that are present-directed and determinate, since putting a mentalese sentence in the planning-box is the work of a moment. It is not clear that decisions to plan on ϕ-ing are high-level, in the way plans themselves are. To be sure, if ϕ is something like 'catch the train', you need to be able to have high-level content about trains in order to have a plan with that content. But the content of the decision to plan may just be to put **that** mental state into the planning box. If this is so, then perhaps all rationalization is low-level in my sense, and so-called high-level planning is a construct built out from it.

prima facie a demanding condition. You might suspect that if I have a perception as of a red ball in front of me, what I learn includes the existence of a red ball. But if I give some small probability to the possibility of having being drugged and hallucinating the ball, or being in abnormal conditions in which a white ball is illuminated with red light, then it seems overly dogmatic to become *certain* that there's a red ball in front of me.[14]

What could this proposition be? It's certainly not one that describes the sensory stimulation of our retinas—*those* aren't the propositions we learn about through immediate perception. The layout of 'sense-data'—visible properties instantiated not by items in the physical world but in a private visual space—was traditionally supposed to be something of which agents could be utterly certain. That fits quite nicely with the seeming Cartesian presupposition of the simple conditionalization model of learning, and since facts about what sense-data I'm related to are not *representational* facts about me, those readers bold enough to believe in sense-data have here a way of trying out a direct substitution for (E) in non-representation terms. But I'm not happy to presuppose the sense-data model of perception, so I'll look elsewhere.

Here is one clue. When we undergo an experience, we end up not just with beliefs about our environment, but also beliefs that we've seen, heard, touched certain things. It's not as though we first of all acquire a belief about the existence of red balls in our environment, cast around for an explanation of the remarkable fact that we've got this information, and then end up inferring that we must have seen it. At least in part, perceptual learning is in

---

[14] More complicated Bayesian models of rational update (e.g. by 'Jeffrey conditionalization') allow for situations in which probabilities in salient propositions are raised, but not all the way to certainty. On one version of this, you again need to pick out a proposition. But you need not become fully certain of its truth—rather, it can rise to a high but not full confidence-level k. Its negation becomes $1-k$. The Bayesian theory predicts how one's credence in all other propositions should then evolve. The price we pay for the generalized model is that there are two parameters to fix: given a physical description of the situation, we need to pick out a proposition and a level of confidence which it is to be given in the updated belief states. It's one thing to say that given an experience as of a red ball in front of me, my confidence that there is a red ball in front of me should rise. It's quite another to predict what level k it should rise to (and you can't expect to read this off the experience: your prior beliefs about what the likelihood is of being drugged or finding oneself in abnormal circumstances will matter a lot). Because of this trouble in figuring out what the rule says, it would be really nice if we didn't have to rely on it. (One prima facie appeal of Jeffrey conditionalization would be if it allowed us to make sense of the claim that we update on the content of experience and not, as suggested below, on the fact we have experienced thus-and-such. But this promise is not fulfilled, for the reasons set out in the next footnote.)

itself learning facts about what we have perceived.[15] The way forward this suggests is the following: rather than conditionalize on the content of our perceptual experience (which led to the problematic dogmatism when combined with the simple Bayesian model of update), let us conditionalize on the *fact* that we are undergoing a perception with that content. Thus, rather than becoming certain of the following post-update:

- There is a red sphere to the front of me.

I suggest we become certain of the following:

- I am undergoing a perception as of a red sphere to the front of me.

Even if you suspect that you have been drugged or are in abnormal circumstances, it's arguable that you should be fully confident of this.[16]

---

[15] Sturgeon (forthcoming) reports an unpublished exchange between Dorothy Edgington and David Lewis where the importance of this came up. Suppose a burglar is about to look to see if a house has an alarm. The burglar's priors are low that he will burgle, if the house is alarmed. The burglar looks, has an experience as of no alarm, and updates accordingly, with the effect he has high credence in the house having no alarm. In the posterior probabilities, the burglar's probability is high that he will burgle if the house is alarmed—after all, he now knows he's likely to burgle, and this is so whether or not the house is in fact alarmed (he's already done all the checking he's going to do, so if he's unlucky, he's unlucky). In order to explain this change in conditional probabilities, the obvious thing is to appeal to the burglar's prior conditional probabilities involving his having the experience as of no alarm: if that proposition is E, the proposition the house is alarmed is A, and the proposition he will break in is B, then the priors are: $p(B|A)$ low, $p(A|E)$ low, and $p(B|A\&E)$ low. So the experience 'screens off' the facts about the alarm, if we represent the burglar as conditionalizing on E (or Jeffrey-conditionalizing with a big upward shift in E) then this predicts the shift in conditional probability of B on A. On the other hand, it is impossible to recover the change in conditional probabilities if we tried to Jeffrey-conditionalize where A itself was one of the possibilities, due to a technical fact about Jeffrey conditionalization: that conditional probabilities on cells of the relevant partition are unchanged through an update. See also Schoenfield (2016) for conditionalization on learning in the context of accuracy-based foundations for rationality.

[16] Lewis (1996) advocates something close to this proposal: '[A] possibility W is uneliminated if the subject's perceptual experience [...] in W exactly match[es] his perceptual experience and memory in actuality. [...] When perceptual experience E [...] eliminates a possibility W that is not because the propositional content of the experience conflicts with W. [...] The propositional content of our experience could, after all, be false. Rather, it is the existence of the experience that conflicts with W: W is a possibility in which the subject is not having experience E. Else we would need to tell some fishy story of how the experience has some sort of infallible, ineffable, purely phenomenal propositional content...' (Lewis 1996, p.553). The elisions in the quote are where Lewis appeals to memory (the context is not just the increment of evidence in diachronic update, but the subject's total evidence). He also suggests that certain sensory faculties might not issue in *experiences* but rather spontaneous judgements—and suggests that memory works like this—and in such cases we might conditionalize not just on the fact we are undergoing such-and-such experience, but on the fact that we

There are parallels between the individuation of update-propositions and the Heddenic individuation of options. You might have expected the following: our options are things like putting one foot in front of another, raising my arm, drinking from the cup, etc. But on Hedden's account, those are not the relata of rationalization; rather, the relata of rationalization are certain mental states which have those behaviours as contents. There is a parallel move here, where the epistemic update becomes a relation to a fact about a perceptual state, not a relation to its content.

9.6 Which Perceptions are Evidence?

Here are three descriptions of my experience upon viewing a banana:

1. I have a perceptual experience with a rich analogue content: a yellow-crescent shaped object mottled with brown, shaded in various ways, set against a variegated backdrop.
2. I have a perceptual experience as of a yellow crescent-shaped thing to my front.
3. I have a perceptual experience as of a banana.

Neither (1) nor (3) slot into the theory as stated very well. In the case of (1), the trouble is that I can't possibly incorporate into my beliefs all the rich detail of my perceptual experience. For example, I take it that my perception represents the banana as having a definite number of brown spots—say, eighteen visible ones. But I can't take that in at a glance. So, it seems, when we give a full specification of the content p of (1), it will be false to say that I updated on the information that I had a perception with the content p—the details are immediately lost.[17]

Description (3) suffers from a different problem. Being a banana is not an intrinsic property of a thing. Something is a banana only if derives from a certain giant herb that exists on Earth. Perhaps duplicates of bananas could grow on some Twin Earth, where they would be the fruit of some other quite different species. Inhabitants of Earth have experiences as of bananas.

---

have spontaneously formed such-and-such judgement. Such adjustments could be implemented in the current model too.

[17] Compare Chisholm (1942).

Inhabitants of Twin Earth have experiences as of twin-bananas. It follows from the fact that I have a perception with the content that *that's a banana* that I live on Earth rather than on Twin Earth. Now, it might well be that I have perceptions with this kind of natural-kind high-level content. But rationality can't require that I become certain of them, just in virtue of having them. After all, my friends may have been slowly convincing me for years that I have been kidnapped and taken to Twin Earth, so that what I'm seeing are twin bananas. I laugh off their attempts, but some small gnawing doubt remains. I can't resolve the doubts simply by looking at a banana and conditionalizing on the resulting high-level content.[18]

So part of this story about rationalization must be a commitment to a level of intermediate-level content—content which is selective (so doesn't include all the detail of (1)) but low-level (so not getting us into the kind of trouble (3) does). Something like content that involves constellations of traditional primary and secondary qualities looks fit for the job. I take it that perceptual states like (1) do exist, and I have no reason to deny that there are also genuinely perceptual states with content like (3)—but the epistemological role of perception, if it to work as described, crucially relies on (2) being available to be updated upon. I presuppose, going forward, that type (2) facts have a distinctive role in mediating between perception and belief, and thus that in tracing Sally's path through space and time, we've earned a right to identify those of her perceptual states that play the role of 'perceptual evidence', and which therefore form the basis for Radical Interpretation.[19] The demand on a metaphysics of source intentionality is that it

---

[18] This problem is perhaps resistable. One might insist on a 'narrow' specification of content of experience, shared by earthlings and twin earthlings; and Jeffrey conditionalization might also be wheeled in to model the update: a partition of different possible experiences according to my prior probabilities of whether I'm in earth or twin earth.

[19] Here's what I suspect we should say: rationalization, in the general case, will not only specify a relation between belief change and a proposition/some propositions on which one updates and directly incorporates into belief. Bayesian conditionalization is not the whole of the story, even if it is a crucial component. Rather, rationalization will relate belief-change to the full analogue perceptual state (i.e. type (1) facts), without assuming the whole of that fact is taken up as belief. An extra parameter is needed: the rational constraint on belief change is that one updates on those aspects of one's experience to which one stands in the right functionally characterized 'uptake' relation. In that case, if q is the full content of Sally's experience, then the interpretation of Sally will be constrained by a complex condition: for Sally to undergo a rational belief change, then there must be some p such that (i) Sally changes her beliefs by updating on the fact she perceived p; (ii) p is entailed by q (iii) Sally is standing in the right functional relation to p—e.g. attending to the p-aspect of her experience. Element (i) will be where Bayesian conditionalization will come in. Element (ii) keeps us honest by requiring that the story doesn't go beyond facts given in experience. Element (iii) will be tailored in different ways to different perceptual architectures.

ground the representation content of these particular perceptual states since they are needed to get the story rolling. Assigning content to higher-level perceptual states can be deferred to a later stage of the story (compare the assignment of content to planning states vs. low-level action guiding states in sections above).

9.7 Conclusion

This chapter has argued that Radical Interpretation needs to appeal to representational facts in its 'basis'. Raw behavioural and facts about sensory stimulation will not do, since they don't plausibly characterize the relata of the relevant kind of rationalization. Further, I've identified two hypotheses about what the relata of rationalization are, once we allow ourselves to appeal to certain low-level representational facts. The targets of first-layer representational facts are set. If we can provide a non-representational metaphysical account for low-level action-guiding states, and for low-level perceptual states, then belief and desire content will have been grounded in perceptual and action-guiding content, which in turn reduces to the non-representational. The final chapter takes up that task.

10

Laying the Foundations

The last chapter characterized the sort of representational facts that feature in the basis of Radical Interpretation. The job now is to look at what account we might give of the metaphysical basis of this kind of source intentionality.

In this chapter, I co-opt and build on Karen Neander's (2017) account of sensory/perceptual representation. This is an account within a tradition often contrasted with Radical Interpretation—a teleosemantic metaphysics of representation. But since Neander explicitly presents her theory just as an account of the intentionality of perception, she is officially silent on the grounding of representation of belief, desire, and language. In this her theory contrasts sharply with those, for example, of Dretske (1981, 1988) and Millikan (1984, 1989a, 1989b), whose accounts are developed with an eye to more general application—generality that comes at a considerable cost in complexity.

Neander's account won't be enough if we can't provide a story about the representational content of action-guiding states. So after presenting Neander's account—which I adopt wholesale—I will show how to generalize this to the case of action-guiding states.

Neander's account appeals to functions and to causation. In adopting and extending her account of source-intentionality, I acquire those commitments. The final section of this chapter takes a final look at these, the ultimate basis for representation on my three-layer story.

10.1 Neander's Theory Gives us an Account of the Intentionality of Perception

I begin the task of reducing source intentionality by reviewing a teleosemantic account of sensory-perceptual content due to Neander. Her story comprises two steps. The first is the following:

A sensory-perceptual representation R in sensory-perceptual system S has [E occurs] as a candidate-content iff S has the function to produce R-type events in response to E-type events (as such).

The Metaphysics of Representation. J. Robert G. Williams, Oxford University Press (2019).
© J. Robert G. Williams.
DOI: 10.1093/oso/9780198850205.001.0001

So let's unpack this. The key notion here is the appeal to the function of something within a certain system. It's this appeal that makes the account part of the teleosemantic tradition. There's a lot that could be said about what grounds facts of the form '*x* has function *y* in system *z*'. All we need, for now, is the assumption that these are grounded prior to, and independently of, any representational facts (Neander will also require that the eventual story makes functions, at least in our own cases, naturalistically respectable features, but as I mentioned back in the introduction, I don't operate under that particular constraint). Still, the non-representational gloss on functions does rule out some candidate theories. For example, a theological account of functions, whereby the function of *x* is to *y* in *z* iff God designed *x* to *y* in *z*, is out, and more subtly, a stance-relative account of functions, whereby the function of *x* in *y* in *z* for a theorist *t* depends on theorist's *t*'s projects and aims, is also out. Neander herself (1991a, b) favours an etiological theory of functions, whereby (roughly) the function of *x* in *y* is *z* iff *x*'s in z were evolutionary selected to do *y*. The details matter, and I will come back to them later. But for now, I'll be treating functions as a working primitive.

Neander's proposal is that once we see Sally's sensory-perceptual system as containing states with a variety of functions, it is 'response functions' that hold the key to analysing perceptual content. The system is functioning 'as designed' when a certain worldly event-type causes a specific state-type to be tokened within it. Consider the following non-biological example. Runners passing a checkpoint throw a tab with their number into a bucket. The system is functioning 'as designed' when runner number 150 passing the checkpoint causes there to be a tab with 150 inscribed upon it in the bucket (the causal mechanism is the runner throwing a random tab from those on a loop on their belt into the bucket). Of course, things can go wrong (the runner can forget to throw the tab, they can miss the bucket, they may have been given a wrongly inscribed tab at the start), but those would be cases of the system malfunctioning.

Designed systems like this, at least, have these response functions. In such cases, it's very tempting to think that it's in virtue of the response function that the contents of the bucket records or represents the runners who have passed. Neander's contention is that biological systems with etiological functions work analogously. Because the grounding of the relevant bio-logical functions are representation-free, this promises a way of grounding such representation in non-representational facts.

One famous challenge to naturalistic theories of representation (especially perceptual representation) was to separate the items in the causal history of an episode of perception into those which figure in the content of the perception, and those that do not. For example, a red cube observed from a given angle causes a certain pattern of retinal stimulation, which in turn causes a certain state R to obtain in the sensory-perceptual system. The perception has a content that concerns red cubes, not retinal stimulations. Yet it's perfectly true that part of a well-functioning sensory-perceptual system is that it responds to retinal stimulations of a certain pattern by producing R. It's also true that that the well-functioning system produces R in response to red cubes at the given angle—indeed, within the system, the response to retinal stimulation is the means by which it responds to 'distal' red cubes. But we had better not analyse perceptual content as anything to which the perceptual system has a function to produce states in response to, or we'll include proximal and distal events together. This is why the gloss above talks of 'candidate contents' not 'contents' simpliciter. Neander (2017, p. 222) appeals to an asymmetric means-end relation in the functioning of the system to narrow things down. Here is my reconstruction of her proposal:

> Among candidate contents E1, E2, let E1 > E2 iff in S, the function to produce R-type events as a response to E2 is a means to produce R-type events as a response to E1 but not vice versa.
>
> The content of R is the >-maximal candidate content (if there are multiple >-maximal contents, then the content of R is indeterminate between them).

Suppose that I perceive a red cube to my right, and suppose that the vehicle of this representation is a single state of my sensory-perceptual system (presumably a state produced after a fair degree of processing has gone on). What grounds the fact that that token state represents what it does? On this account, it is because in the evolutionary history of this biological system, states of that type were produced in response to the presence of red cubes to the right of the perceiver, and this feature was selected for. The process by which the states were produced includes intermediary objects and properties, and the sensory-perceptual state was produced in response to those no less than it was in response to the red cube (perhaps the intermediary states include three mutually orthogonal red surfaces orientated towards the subject, a certain pattern of retinal stimulation in the subject, etc.). However, the function to respond to such intermediaries is a mere means to the end of responding to the presence of *red cubes to the right*.

I will be using Neander's theory as my account of the first-layer intentionality in perception. When we see appeal, in Radical Interpretation, to rationalizing dispositions to act given the experiences undergone, these 'experiences' are to be cashed out in terms of teleoinformational contents. But we needed more than just experience: we needed action-guiding states under intentional descriptions. The next section shows how we can secure these in parallel fashion.

10.2 We Can Extend This Account to Ground the Intentionality of Action-guiding States

Neander gives a theory of the representational contents of sensory-perceptual systems. She is explicit that this account is aimed to ground 'original intentionality' in contrast to 'derived intentionality', where:

> [D]erived intentionality [is defined] as intentionality derived (constitutively) from other independently existing intentionality, and original intentionality [is defined as] intentionality not (constitutively) so derived.
>
> (Neander 2017, p.9)

Neander's view is that original intentionality belongs at least to sensory-perceptual states '...and might only belong to them'. However, I want to argue that certain other states have almost exactly this sort of original or source intentionality.

I will assume that our agents' cognitive architecture includes an intentional-motor system, which takes as input representations from a central cognitive system (intentions to do something). I assume it has as output some states to which we may have limited or no conscious access, but which control the precise behaviour needed to implement the intention. I suggest that original intentionality belongs also to these intentional-motor states, and the metaphysics of this sort of representation is again teleoinformational. Indeed, it will be a mirror-image of the story of the grounding of representation in sensory-perceptual states—the differences traceable simply to the distinct directions of fit of perception and intention.

I offer the following:

> An intentional-motor representation R in intentional-motor system M has [E occurs] as a candidate-content iff M has the function to produce E-type events (as such) as a result of an R-type state occurring.

This time, representation is analysed as a matter of a production-function rather than a response-function, but this simply amounts to reversing the direction of causation that appeared in the account of perceptual content.

We can illustrate this again with a non-biological example. Every shopper in a store has a half-ticket-stub, and as their goods are brought up from storage, the other half of their ticket is hung up on a washing line in front of the desk. The system is functioning 'as designed' when hanging up half of ticket number 150 causes the shopper with ticket number 150 to move forward and collect their goods. (The causal mechanism is the shopholder collecting the goods, bringing them to the desk, and hanging up the matching ticket.) This is a designed system where certain states, namely tickets hanging on the line, have production functions.

A perceptual state has many causal antecedents, and many of these causal antecedents are intermediaries that produce the state 'by design'. Just so, an intentional-motor state has many causal consequences, many of which produce the state 'by design'. An intention to hail the taxi (or even: to raise and wave one's arm) will produce motor states controlling the fine details of the way the arm is raised and waved, as well as the bodily motion of the arm waving and finally the taxi being summoned. The more proximal states produced 'by design' are means to an end: producing the most distal state. To capture this, we mirror the account given in the case of perception:

> Among candidate contents E1, E2 of an intentional-motor state R, let E1 > E2 iff in S, the function to produce E1-type events as a result of an R-type state occurring is a means to the end of producing E2-type events as a result of an R-type state occurring, but not vice versa.
>
> The content of R is the >-minimal candidate content (if there are multiple >-minimal contents, then the content of R is indeterminate between them).

Suppose that I intend to grasp a green sphere to my right, and suppose that the vehicle of this representation is a single state of my intentional-motor system (a state whose formation will trigger a good deal of further processing before bodily motion occurs). What grounds the fact that that token state represents what it does? On this account, it is because in the evolutionary history of this biological system, states of that type produced a hand prehending and attaching itself to some green sphere to the right of the perceiver—and this feature was selected for. Though there were other causal consequences of that states that were also selected for, they were selected as a means to the end of producing right-green-sphere-graspings.

I will be using this teleoinformational account as my treatment of the first-layer intentionality of action. So when we see appeal, in Radical Interpretation, to rationalizing dispositions to act given the experiences undergone, the 'actions' are to be cashed out in terms of teleoinformational contents.

The focus here has been the contents of certain mental states—intentions, motor states, and the like. Typical actions (raising an arm, hailing a taxi, etc.) in part consist of physical movements of the body, so I haven't yet quite earned the right to get from Sally-as-a-physical-system to Sally-as-acting-in-the-world. Further, there's nothing in the account above that guarantees that states with content grounded in this way are personal-level and rationalizable, rather than subpersonal and arational. The exact prehension of my hand as it reaches for a cup is controlled, presumably, by states of my nervous system, and these states may have a function to produce the subtle movements. They are representational states in the current sense. But these details are not chosen by me or under my rational control. I don't, for example, believe that by moving my fingers *just so* I will grasp the cup, and hence form a person-level intention to move my fingers like that. Rather, I intend to grasp the cup, and rely on downstream processing to take care of the fine details. So just as in the case of perception, we have secured representational resources, but there's work to do in shaping the raw material of first-layer intentionality into a form where it can feed into the second-layer story about Radical Interpretation that I am putting forward.

10.3 Perceptual and Action-guiding States with the Right Causal Role Rationalize

In the last two sections, I have presented an account of the representational properties of sensory-perceptual states on the one hand, and intentional-action-guiding states on the other, by appeal to biological function and causation. Perceptual and action-guiding states in normal conditions, and absent malfunction, will respectively be brought about by/will bring about the states of affairs that are their contents. The same cannot be said for beliefs in general. The fact that *a majority of the population supports the monarchy* isn't itself part of the causal history of my belief that this is so. I form this belief from testimony, which is ultimately rooted in an inference based on sampling individual members of the population—and the views of individual members support the generalization, but are not caused by it. So in general, and without abnormality or malfunction, a belief isn't *brought about by/produced/caused* by its content specifically. Likewise, my desire (even my plan) to *establish a republic* does not have the function to bring about the satisfaction of its content. An inability to find means to implement a plan or desire, or false beliefs about effective means, does not require malfunction or abnormality—it is the human condition. Perceptual and action-guiding states are the points at which our mind most immediately reflects or shapes the external environment, and this makes them uniquely suited to the treatment just laid out. My conjecture, of course, is that we need quite different treatment of the representation in belief and desire.

In the previous chapter, I talked about the kind of facts about perceptual and action-guiding representation that are part of the basis of Radical Interpretation. In the case of perception, I targeted low-level but selective perceptual states—for example, the visual perception that there is a yellow crescent-shaped object to the front. This level of perceptual representation contrasts with much more fine-grained 'analogue' contents that would include, e.g. information about the exact mottling of the object's surface. In the case of action-guiding states, I targeted low-level contents once again—as in a decision to reach out with my arm, grasp the object to the front of me, and bring it to my mouth. The states of this kind that we can form in a given decision situation are our options in that situation.

These kind of states are good candidates for the story of the last two sections. But the story of the last two sections doesn't only ground the content of those states. Subpersonal states of the visual system, as well as the person-level states involved in the finer-grained perception of the mot-tled surface of the banana, will have the function to be brought about by their content (many of Neander's examples are of subpersonal states). Likewise, the subpersonal motor states that are triggered by a person's decisions to reach out and grasp, which control the fine-grained prehension of the fingers, have a function to bring about states of the world that will therefore, by the story given, constitute their content. So we do not establish the basis of Radical Interpretation simply by pointing to an array of repre-sentational facts caught up in some way or other in perception and action. The basis for Radical Interpretation must be selected from among that array. My proposal is that this be done on the basis of functional/causal role. The relevant perceptual states are the terminal states of the sensory-perceptual system which are direct inputs to belief-systems (themselves identified by causal role). The relevant action-guiding states are direct outputs of belief and desire systems, and trigger further motor control processing. It is states that occupy these causal roles which are then the basis for rationalization in Radical Interpretation, and those states, say I, have their content fixed by the teleoinformational story of this chapter.

I emphasized perceptual and action-guiding states with low-level content, e.g. configurations of objects in the immediate environment with observable primary and secondary qualities, or movements of limbs. The reason for this is to keep (at least initially) to cases where it is most plausible that the states in questions have the function to produce/be produced by their content. There are some fascinating questions about how and whether this can be extended to high-level content—perceptions or action-guiding states whose content involves natural or artificial kinds (banana, water, train). On this turns the question of whether a perception that *there is a banana in front of me* or an action-guiding-intention *to board the train* can be grounded in the way described.

It's important to distinguish two questions here. The first is whether states with high-level content can play the epistemological/practical role of rationalizing belief-change or being rationalized by beliefs/desires. The second is whether, if they do play that epistemological/practical role, the needed content can be grounded via the teleoinformational theory of the last two sections.

There is a vulnerability here for Radical Interpretation. Argue that states with high-level content play the epistemological/practical role, and that they can't be grounded in the fashion described here, and the teleoinformational foundations will not be an adequate basis for Radical Interpretation.

However, the story of the last chapter had it that such high-level states were not relata of rationalization in the relevant sense, which means that to exploit this vulnerability, one will need to pinpoint what goes wrong in that discussion. The lack of a role for high-level content in rational update and choice is quite compatible with a variety of senses in which there may be genuine high-level perceptual content. High-level content might make a difference to perceptual phenomenology. It might influence the aspects of low-level perceptual content we (are able to) attend to and so update upon. And it might feature in informative summaries of low-level content that allow us to convey to each other what we have seen or heard.[1] So the

---

[1] As sketched earlier, it's certainly possible that to update by conditionalization on the fact that one has perceived such-and-such low-level content is formally identical to updating by Jeffrey conditionalization (suitably weighted) on such-and-such high-level content. The weights in question would be fixed by the prior beliefs and low-level content.

Bayesian position I am working with isn't committed to the claim that there is no high-level content to perception, strictly construed, though it is of course compatible with that claim. Instead, it just says that such perceptual states aren't the immediate objects of rationalization. (Analogous remarks apply to action-guiding states with high-level content.)

On the second question, in order for perceptual or action-guiding states to have high-level content, it would have to be the function of a state, e.g. a decision to board the train, to bring about this state of affairs: that I board the train. There is no principled reason why a system couldn't include a state with the function to bring about exactly this state of affairs. We could, for example, design an artificial system where the press of a button led to a trapdoor opening underneath the presser's feet which tipped them down a slide into a waiting train. Pressing the button would have the function to bring about train-boarding. As this case illustrates, a state within a system doesn't need 'conceptual structure' involving the high-level concept 'train' in order to possess the content in question. Even if, in our own case, action-guiding states involve mentalese sentences and contain our concept for 'train', the content of the state as a whole could still be fixed by the fact that it has the function to bring about a train-boarding state of affairs (a story that doesn't mention the concept or its content at all).[2]

The main challenge, however, is to say whether *biological* states have a function to bring about high-level content. For example, one account of the functions of biological states appeals to the way states of that type worked in evolutionary history. But the evolutionary history of humans didn't involve interaction with trains. Nor did it involve interaction with natural kinds that were not present in the evolutionary environment (kiwi fruits weren't present in the neighbourhood of my ancestors, for example). Once one starts appealing to contents that are not part of the human condition, one starts loading weight on the theory of function, and this is something of a theoretical gamble. That's why I've presented an account on which low-level content involving primary and secondary qualities of medium-sized dry goods and movements of body parts have played the starring role.

Despite this, it's still possible that high-level contents of perception and action-guiding states have the function to be produced by/produce their

---

[2] Only if you add the assumption that the contents of action-guiding states involving concepts are metaphysically grounded in the contents of those concepts, would there be a tension with my story. And perhaps the archetypical metaphysical manoeuvre of the radical interpreter is to deny and then reverse such putative orders of explanation.

content. I myself would like a metaphysics of biological function that was able to underwrite *acquired* functions as well as innate ones. The terminal *person-level* action-guiding state can, I think, can change as we acquire skills. This can happen either as we learn to put together sequences that produce an effect while letting subpersonal systems fill in the elements of the sequence (running at high speed, with control, down a rough scree-slope), or as we learn to attend to and control individual elements of what was once a single action (the foot-plant, cadence, and stride-length of an individual running stride). Likewise, in perception, one might acquire perceptual skills to recognize patterns in one's environment—e.g. the changes in colour in vegetation that indicate boggy ground, or the linear variation in shading in grass that indicates a runner's trod. A theory of functions, I think, should underwrite ways in which states can acquire functions through skill-acquisition. If that path is open, the main *principled* barrier to high-level content being grounded in this way is overcome.

10.4 The Basis of the Basis

Linguistic content is grounded, via convention, in the mental content of belief and desire. The representational content of belief and desire is grounded, via normativity, in the low-level content of sensory-perceptual and intentional-motor states. The whole structure is grounded by functions to respond to, or produce, certain states of the world. In these closing sections, I'll examine the metaphysics of these ultimate bases: the functions themselves.

Here is a warm-up case. A watch can be used to keep time. An exact physical duplicate of the watch can be used to keep time just as well as the original, even if the duplicate is created by statistical mechanical fluke or lightning strike in a swamp, rather than through a careful design and manu-facture process.[3] A broken watch can't be used to keep time until it is fixed.

---

[3] The miraculous creation by lightning strike evokes the swampman case of (Davidson 1987) which is itself discussed later in this section. For the kind of statistical mechanical flukes I have in mind, see e.g. Carroll (2017) on Boltzmann brains. It should be noted that in the latter case, serious physical theories of the actual world seem to entail the actual existence of replicas of watches and people, so unless (as Carroll argues) these theories themselves should be dismissed because they are not stably believable, then we shouldn't assert too hastily that these cases are recherché possibilities.

We might introduce a notion of 'timekeeping device' in a way that was tied to the current capacity of a thing to keep time. Then the watch, a sand glass on my shelf, and the swamp-watch would all be timekeeping devices. So construed, the broken watch would not count as a timekeeping device. This would be a bit of a departure from the ordinary way we use those words. Alternatively, we might introduce a notion of 'timekeeping device' in a way that was tied to the design and manufacture: the broken watch was designed and made *for* keeping time. Then the watch and sand-glass as well as the broken watch would be timekeeping devices, but the swamp-watch would not be. This again involves a departure from the ordinary sense of the words, since prima facie a swamp-watch, irrespective of the circumstances of its creation, would count as a timekeeping device.

With just the resources to hand, there's an obvious third candidate notion of 'timekeeping device' to consider. This is the following: a timekeeping device is something with the capacity to keep time, or at least, something that was designed and manufactured in order to have that capacity. On this characterization, things that have the capacity to keep time get counted as timekeeping devices straight away. For things that lack the capacity to keep time, one has to look to their history to determine classification. This is a definition that is disjunctive in form, but it is far from a 'disjunctive' definition in the sense that suggests an arbitrary gerrymander, since the disjuncts stand in a tight relation to one another.

With this in mind, let's turn back to the case at hand: the appeal to functions in the teleoinformation treatment of source intentionality of this chapter. Sensory-perceptual states have the function to be produced in response to such and such. Intention-motor states have the function to produce so-and-so. What does it take for then to have 'the function' in this sense?

Here are two broad traditions of understanding function-talk. In one corner, there are those who emphasize intrinsic features of cognition: the details of the way that Sally's perceptual or motor systems work and allow her to make her behaviour depend on the way the environment is. In a bit more detail, 'Cummins functions' are to be fixed by looking to a functional explanation of how a system overall does what it does—if the capacity of a sensory-perceptual state to be produced by a state of the world is appealed to in such an explanation, then it the state has that as its function.[4]

---

[4] Cummins (1975). A recent defender of this style of view is Davies (2000), who argues that etiological functions are simply a special case.

In the other corner, we have 'etiological' theorists, who link the 'proper functions' of biological systems and states to historical facts about evolutionary selection. Neander (1991a, p.174) characterizes the view as follows:

> It is the/a proper function of an item (X) of an organism (O) to do that which items of X's type did to contribute to the inclusive fitness of O's ancestors, and which caused the genotype, of which X is the phenotypic expression, to be selected by natural selection.[5]

This is not the place to analyse in great depth the comparative merits of the two approaches—a topic that would take me well beyond representation to consider functions and teleology in general. I do, however, want to indicate my favoured line on a pair of issues that are prominent in the discussions.

The first is a problem for deploying Cummins functions within a teleoinformational account like the one above. It struggles to allow for a phenomenon that certainly seems possible: misrepresentations that are induced by malfunctions. The most compelling examples would involve cases where a whole state type functions in an unusual way, as a result e.g. of a brain lesion (the Cummins theorist can allow for token malfunctions so long as functioning is the rule). So e.g. consider synaesthesia produced by brain damage, in which red experiences may—with external conditions perfectly standard—be produced in response to square-shaped things—and let's suppose that at the same time, damage to the retina produces colour-blindness, so that coloured surfaces no longer prompt red experiences. The squares, it seems, are still being represented as red. The same goes for action-guiding states and their contents. In cases of paralysis, action-guiding states will no longer lead to the bodily movements that (one would think) it is their function to produce. But in the absence of these state-types playing a role in the explanation of actual functioning, they will not have Cummins functions. So it will not be the case that the red experiences have the Cummins function to be produced by an instances of a certain colour, nor that a decision to raise one's arm has the Cummins function to produce one's arm rising. But that is a counterexample to the thesis that the contents of such states are to be identified with what they have the function to produce/be produced by, under the present gloss on 'function'.

---

[5] See also Wright (1973), Millikan (1984,1989b),

The second is a problem for deploying etiological functions within a teleoinformational account like the one above. Consider again the creation of items by a statistical-mechanical fluke within a Boltzmann bubble, or by a freak lightning strike. Not just duplicates of watches, but duplicates of biological creatures like you or I could be so formed (Davidson's 'swampman'). Lacking an evolutionary history, Swamp Sally's brain states will have no proper functions, if those are understood in the etiological theorist's sense. In the current context, this implies that she perceives nothing and intends nothing, and because of the way that belief and desire are grounded in such states, she has no mental life. Given that leading teleoinformational theorists, such as Neander and Millikan, embrace the etiological theory and do accept the Swamp Sally verdicts, I could follow them and be no worse off, dialectically. But I can't myself shake the feeling that this is simply a counterexample to the combination of teleoinformational and etiological accounts. Papineau (2001) attributes a particularly convincing version of the worry to Eilert Sundt-Ohlson: insofar as mental representation matters for wider theory and practice, and in particular moral standing, then denying that the living, breathing Swamp Sally has perceptions, plans, beliefs and desires, will ramify. Surely eating Swamp Sally would be wrong—but we lose the obvious explanation of this if we follow this line.[6] And it's really hard to see how any purely etiological theory will avoid counterexamples of this sort, given the central role given to the extrinsic feature of 'selection'—even if not understood along strict evolutionary lines, the whole idea of the set-up relies on features that are not present in Swamp Sally.

The discussion of timekeeping devices suggests a way forward. That gave us an exactly parallel tension between a pure classification based on intrinsic workings of the items under investigation (which fails to deal adequately for 'broken' or malfunctioning cases) and a pure classification based on historical features (which deals nicely with 'broken' cases but fails to carve the obvious distinctions among accidental duplicates). Since the counterexamples in each case are a problem of *lack of coverage*—non-necessity rather

---

[6] Papineau (2001) suggests that to deal with swamp person cases, we should appeal to the role-realizer distinction. Having something that plays the belief-role is what matters for morality, say, but the core etiological teleosemantic claim, according to Papineau, is about what realizes that role in the actual world. Unfortunately, he does not say much about how to understand the idea of a 'belief role', where that encompasses the role of something having a particular *content*—I do not see how to apply the standard functionalist machinery to this case. However, the idea of the etiological claim being just one way among several of making it true that our subject is in a belief state with specific content is something that Papineau's idea shares with the disjunctive proposal below.

than insufficiency of the criteria—the obvious thought was to pool the explications. I propose to do the same for functions.

So the pattern that I suggest is the following:

An item *s* has uber-function to F (within a system with S which has the capacity to C) iff either *s* has a Cummins-function to F (relative to S/C) or *s* has the etiological-function to have that Cummins-function to F

(relative to S/C).

Just as with the pooled characterization of timekeeping devices, this is disjunctive in form, but by no means gerrymandered—since the disjuncts are intimately related.[7] The characterization covers both Swamp Sally (in virtue of her perceptual and motor states satisfying the first disjunct) and actual cases of malfunctioning systems (where the second disjunct kicks in).

Let's consider a different case. Let Suzy be the colour-blind synaesthete discussed earlier, whose perceptual states ('red experiences') have their functions in virtue of evolutionary history rather than current activity. Swamp Suzy, then, can duplicate Suzy precisely, but the states that are triggered by squares—which in Suzy and us represent the colour red—will not have the function to be produced by red things when they occur in Swamp Suzy, since that is no part of the way that Swamp Suzy actually functions, nor is it groundable in her lineage (since she lacks a lineage). But at this point, I don't see this as a counterexample at all. It's of course natural to treat Swamp Suzy as if she were human, and so understand her perceptual architecture as a deviation from the human norm. But one could equally see her as a deviation from some other merely possible creatures for whom chromatic quale are systematically produced by shapes, where it would be not natural at all to think that such experiences represent certain properties of the textures of surfaces. So the verdict of the overarching theory seem perfectly plausible in this case.

Let me say what I have and haven't done. I haven't cracked open the metaphysics of functions, or defended either a detailed version of the Cummins function view, or the etiological view, which are components of what I am suggesting.[8] An assumption of what I have said about source

---

[7] Millikan's notion of function is already disjunctive, in an equally non-arbitrary way, to allow for both 'direct' and 'derived' functions.

[8] One feature of the Cummins-style account—which Neander (2017) highlights—is that things have Cummins-functions relative to a specific capacity of the containing system, and on many ways of developing the account (e.g. Davies 2000), this is glossed as depending on

intentionality is that these two approaches are not holed below the water line for reasons quite other than those which I have discussed (the same could be said about many others of my working primitives—every project has its starting points). What I have done is motivate an overall shape of theory that will avoid both counterexamples from swamp people and from malfunction.

Let me end by sketching the relevance of this to one of the issues about the nature of functions that I flagged above, concerning functions in the context of skilful action and perception. Concentrating on action-guiding states, let's suppose that skill works like this: that we internalize the capacity to intervene at the personal level either at a more or less distal stage of processing. E.g. the skilful runner or cellist can decide to descend the hill fast, or play an arpeggio, and delegate the implementation to subpersonal states, while the learner has to attend to each step or finger movement. But equally, we may gain the potential to exercise person-level control over more fine-grained aspects of an action which the unskilful person is forced to delegate to subpersonal states. But since the sequence of movements that constitute playing an arpeggio is not plausibly selected for that purpose in evolutionary history, if I relied on the straight etiological account as set out above, there would be difficulties.[9] On the other hand, the Cummins-style treatment, with its focus on explaining current capacities, should face no new problems in covering acquired functions of this kind. The overarching account I've been suggesting should inherit the strengths of the Cummins-style account, and it is not clear to me that there's any pressure to adjust the etiological theory to cope with such cases—that is motivated only if we imagine a certain state acquires a function to produce some skilful behaviour, and can *retain* that function even if the state-type never produces that behaviour. But the most natural description of such cases is that the relevant skill is lost— that the state which once had the function to produce the behaviour no longer does so. So it seems to me that the overarching theory I have

---

theorist's projects and interests—hardly appropriate for a reductive theory of content! It seems to me that the appeal to theorist's interests is easily sidestepped, since we can simply build our analysis of perceptual/action-guiding content not on the notion of function simpliciter, but function-relative-to-C, where C is the relevant capacity of perceptual/action systems. A remaining challenge, though, is to spell out what C is without mentioning representation in the specification. This is the kind of issue that I'm forswearing here!

[9] Millikan (1984, 1989b) introduces a class of 'derived functions' which are possessed by items which are produced by systems that have etiological functions in the original sense. This allows her to account for states with functions even where those states themselves do not figure in evolutionary history, so long as they have the right ties to systems that do.

suggested fits neatly with the kind of malleable view of the action-guiding and perceptual states that form the basis of Radical Interpretation that I put forward in the main text.

10.5 Conclusion

In the previous chapter, I identified the facts that form the basis of Radical Interpretation: certain perceptual states, and certain action-guiding states. In this chapter, I've advocated a teleoinformational theory of the metaphysical grounding of such states. The working primitives in this account are the functions of states of biological systems, and causation. Both of these are features of the world that are independent of representation—even if there were no representations, hearts would have the function to circulate oxygenated blood around the body, and the expansion of ice would cause the splintering of rocks. Put together these two non-representational kinds of fact, however, and we get the source intentionality we need to run Radical Interpretation.

Causation and function are the ultimate grounds for representational content, on this story. The last thing I've done is to propose a way of combining two existing theories of functions that avoids what I see as the problematic features of both. I do not claim to have given you a full metaphysical story about causation, nor a full metaphysical story about functions. A theory of representation is part of, but not coextensive with, the theory of everything.

Overall Conclusions

Scope and Limits

All three layers of representation described in the manifesto are in place. Part III started from functions and causes, assumed to be part of the pre-representational, natural world, and follows the teleosemanticists in using them to identify a primordial kind of 'source' intentionality. This lays the basis for running the metaphysics of belief and desire content explored in Part I and inflected and extended in Part II. The story is not obviously naturalistic at these later levels, since essential appeal is made to normative facts in the transition from source intentionality to belief and desire. But it is still a metaphysics on which the representational is grounded in the non-representational.

In the conclusion to Part I, I suggested a number of ways in which to generalize the project carried therein, of predicting and explaining local patterns of reference on the basis of Radical Interpretation (and assumptions about cognitive architecture, and first-order claims about how we ought to believe and when we ought to act and feel). We might do the same at a larger scale here. I see the three layers discussed here as a common core, but there are plenty of representational phenomena that await discussion—photographs and memories, to take just two. One such generalization is given in the first chapter of Part II, where I discussed the generalization of the convention-based story about linguistic representation from cases where the sentences express mental states of belief, to where they express mental states of other kinds (plans, conditional beliefs, uncertainty, and the like).

I've covered the representational features of individuals, human beings like you or I or Sally. One question is whether the metaphysics generalizes beyond this, and could be used to understand what it takes for other kinds of entities to believe or desire this or that. One obvious target case is collective entities: from small interactive social groups to whole nations. We have a common practice of using belief and desire talk to describe such entities—talking of what a nation desires, or what a committee believes and has collectively decided. Radical Interpretation is an attractive way to start

The Metaphysics of Representation. J. Robert G. Williams, Oxford University Press (2019).
© J. Robert G. Williams.
DOI: 10.1093/oso/9780198850205.001.0001

thinking about what might make such attributions true—providing a continuity with the case of individuals, so that it is no mystery why we use the same terms for belief/desire in each case, while resting on a theory that does not itself appeal to factors obviously missing from the group case—nations do not have anything like a group brain![1] Understanding more deeply what is involved in the individual case is a prerequisite for evaluating such generalizations. For example, it is far from clear what story to give about source intentionality for collectives—nations or committees don't have visual or action systems with inner states in the way that you or I or Sally do. Yet still, if the story is to be run, some account of those raw materials must be provided.[2] And if it is right, as suggested above, that the expression of thoughts in a public medium of communication is not only grounded in a prior level of mental content, but also inflects that very content, then it suggests that thinking about the ways that different kinds of groups do or do not collectively express their attitudes would be crucial.

I've told an integrated story about the foundations of (individual) perceptual and agential, mental, and linguistic content. Various elements of this story might be pulled apart and replaced or recombined. If the teleosemantic theory of experience and action is not acceptable, something else might do the job—I mentioned but then set aside Pautz's primitivism. If linguistic conventions aren't where it's at, for theorizing linguistic meaning, we can go looking for other accounts of linguistic representation grounded on mental content. Throughout my discussions of the detailed predictions of Radical Interpretation, I was relying on first-order normative theory, and these predictions should be responsive to best theory in philosophy of logic, in epistemology, in first-order moral theory, and beyond. Like a slot machine, you can hold fixed many parts of my story, while spinning others, so long as you keep an eye on dependencies between layers and theses, where they exist. As well as being my own best guess at how all this fits together, I would hope that it provides a baseline for others to devise and explore their own variations.

---

[1] See List and Pettit (2011, chapters 1 and 2) and Tollefsen (2015). Tollefsen endorses a Dennettian 'intentional stance' treatment of group belief ascriptions. See the discussion in the preface for the relation, or lack of it, between that approach and the more straightforwardly metaphysical project of this monograph.

[2] One option is to look to the literature on collective intention and action, especially where that is characterized in terms of individual intention (Bratman 2014—see also discussion in List and Pettit, 2011).

Bibliography

Block, Ned (1978). Troubles with Functionalism. *Minnesota Studies in the Philosophy of Science* 9: 261–325.

Boyd, Richard (1979). Metaphor and Theory Change. In Ortony, A. (ed.), *Metaphor and Thought*, Cambridge University Press.

Boyd, Richard (1982). Scientific Realism and Naturalistic Epistemology. *PSA: Proceedings of the Biennial Meeting of the Philosophy of Science Association* 1980 (2): 613–62. The Philosophy of Science Association.

Boyd, Richard (1988). How to Be a Moral Realist. In Sayre-McCord, Geoffrey (ed.), *Essays on Moral Realism*, Cornell University Press, 181–228.

Bratman, Michael (1987). *Intention, Plans, and Practical Reason.* Center for the Study of Language and Information.

Bratman, Michael E. (1992). Practical Reasoning and Acceptance in a Context. *Mind* 101 (401): 1–16.

Bratman, Michael E. (2014). *Shared Agency: A Planning Theory of Acting Together.* Oxford University Press USA.

Buchak, Lara (2013). *Risk and Rationality.* Oxford University Press.

Burge, Tyler (1979). Individualism and the Mental. *Midwest Studies in Philosophy* 4 (1): 73–122.

Camp, Elisabeth (2007). Thinking with Maps. *Philosophical Perspectives* 21 (1): 145–82.

Campbell, J. (2002). *Reference and Consciousness.* Oxford University Press.

Carey, Susan (2009). *The Origin of Concepts.* Oxford Chicago Press.

Carnap, Rudolf (1950). *The Logical Foundations of Probability.* University of Chicago Press.

Carroll, Sean (2017). Why Boltzmann Brains are Bad. https://arxiv.org/pdf/1702.00850.pdf. Downloaded 29 October 2017.

Chalmers, David J. (2002). The Components of Content. In Chalmers, D.J. (ed.), *Philosophy of Mind: Classical and Contemporary Readings.* ed. Chalmers, D.J. Oxford University Press.

Chang, Ruth (2002). The Possibility of Parity. *Ethics* 112 (4): 659–88.

Chang, Ruth (2005). Parity, Interval Value and Choice. *Ethics* 115 (2): 315–50.

Chisholm, Roderick (1942). The Problem of the Speckled Hen. *Mind* 51 (204): 368–73.

Christensen, David (2004). *Putting Logic in its Place: Formal Constraints on Rational Belief.* Oxford University Press.

Clarke, Roger (2013). Belief Is Credence One (in Context). *Philosophers' Imprint* 13 (11): 1–18.

Cohen, Jonathan and Meskin, Aaron (2006). An Objective Counterfactual Theory of Information. *Australasian Journal of Philosophy* 84 (3): 333–52.

Cummins, Robert C. (1975). Functional Analysis. *Journal of Philosophy* 72 (November): 741–64.

Dancy, Jonathan (2000). The Particularist's Progress. In Hooker, B.W. and Little, M. (eds.), *Moral Particularism* (Oxford University Press), 130–56.

Dancy, Jonathan (2004). *Ethics without Principles*. Clarendon Press.

Darwall, Stephen (2010). But It Would Be Wrong. *Social Philosophy and Policy* 27 (2): 135–57.

Davidson, D. (1977). Reality without Reference. *Dialectica* 31 (1): 247–53.

Davidson, Donald (1979). The Inscrutability of Reference. *Southwestern Journal of Philosophy* 10 (2): 7–19.

Davidson, Donald (1980). Toward a Unified Theory of Meaning and Action. *Grazer Philosophische Studien* 11: 1–12.

Davidson, Donald (1984). *Inquiries into Truth and Interpretation*. Oxford University Press.

Davidson, Donald (1987). Knowing One's Own Mind. *Proceedings and Addresses of the American Philosophical Association* 60: 441–58. Reprinted in *Subjective, Inter-subjective, Objective*, Oxford University Press, 15–38.

Davies, Paul Sheldon (2000). The Nature of Natural Norms: Why Selected Functions are Systemic Capacity Functions. *Noûs* 34 (1): 85–107.

Dennett, Daniel C. (1978). *Brainstorms*. MIT Press.

Dennett, Daniel C. (1987). *The Intentional Stance*. MIT Press.

Dickie, Imogen (2015). *Fixing Reference*. Oxford University Press.

Dowell, Janice (2016). The Metaethical Insignificance of Moral Twin Earth. In Shafer-Landau, Russ (ed.), *Oxford Studies in Metaethics*. Oxford University Press, ch. 1.

Dretske, Fred (1981). *Knowledge and the Flow of Information*. MIT Press.

Dretske, Fred (1988). *Explaining Behavior: Reasons in a World of Causes*. MIT Press.

Dunaway, Billy and McPherson, Tristram (2016). Reference Magnetism as a Solution to the Moral Twin Earth Problem. *Ergo, an Open Access Journal of Philosophy* 3 (25): 639–75. http://quod.lib.umich.edu/e/ergo/12405314.0003?rgn=main;view=fulltext.

Elliott, Edward (2017). Probabilism, Representation Theorems, and Whether Deliberation Crowds Out Prediction. *Erkenntnis* 82 (2): 379–99.

Elstein, Daniel Y. and Hurka, Thomas (2009). From Thick to Thin: Two Moral Reduction Plans. *Canadian Journal of Philosophy* 39 (4): 515–35.

Enoch, David and Schechter, Joshua (2008). How Are Basic Belief-Forming Methods Justified? *Philosophy and Phenomenological Research* 76 (3): 547–79.

Evans, Gareth (1973). The Causal Theory of Names. *Aristotelian Society Supplementary Volume* 47 (1): 187–208.

Evans, G. (1981). Semantic Theory and Tacit Knowledge. In Holtzman, S. and Leich, C. (eds.), *Wittgenstein: To Follow a Rule*. Routledge and Kegan Paul. Reprinted in McDowell, John (ed.), *Gareth Evans: Collected Papers* (Clarendon Press, Oxford), 322–42.

Evans, Gareth (1982). *Varieties of Reference*. Oxford University Press.

Field, Hartry (1972). Tarski's Theory of Truth. *Journal of Philosophy* 69 (13): 347.

Field, Hartry (1977). Logic, Meaning, and Conceptual Role. *Journal of Philosophy* 74 (July): 379–409.

Field, Hartry H. (1978). Mental Representation. *Erkenntnis* 13 (1): 9–61. Reprinted in Field, *Truth and the Absence of Fact* (Oxford University Press, 2001), 30–67.

Field, Hartry. H. (2001). *Truth and the Absence of Fact.* (Oxford University Press).

Fodor, Jerry A. (1975). *The Language of Thought.* Harvard University Press.

Fodor, Jerry (1987). *Psychosemantics.* MIT Press.

Gibbard, Allan (1990). *Wise Choices, Apt Feelings: A Theory of Normative Judgment.* Harvard University Press.

Gibbard, Allan (2003). *Thinking How to Live.* Harvard University Press.

Gibbard, Allan (2012). *Meaning and Normativity.* Oxford University Press.

Godfrey-Smith, Peter (2002). Goodman's Problem and Scientific Methodology. *Journal of Philosophy* 100 (11): 573–90.

Goodman, Nelson (1954). *Fact, Fiction and Forecast.* Athlone Press.

Greco, Daniel (2015). How I Learned to Stop Worrying and Love Probability 1. *Philosophical Perspectives* 29 (1): 179–201.

Grice, H. Paul (1975). Logic and Conversation. In Cole, Peter and Morgan, Jerry (eds.), *Speech Acts [Syntax and Semantics 3].* Academic Press, 41–58.

Grünwald, Peter (2004). Introducing the Minimum Description Length Principle. In Grünwald, P.D., Myung, J.I., and Pitt, M.A., *Advances in Minimum Description Length: Theory and Applications.* MIT Press, 3–21.

Hare, R.M. (1952). *The Language of Morals.* Oxford University Press.

Harman, Elizabeth (2011). Does Moral Ignorance Exculpate? *Ratio* 24 (4): 443–68.

Harman, Gilbert (1965). The Inference to the Best Explanation. *Philosophical Review* 74: 88–95.

Harris, John H. (1982). What's so Logical about the 'Logical' Axioms? *Studia Logica* 41 (2–3): 159–71.

Hattiangadi, Anandi (2007). *Oughts and Thoughts: Rule Following and the Normativity of Content.* Oxford University Press.

Hawthorne, John (1990). A Note on Languages and Language. *Australasian Journal of Philosophy* 68 (1): 116–18.

Hedden, Brian (2012). Options and the Subjective Ought. *Philosophical Studies* 158 (2): 343–60.

Heim, Irene (1982). *The Semantics of Definite and Indefinite Noun Phrases.* Dissertation, UMass Amherst.

Heuer, Ulrike (2010). Wrongness and Reasons. *Ethical Theory and Moral Practice* 13 (2): 137–52.

Hodes, Harold T. (1984). Logicism and the Ontological Commitments of Arithmetic. *Journal of Philosophy* 81 (3): 123–49.

Holton, Richard (forthcoming). Intention as a Model for Belief. In Vargas, Manuel and Yaffe, Gideon (eds.), *Rational and Social Agency: Essays on the Philosophy of Michael Bratman.* Oxford University Press.

Horgan, Terence and Timmons, Mark (1992). Troubles on Moral Twin Earth: Moral Queerness Revived. *Synthese* 92 (2): 221–60.

Jackson, Frank (1975). Grue. *Journal of Philosophy* 5: 113–31.

Jackson, Frank (1977). *Perception: A Representative Theory*. Cambridge University Press.

Jeffrey, Richard (1965). *The Logic of Decision*. University of Chicago Press.

Joyce, James M. (1999). *The Foundations of Causal Decision Theory*. Cambridge University Press.

Kolodny, Niko (2005). Why be Rational? *Mind* 114 (455): 509–63.

Kripke, Saul A. (1980). *Naming and Necessity*. Harvard University Press.

Kripke, Saul A. (1982). *Wittgenstein on Rules and Private Language*. Harvard University Press.

Leckie, G. and Williams, J.R.G. (2019). Words by Convention. In Lepore, Ernie and Sosa, David (eds.), Oxford Studies in Philosophy of Language, Volume 1. Oxford University Press.

Lepore, Ernest and Kirk, Ludwig (2005). *Donald Davidson: Meaning, Truth, Language, and Reality*. Oxford University Press.

Lewis, David (1969). *Convention: A Philosophical Study*. Harvard University Press.

Lewis, David (1970). How to Define Theoretical Terms. *Journal of Philosophy* 67 (13): 427–46.

Lewis, David (1974). Radical Interpretation. *Synthese* 27 (July–August): 331–44.

Lewis, David (1975). Languages and Language. In Gunderson, Keith (ed.), *Minnesota Studies in the Philosophy of Science* 7. University of Minnesota Press, 3–35.

Lewis, David (1978). Truth in Fiction. *American Philosophical Quarterly* 15 (1): 37–46.

Lewis, David (1980). A Subjectivist's Guide to Objective Chance. In Jeffrey, Richard C. (ed.), *Studies in Inductive Logic and Probability*. University of California Press, 83–132.

Lewis, David (1981). Causal Decision Theory. *Australasian Journal of Philosophy* 59 (1): 5–30.

Lewis, David (1983). New Work for a Theory of Universals. *Australasian Journal of Philosophy* 61 (4): 343–77.

Lewis, David (1984). Putnam's Paradox. *Australasian Journal of Philosophy* 62 (3): 221–36.

Lewis, David (1992). Meaning without Use: Reply to Hawthorne. *Australasian Journal of Philosophy* 70 (1): 106–10.

Lewis, David (1994a). Reduction of Mind. In Guttenplan, Samuel (ed.), *Companion to the Philosophy of Mind*. Blackwell, 412–31.

Lewis, David (1994b). Humean Supervenience Debugged. *Mind* 103 (412): 473–90.

Lewis, David (1996). Elusive Knowledge. *Australasian Journal of Philosophy* 74 (4): 549–67.

List, Christian and Pettit, Philip (2011). *Group Agency: The Possibility, Design, and Status of Corporate Agents*. Oxford University Press.

Logue, Heather (2014). Experiential Content and Naïve Realism: A Reconciliation. In Brogaard, Berit (ed.), *Does Perception Have Content?*, Oxford University Press, 220–41.

Ludwig, Kirk A. (1994). Blueprint for a Science of Mind: A Critical Notice of Christopher Peacocke's *A Study of Concepts*. *Mind and Language* 9 (4): 469–91.

Macfarlane, John (2016). Vagueness as Indecision. In *Proceedings of the Aristotelian Society, Supplementary Volume*.

Mandelkern, Matthew, Schultheis, Ginger, and Boylan, David (2017). Agentive Modals. *Philosophical Review* 126 (3): 301–43.

Marmor, Andrei (2009). *Social Conventions*. Princeton University Press.

McDowell, John (2011). Some Remarks on Intention in Action. *The Amherst Lecture in Philosophy* 6: 1–18. <http://www.amherstlecture.org/mcdowell2011>.

McGee, Vann (2000). Everything. In Sher, Gila and Tieszen, Richard (eds.), *Between Logic and Intuition*. Cambridge University Press, 54–78.

McGee, Vann (2005). Inscrutability and its Discontents. *Noûs* 39 (3): 397–425.

McGlynn, Aidan (2012). Interpretation and Knowledge Maximization. *Philosophical Studies: An International Journal for Philosophy in the Analytic Tradition* 160 (3) (September): 391–405.

Mill, John Stuart (1863). *Utilitarianism*. Parker, Son and Bourn, West Strand.

Millikan, Ruth G. (1984). *Language, Thought and Other Biological Categories*. MIT Press.

Millikan, Ruth G. (1989a). Biosemantics. *Journal of Philosophy* 86 (6): 281–97.

Millikan, Ruth G. (1989b). In Defense of Proper Functions. *Philosophy of Science* 56 (2): 288–302.

Neander, Karen (1991a). Functions as Selected Effects: The Conceptual Analyst's Defense. *Philosophy of Science* 58 (2): 168–84.

Neander, Karen (1991b). The Teleological Notion of 'Function'. *Australasian Journal of Philosophy* 69 (4): 454–68.

Neander, K. (1995). Misrepresenting and Malfunctioning. *Philosophical Studies* 79 (2): 109–41.

Neander, Karen (2004). Teleological Theories of Mental Content. In Zalta, Edward N. (ed.), *Stanford Encyclopedia of Philosophy* (Spring 2018 edition). Available at https://plato.stanford.edu/archives/spr2018/entries/content-teleological.

Neander, Karen (2017). *A Mark of the Mental: In Defense of Informational Teleosemantics*. MIT Press.

Papineau, David (2001). The Status of Teleosemantics, or How to Stop Worrying about Swampman. *Australasian Journal of Philosophy* 79 (2): 279–89.

Pautz, Adam (2013). Does Phenomenology Ground Mental Content? In Kriegel, Uriah (ed.), *Phenomenal Intentionality*, Oxford University Press, 194–234.

Peacocke, C. (1992). *A Study of Concepts*. MIT Press.

Peacocke, Christopher (1987). Understanding Logical Constants: a Realist's Account. *Proceedings of the British Academy* 73: 153–200.

Perez Carballo, Alejandro and Santorio, Paolo (2016). Communication for Expressivists. *Ethics* 126 (3): 607–35.

Pollock, John (2006). *Thinking About Acting: Logical Foundations for Rational Decision Making*. Oxford University Press.

Putnam, Hilary (1975). The Meaning of 'Meaning'. *Minnesota Studies in the Philosophy of Science* 7: 131–93.

Putnam, Hilary (1980). Models and Reality. *The Journal of Symbolic Logic* 45 (3): 464–82. Reprinted in Benacerraf and Putnam (eds.), *Philosophy of Mathematics: Selected Readings*, Second Edition. Cambridge University Press, 1983, 421–46.

Putnam, Hilary (1981). *Reason, Truth and History*. Cambridge University Press.

Quine, W.V. (1960). *Word and Object*. MIT Press.

Railton, Peter(1986). Moral Realism. *The Philosophical Review* 95 (2): 163–207.

Restall, Greg (2015). Assertion, Denial, Acceptance, Rejection, Symmetry, and Paradox. In Caret, Colin R. and Hjortland, Ole T. (eds.), *Foundations of Logical Consequence*. Oxford University Press, 310–21.

Rips, Lance J. (2008). Logical approaches to human deductive reasoning. In Adler, J.E. and Rips, L.J. (eds.), *Reasoning: Studies of Human Inference and its Foundations*, Cambridge University Press, 187–205.

Ross, Jacob and Schroeder, Mark (2014). Belief, Credence, and Pragmatic Encroachment. *Philosophy and Phenomenological Research* 88 (2): 259–88.

Russell, Bertrand (1912). *The Problems of Philosophy*. Home University Library.

Savage, Leonard J. (1954). *The Foundations of Statistics*. Wiley Publications in Statistics.

Scanlon, T.M. (2007). Wrongness and Reasons. In Schafer-Landau, R. (ed.), *Oxford Studies in Metaethics 2*. Oxford University Press, 5–20.

Schoenfield, M. (2016). Conditionalization Does Not (in General) Maximize Expected Accuracy. Mind 126 (504): 1155–87.

Schroeter, Laura and Schroeter, Francois (2003). A Slim Semantics for Thin Moral Terms? *Australasian Journal of Philosophy* 81 (2): 191–207.

Schwarz, Wolfgang (2014). Against Magnetism. *Australasian Journal of Philosophy* 92 (1): 17–36.

Searle, John R. (1979). The Intentionality of Intention and Action. *Inquiry: An Interdisciplinary Journal of Philosophy* 22 (1–4): 253–80.

Shapiro, Stewart (1991). *Foundations Without Foundationalism: A Case for Second-Order Logic*. Oxford University Press.

Sider, Theodore (2009). Ontological Realism. In Chalmers, David John, Manley, David, and Wasserman, Ryan (eds.), *Metametaphysics: New Essays on the Foundations of Ontology*. Oxford University Press, 384–423.

Sider, Theodore (2011). *Writing the Book of the World*. Oxford University Press.

Skolem, T. (1920). Logico-Combinatorial Investigations on the Satisfiability or Provability of Mathematical Propositions: A Simplified Proof of a Theorem by Loewenheim. In van Heijenoort, Jean (ed.), *From Frege to gödel: A Source Book in Mathematical Logic, 1879–1931*. Harvard University Press.

Skorupski, John M. (2010). *The Domain of Reasons*. Oxford University Press.

Smith, Michael (1994). *The Moral Problem*. Blackwell.

Sober, Elliott (2008). *Evidence and Evolution: The Logic Behind the Science*. Cambridge University Press.

Sober, Elliott (2015). *Ockham's Razors: A User's Manual*. Cambridge University Press.

Stalnaker, Robert (1984). *Inquiry*. Cambridge University Press.

Stalnaker, Robert (1999). *Context and Content*. Oxford University Press.

Sturgeon, Scott (forthcoming). Undercutting Defeat and Edgington's Burglar. In *Conditionals, Probability, and Paradox: Themes from the Philosophy of Dorothy Edgington*. Walters, Lee and Hawthorne, John (eds.). Under contract with OUP.

Tasker, Nick (2017). *The Foundations of Public Language: Words as Social Artefacts*. PhD thesis, University of Leeds.

Tollefsen, Deborah (2015). *Groups as Agents*. Polity Press.

van Fraassen, Bas C. (1984). Belief and the Will. *Journal of Philosophy* 81: 235–56.

van Roojen, Mark (2006). Knowing Enough to Disagree: A New Response to the Moral Twin Earth Argument. *Oxford Studies in Metaethics* 1: 161–94.

van Roojen, Mark (2018). Rationalist Metaphysics, Semantics and Metasemantics. In Jones, Karen and Schroeter, Francois (eds.), *The Many Moral Rationalisms*. Oxford University Press.

Vogel, Jonathan (1990). Cartesian Skepticism and Inference to the Best Explanation. *Journal of Philosophy* 87 (11): 658–66.

Wallace, John (1977). Only in the Context of a Sentence Do Words Have Any Meaning. *Midwest Studies in Philosophy* 2 (1): 144–64.

Walton, Kendall L. (1990). *Mimesis as Make-Believe: On the Foundations of the Representational Arts*. Harvard University Press.

Weatherson, Brian (2003). What Good are Counterexamples? *Philosophical Studies* 115 (1): 1–31.

Weatherson, Brian (2013). The Role of Naturalness in Lewis's Theory of Meaning. *Journal for the History of Analytical Philosophy* 1 (10): 1–19.

Wedgwood, Ralph (2001). Conceptual Role Semantics for Moral Terms. *Philosophical Review* 110 (1): 1–30.

Williams, Bernard (1981). Persons, Character and Morality. In Williams, B., *Moral Luck*, Cambridge University Press, 1–19.

Williams, J. Robert G. (2007). Eligibility and Inscrutability. *Philosophical Review* 116 (3): 361–99.

Williams, J. Robert G. (2008a). Permutations and Foster Problems: Two Puzzles or One? *Ratio* 21 (1): 91–105.

Williams, J. Robert G. (2008b). The Price of Inscrutability. *Noûs* 42 (4): 600–41.

Williams, J. Robert G. (2010). Fundamental and Derivative Truths. *Mind* 119 (473): 103–41.

Williams, J. Robert G. (2012). Requirements on Reality. In Correia, Fabrice and Schnieder, Benjamin (eds.), *Metaphysical Grounding: Understanding the Structure of Reality*, Cambridge University Press, 165–85.

Williams, J. Robert G. (2013). Davidson on Reference. In Ludwig, Kirk and Lepore, Ernest (eds.), *A Companion to Donald Davidson*. Blackwell.

Williams, J. Robert G. (2015). Lewis on Reference and Eligibility. In Loewer, B. and Schaffer, J. (eds.), *Companion to David Lewis*. Wiley, 264–86.

Williams, J. Robert G. (2016a). Probability and Nonclassical Logic. In Hajek, Alan and Hitchcock, Christopher (eds.), *The Oxford Handbook to Probability and Philosophy*. Oxford University Press, 248–76.

Williams, J. Robert G. (2016b). Angst, Indeterminacy and Conflicting Values. *Ratio* 29, Issue 4 December.

Williams, J. Robert G. (2016c). Vagueness as Indecision. In *Proceedings of the Aristotelian Society, Supplementary Volume*.

Williams, J. Robert G. (2016d). Representational Scepticism: The Bubble Puzzle. *Philosophical Perspectives* 30 (1): 419–42.

Williams, J. Robert G. (2017). Indeterminate Oughts. *Ethics* 127: 645–73.

Williams, J. Robert G. (2018a). Normative Reference Magnets. *Philosophical Review* 127 (1): 41–71.

Williams, J. Robert G. (2018b). Rational Illogicality. *Australasian Journal of Philosophy* 96 (1): 127–41.

Williamson, T. (2007). *The Philosophy of Philosophy*. Blackwell.

Wright, C. (1981). Rule-Following, Objectivity and the Theory of Meaning. In Holtzman, S. and Leich, C. (eds.), *Wittgenstein: To Follow a Rule*, Routledge, 99–117.

Wright, C. (1987). Theories of Meaning and Speaker's Knowledge. In Wright, Crispin *Realism, Meaning and Truth*, Blackwell, 204–38.

Wright, Larry (1973). Functions. *Philosophical Review* 82 (2): 139–68.

Index

For the benefit of digital users, indexed terms that span two pages (e.g., 52–53) may, on occasion, appear on only one of those pages.